CHARITY ENTREI

# How to launch a
# HIGH-IMPACT
# FOUNDATION

First edition
Published 2023

By Joey Savoie, Aidan Alexander,
Judith Rensing and Will Troy

CHARITY ENTREPRENEURSHIP

# How to launch a
# HIGH-IMPACT
# FOUNDATION

First edition | Published 2023

Learn more about our grantmaking program at www.impactfulgrantmaking.com

Learn more about us at www.charityentrepreneurship.com

Disclaimer: while the information in this book is correct at the time of publication to the best of our knowledge, it is not (and should not be treated as) a substitute for legal advice. We accept no liability whatsoever (regardless of whether such liability arises in tort, contract, or in any other way and whether or not caused by negligence or misrepresentation) for any losses which you may suffer as a result of acting on the information in this book except to the extent that the exclusion of such liability is prohibited.

# ACKNOWLEDGEMENTS

If it takes a village to raise a child, it takes an army to write a book. Publishing this handbook wouldn't have been possible without the contributions of a long list of individuals who offered their perspectives and their time.

Firstly, a massive thanks to Charity Entrepreneurship's copyeditor Kylie Abel, who helped us turn over 100,000 words of chaos into something resembling a coherent book.

We extend our thanks to everyone who reviewed and provided feedback on our draft versions, especially Morgan Fairless, Leonie Falk, and Steve Thompson.

Thank you to the first two cohorts who participated in our Grantmaking Program for enduring our unpolished early drafts, providing invaluable feedback, and helping us to refine our thinking on grantmaking theory and practice.

Finally, we express our gratitude to the entire Charity Entrepreneurship team. Many members contributed directly to this handbook, and everyone played a part in building the rich foundation of organizational knowledge that this book draws from.

Due to your collective efforts, we now have a finished product that we sincerely believe can play a significant role in bettering our world.

# TABLE OF CONTENTS

| | |
|---|---|
| PREFACE: SAVING A LIFE | 1 |
| 1. INTRODUCTION | 3 |
| 1.1. Why read a book on foundations? | 4 |
| 1.2. Who is this book for? | 5 |
| 1.3. How this book is different | 6 |
| 1.4. How this book is laid out | 8 |
| 2. WHY START A FOUNDATION? | 11 |
| 2.1. Why start a foundation instead of a charity or business? | 12 |
| 2.2. Why start a foundation vs. giving your money to the best existing ones? | 15 |
| 2.3. Why start a foundation with a relatively small amount of money? | 23 |
| PART A: MAKING GOOD DECISIONS | 27 |
| 3. FORMS OF EVIDENCE | 37 |
| 3.1. Rationality | 43 |
| 3.2. Scientific Evidence | 53 |
| 3.3. Independent Experts | 63 |
| 3.4. Heuristics | 77 |
| 4. WAYS OF AGGREGATING EVIDENCE | 89 |
| 4.1. Cost-effectiveness analysis | 91 |
| 4.2. Weighted-factor models | 113 |
| 5. BEST PRACTICE CHARITY DECISION-MAKING PROCESSES | 129 |
| 5.1. Theory of change | 131 |
| 5.2. Monitoring and evaluation | 147 |
| 5.3. Benchmarking | 169 |

**PART B: KEY DECISIONS FOR NEW FOUNDATIONS** 175

**6. SCOPE** 179

6.1. Values 183

6.2. Cause areas 197

6.3. Geography 213

6.4. Grantee size and maturity 217

6.5. Identifying funding gaps 223

**7. STRUCTURE** 231

7.1. Wealth 233

7.2. Wisdom 251

7.3. Work 265

**8. STRATEGY** 273

8.1. Evidence vs. hits-based grantmaking 275

8.2. Active vs. passive grantmaking 289

8.3. Open vs. closed application process 303

8.4. Creating leverage 309

8.5. Counterfactuals 319

8.6. Neglected strategies 327

**PART C: CHOOSING WHO TO HIRE AND WHO TO FUND** 339

**9. SELECTING TRAITS TO LOOK FOR** 343

9.1. Selecting traits to vet for in hiring 343

9.2. Traits to look for when grantmaking 347

**10. DESIGNING A BEST-PRACTICE VETTING PROCESS** 363

10.1. Principles for vetting processes 363

10.2. Structuring the vetting processes 369

**11. PUTTING IT ALL INTO PRACTICE** 381

11.1. Learn decision-making skills by doing 382

11.2. Make preliminary decisions 382

11.3. Goals for a foundation in its first year 386

11.4. Final remarks 388

# PREFACE

# Saving a life

*Yuko felt the smoke first; it stung her eyes and filled her lungs. As she turned the corner, a house on fire lit up the night. She saw bright flames through the windows and black smoke billowing from cracks in the walls. Hearing a scream from inside the house, Yuko didn't think twice. No one else was around; she knew she had to help.*

Few people have saved someone's life. Those who have say it's a profound and surreal experience to know someone would not be alive if it weren't for their actions. And the impact doesn't stop there: from their friends and family to passing acquaintances, dozens of lives are affected. You might get a single opportunity in your lifetime to save another individual, such as running into a burning building at great personal risk. You might be lucky enough to have a job where these kinds of opportunities are fairly common, like being a paramedic, but this applies to very few of us.

What about saving a life every day? This is a tier reserved for only the most talented scientists, the most well-known political activists, the most successful charity founders, and the wisest foundations. Foundations have the ability to catalyze a movement and transform the state of play in a given cause area. Foundations that prioritize impact, make good decisions, and apply their time strategically can save a life for every day they operate or even every hour.

Helping this many people is a task normally reserved for superhero movies, yet this feat can be achieved with a lot of hard work and a little luck. This is the main reason to consider starting a foundation. Historically, foundations have made a massive difference in countless lives and tackled incredibly important problems that would have otherwise been forgotten.

If your choices are backed by strong research and a good set of decision-making tools, founding a high-impact foundation is an achievable goal and may lead to the greatest good you could possibly achieve with your time.

**This handbook is about how to become that founder.**

# 1. Introduction

*Yuko burst through the front door and ran up the stairs. A terrified family was huddled together, choking on the smoke. One by one, she guided them out of the house. Finally, she went back for the two family dogs, carrying them out one at a time.*

*While they waited for the emergency services, she comforted the shocked family. As the magnitude of her accomplishment sank in, she began to cry... but before she could even wipe away her tears, she heard another piercing scream some distance behind her. Her heart dropped. She turned around and stared, slack-jawed with disbelief – three other homes, all on this same street, completely engulfed in flames. Where are the fire fighters? Who is going to save these people? Before she knew it, she was kicking in the door of the closest building and rushing into the smoke-filled room.*

*One by one, she rescued each person of all three families out of their burning homes. Exhausted and coughing, she stumbled out of the third house with the last family member - a fluffy little house cat named Billy - but her relief turned to shock.*

*The entire neighborhood around her was on fire. The families she had already rescued looked at her pleadingly. They thought she was superhuman. "I can't save the whole neighborhood!" thought Yuko. She looked up and saw, in the clouds, whole cities on fire in the sky. She felt the heat of the flames on her skin.*

*Yuko bolted awake, covered in sweat. That same dream again. But what does it mean? She took some deep breaths and reminded herself that it wasn't real. She felt relief... and disappointment.*

*Sitting down to her first cup of coffee, Yuko looked over the applications pouring in for her most recent round of funding. She had taken this new job at a foundation just over a month ago and was still getting used to it. Looking through each proposal, she felt a familiar feeling of excitement and dread.*

*A shiver ran up her back. She wondered which fires she would put out first.*

# 1.1. Why read a book on foundations?

**Starting a great foundation is challenging.** It can be a lonely path, fraught with high stakes but ambiguous decisions, seemingly endless competing possibilities, and no shortage of complexity.

Despite good intentions, many foundations don't spend their money well, resulting in little or no impact. Some even do harm.

If a for-profit is doing a bad job, eventually the market will put them out of business. But the nonprofit world doesn't have this same accountability mechanism. Legal due diligence is required, but in real terms, being ineffective won't get you shut down. Ineffective charities can limp along for years despite having minimal impact, so long as they're persuasive fundraisers. The situation is worse for donors. It's a well-known aphorism that once you start giving away money, you'll never tell a bad joke again. Few charities would dare to criticize their sources of financial support, and foundations don't often critique other foundations. People change around money. Honest feedback becomes hard to come by. This lack of accountability and feedback makes founding and running a high-performing foundation challenging.

Besides this, there are many challenges that a foundation faces on its path to impact. Some are similar to what any NGO or for-profit faces, like attracting and retaining an excellent team or making high-stakes decisions with limited information. Other challenges affect foundations more than most types of organizations. For example, measuring a foundation's impact is particularly challenging as it requires understanding the impact of each project they have funded and whether those projects would have been funded anyway. **But we believe it's possible,** with the help of this book, to position your foundation for exceptional impact. You have the potential to reshape entire fields and achieve lasting changes. Half the battle is just having clarity about what the most important decisions are! We set these out and then walk through each of them.

**This handbook aims to make it easier.** We'll provide some tools, best practices, and key considerations to help you meet some of the most difficult challenges and decisions head-on. We believe reading and internalizing this handbook's content will enable your foundation to do significantly more good in the world.

This book does not aim to give prescriptive advice like "You should donate 20% of your assets to vaccine interventions in Kenya." Rather, we set out how to leverage the best decision-making tools to find the best answers for *you*. We've studied the DNA of the most effective charities on the planet. And in this book, we'll help you understand the difference between good and exceptional, so you can have the most impact possible.

This book was inspired by interest in our *How to Start a High-Impact Nonprofit* book and our Charity Incubation Program. A number of grantmakers have told us that foundations severely lack resources to learn how to *really* make a difference. Our team has been incubating, teaching, and recommending grants to charities for over five years, and a number of them have gone on to become leaders in their field. We believe that many of the decision-making tools we teach to implementing charities also apply to grantmaking foundations. Our goal in creating this book is to do the most good possible. We hope that this book, which also serves as the textbook for our Grantmaking Program, plays a role in enabling grantmakers to more effectively help those in need and improve lives.

## 1.2. Who is this book for?

This book is for anyone who wants to understand how to be an impactful grantmaker. Perhaps you've started a foundation or work for one and want to ensure you do a great job. Perhaps you've sought advisors to tell you the answers, but some key open questions remain. Perhaps you're unsure if you want to start a foundation or where to start. Or you're feeling imposter syndrome – that you're simply not qualified to make such high-stakes decisions under such high levels of uncertainty. Maybe you're not directly involved in a foundation at all but want to understand what grantmaking is all about. If any of these descriptions rings true, this book is for you.

Whilst we have directed our writing at those who are starting or running a foundation personally, this is purely for the purposes of communicating clearly and succinctly without having to constantly clarify who we are speaking to. Suppose you are simply interested in how foundations can make the biggest difference possible with the money they give away. In that case, we are also writing to you. We believe the content in this book will prove highly valuable to many categories of people in the philanthropic world beyond founders. Additionally, there are many different types of philanthropic and grantmaking entities. For clarity's sake, we use the term "foundation" to refer to all of them.

This book is not targeted at foundations of a specific size or working in a specific cause area or geography. It also isn't aimed at readers with specific types of prior experience or ways of thinking. Rather, we aim to help foundations identify what makes them atypical and to turn this into their comparative advantage. If all foundations thought this way, they could slot together like puzzle pieces to address the most important problems in the world together, without gaps, considering a wide range of complementary perspectives.

To this end, we will review a diverse set of real foundations and explore what caused their successes and failures. We will also explore the range of possible scope, structural and strategic 'settings' that foundations can choose from and the considerations that would make one setting more appropriate than another for a given foundation. This will allow foundations to identify a combination of settings that makes sense for them.

Many of the founders we've worked with report strong feelings of isolation. Very few people understand the challenges they face. Because founders often care deeply about doing a good job, they put so much pressure on themselves. We want to help you channel that pressure, so you make the best possible decisions rather than letting it paralyze you.

To get the most out of this process, readers will not only need to be humble and honest about their weaknesses but also be brave enough to lean into their strengths and carve out a niche other actors in the philanthropic landscape have overlooked.

# 1.3. How this book is different

**This book is different from most others written on foundations and philanthropy.** In many such books, the primary goal is described (implicitly or explicitly) in terms of benefits to the philanthropist. Advice is given on how they can use giving to shape the world to their preferences. This book will come from a different perspective. It will assume that a foundation's primary goal is to cause the most good it can in the world. In some ways, this might seem like an obvious goal; impact is one of the explicitly stated values of many foundations across the world. However, there is a large difference between something being one of a set of competing goals, and it being the primary goal. For example, having impact as your primary goal will lead you to pick a cause area based on evidence rather than because you were personally affected by it. It will lead you to choose a grantmaking process that has a track record of working well rather than a process that is the easiest or most enjoyable.

The goal of causing as much good as possible can be broken down into three principles:

1. **Maximal impact:** Saving two lives is better than saving one. Helping three people is better than helping two. Helping someone immensely is better than helping them a little bit. By extension, our goal should be to help as many humans and animals as we can, as much as we can. Therefore, when spending resources like time and money, the question isn't 'Will this do good,' or even 'Will this do a lot of good.' Instead, it is, 'Will this do the most good out of all the available options?' Aiming to maximize impact sounds self-evident. But in practice, it's quite uncommon because it can have inconvenient implications, like only funding charities in low-income countries you have no strong feelings about or working on diseases you have never heard of.

2. **Impartiality:** When our primary aim is to improve the world, who the beneficiaries are or who gets to claim credit for the improvement is irrelevant. Hence, we should be impartial about such factors. Lives have equal moral value, regardless of whose they are or what problem affects them (e.g. someone dying of malaria is equally important to someone dying of tuberculosis, all else equal). It doesn't matter whether we save a life with our own hands or whether our unrecognized contribution enables someone else to do so; the life saved is the important thing. Being impartial is not always easy. It requires setting aside our aesthetic preferences and our ego and seeking to help the greatest number, to the greatest extent.

3. **Counterfactual impact:** This concept will often be considered throughout the handbook. Thinking counterfactually means thinking about what would have happened otherwise. For example, suppose another foundation would

have covered the costs of a project. In that case, it might be less impactful to fund that project vs. one that would not be able to exist without your funding. Aiming to actually cause as much good as possible means factoring in the opportunity costs of your actions and what would happen absent your involvement.

# 1.4. How this book is laid out

The intended readership of this book is diverse. Therefore, some parts may be more or less relevant than others depending on your current circumstances. Whilst the book has been written sequentially, we invite you to think of it as a menu; read it in the way that best supports your grantmaking journey.

This book is made up of three parts:

## Part A: Tools for making good decisions

Relative to other NGOs, foundations spend a lot less time on execution and a lot more time on decision-making. Good decision-making is pivotal to a foundation's eventual impact, whether it's considering what grant to give, what staff to hire, or what area to focus on. Throughout this handbook, we will focus on different tools or approaches that can be combined into a coherent and systematic plan to make great decisions. Everything from when to use cost-effectiveness analysis to how much to trust an expert in the field. We take a broad but analytical approach to the tools that can be used and include case studies of when each tool has been used in the field. We will cover three categories of tools that can be used.

1. **Forms of evidence:** How should you value different types of evidence? What role might each play in your decision-making as a foundation? What are the relative advantages of experts vs. scientific studies vs. rationality vs. heuristics?
2. **Ways of aggregating evidence:** How do you combine different types of evidence to make a decision? How do you navigate situations when the evidence points in different directions? What role should cost-effectiveness analyses play in a foundation's decision-making?
3. **Best practice processes:** What is your foundation's theory of change? How much monitoring and evaluation (M&E) should you expect from a charity?

Why and how should you choose and use a benchmark to compare grant options?

## Part B: Key decisions for new foundations

We then explore the key decisions that need to be made to start deploying funds effectively.

1. **Scope**: What counts as 'impact,' given your values? Which cause areas, locations, and types of recipients will you focus on so that you can have as much impact as possible?
2. **Structure**: How should your foundation be organized to effectively make change within its scope? For example, how quickly will you aim to deploy your funding? How much will you spend on grantmaking staff vs. the grants themselves? How personally involved should foundation leaders be in grantmaking decisions?
3. **Strategy**: How will you operate your foundation to achieve impact? For example, how much risk will you take with your grants? Will you source grantees through open applications or privately through your network? How will you incorporate considerations like 'counterfactuals' and 'leverage?'

Each decision involves making difficult trade-offs. Some decisions are better than others, but overall, we don't believe there is a correct set of 'settings' that all foundations should adopt. Rather, each foundation will have its own comparative advantages that make a certain scope, structure, and strategy the most impactful choice for *them*. Part B is about discovering those comparative advantages and making your key decisions accordingly.

## Part C: Vetting people and organizations

The final section of the handbook is focused on vetting. A well-designed vetting process is the most concrete output a foundation needs before it starts grantmaking. This process will allow you to separate the best organizations, projects, and grant applications to fund from the worst.

Grantmaking is an area with relatively low levels of research and historical accountability. This means it's hard to find research on processes that have over-performed relative to others. However, there is a nearby area that deals with many of the same challenges and has stronger feedback loops[1]: hiring. We will discuss some of the best practices for hiring staff, backed by strong empirical evidence, and explain how these best practices can be used to build an excellent grantmaking team and be adapted to make the best grants. We will lay this out in two steps:

1. **Selecting traits to look for:** What traits should you look for when hiring, and how does this change as your organization matures? Based on your foundation's scope and strategy, what traits should you look for when grantmaking?

2. **Designing a best-practice vetting process:** What are the best practices for getting the most out of the limited time you have for vetting? How should your vetting process be structured, and how might it vary between hiring, grantmaking, and choosing advisors?

**But before we get into the 'how'** of launching a grantmaking foundation, we need to discuss some of the concerns you may have right now about whether launching a foundation makes sense for you – we need to talk about the 'why.'

---

[1] We will refer to 'feedback loops' often in this book. By 'feedback loops' we mean scenarios where you can monitor signals about the outputs of a system, to determine whether the system is working well or not. For instance, in a car factory, the defect rate detected by your quality control team is a signal that helps you determine whether you're manufacturing cars well and can help you determine how to improve the system. Feedback loops are said to be 'strong' when the signals are accurate, granular, and cover many parts of the system. Feedback loops are said to be 'short' when you don't have to wait long to get a signal on a particular part of the system.

# 2. Why start a foundation?

This chapter aims to address one of the key questions you may have right now: Does it make sense for me, personally, to start a foundation?

The world is big and full of problems, from global poverty to factory farming to risks from pandemics. There are hundreds of issues where philanthropy could be used as a major lever for change that rarely get focused on or addressed. It's fairly clear that there's a vital role for grantmaking foundations to play in providing funding for essential and neglected work that markets and governments won't or can't address.

But there are some common questions that those in the unique position of considering starting a foundation often ask themselves: Is starting a foundation the best way for me to make a difference? Should I start an implementing charity instead? Or are my skills better suited to doing good by starting a business or a social enterprise? Why don't I just give the money to an established and credible existing foundation, and they can deploy it for me using their expertise? Are there really gaps that are not covered by others? Can a small foundation have a significant impact, given the very large philanthropic funds out there?

This chapter will explore the need for more grantmaking foundations[2] and why for some people it's the best way to contribute to making the world a better place.

---

[2] For simplicity's sake, in this handbook we have chosen to use the term "foundation" to refer to all legal structures for philanthropy, from foundations to Donor Advised Funds, to giving straight from a personal bank account.

# 2.1. Why start a foundation instead of a charity or business?

A charitable foundation is a vehicle for using time and money to create positive change in the world. But it's far from the only one, as for-profit and impact investing are competing ways to invest money. Charity entrepreneurship and founding or working for a for-profit to earn more money to give away are alternative ways to invest time. All of these options make claims to impact. In this section, we explain some of the differences between them and when it makes sense to pick the path of starting a foundation.

## Ways to use money to have an impact

If impact is the main goal, we think foundations perform the best overall compared to the other options available. They have the most direct path from action to impact and the lowest risk of being distracted by other outcomes (like profit).

Below we compare three different methods of making a difference.

| | Foundations | Impact investing | For-profit investing |
|---|---|---|---|
| **Definition** | A grantmaking organization focused on granting to charitable organizations | Investments with the intention to generate a beneficial social or environmental impact, alongside a financial return | Investments primarily focused on making a financial return |
| **Examples** | Gates Foundation, Mulago, Rockefeller Foundation | One Acre Fund, Vital Capital, Green Angles | Most major financial institutions |
| **Bottom line** | Impact | Double bottom line of profit and impact | Profit |
| **Unique strengths** | • Can help low-income beneficiaries (people in poverty; animals)<br>• Can partner with governments and other foundations<br>• More neglected<br>• Can focus model solely on impact<br>• Historically has created huge amounts of impact per $ invested | • Can, in theory, create an ongoing impact without ongoing donations<br>• Some opportunities might be nearly as profitable as straight profit but have non-trivial social goods and extra flow-through benefits (e.g.,Wave)<br>• Allows for higher scalability | • Can create more income for future donations<br>• Has been a major source of development overall<br>• Success is easier to measure<br>• Has a far more developed ecosystem with a range of investment vehicles |
| **Unique weaknesses** | • Poor feedback loops<br>• Less guidance and structures<br>• Possible disconnect between funders and beneficiaries<br>• More challenging monitoring and evaluation | • Divided focus makes it hard to compete on impact or profit metrics<br>• More limited pool of investors<br>• Mixed track record (e.g., microloans)<br>• Complex tax structures depending on the country | • In many ways just passes the buck of impact to the future<br>• Depends largely on your value of the impact of donating now vs later<br>• Higher risk of value drift |

## Ways to use time to have an impact

If your goal is to have the biggest impact, a highly important decision is how to spend your time as well as money. These decisions can be independent; you can decide that the best use of your funds is to start a foundation but that running a foundation is not the best use of your time relative to founding a charity or working to create even more funding. (We discuss why and how you might decide to use your money to start a foundation but have someone else lead it in Chapter 7.3.1).

Suppose you have the option of founding a foundation. In that case, you are in a unique situation where you have the available capital and can focus your time primarily on decision-making. This is not an option for most people and, perhaps unsurprisingly, it compares quite favorably to other possible career paths in terms of impact:

| | Grantmaking | Charity founding | For-profit work |
|---|---|---|---|
| **Definition** | Starting a foundation focused on dispersing funding to charitable organizations | Founding a charity focused on direct implementation, using your capital as one of the first donors | Using your time to generate more capital which can be deployed by others to have an impact |
| **Competitive advantage** | Starting a foundation is only a possible path for those with funding and so is highly neglected | Being able to be unconcerned with fundraising in the early stages gives a charity a significant advantage | If you have capital it allows access to unique investment opportunities increasing the amount you can earn |
| **Unique strengths** | • Can spread impact across a large number of projects, lowering risk profile<br>• Can accommodate better work-life balance<br>• If you are part of a broader family fund, you can encourage them to give more, or more effectively | • Can allow projects to get founded that would not get started otherwise due to needing large upfront capital<br>• Arguably the best way to utilize your talent for execution<br>• Lowest barriers to entry (e.g. wealth, credentials) | • Hardest career path to mislead yourself into thinking you are having success when you are not<br>• Moving up a wealth class can provide access to new people to influence towards impactful giving (e.g. joining Founders Pledge) |
| **Unique weaknesses** | • Foundations require the strongest decision making<br>• There is a high risk of nepotism and deploying funding in ways uncorrelated with impact | • Removing the need to fundraise removes some accountability<br>• Implementation charities can and often do fail to have an impact even when funded | • Depends largely on your view on the value of donating now vs. later<br>• Highest risk of value drift |

None of these paths are mutually exclusive, and it's common for an individual to spend some time in each of these areas over the course of their career. Overall, running or working on your foundation (particularly for the first few years as it gets founded) seems like a uniquely impactful path for those with the option.

## 2.2. Why start a foundation vs. giving your money to the best existing ones?

Those who are sold that a foundation is one of the best ways to have an impact may still have a lingering doubt about whether to start a new foundation or support an existing one. Warren Buffet, a notoriously astute investor, has donated a huge amount of funding, not to his own foundation but to the Gates Foundation, asserting that he was more confident in supporting that foundation than setting up his own.[3] Why start a new foundation when you could just pick the best existing one to support with more funding? There are strong reasons to choose either option, depending on the specifics.

### 2.2.1. Donating to another foundation

The case:

**It's quicker and more efficient to leverage the work of others:** Other foundations can absorb a large amount of funding and already have existing expertise, staff teams, processes, and methodologies. This means they can result in much quicker deployment of large funding pools relative to slowly building up a team and a body of knowledge. From the outside, the best foundations look like they have it all figured out; it can be appealing to just pick a winning organization to support.

**It's better for donor coordination:** When many different actors are trying to distribute a pool of funding for the common good, it's hard to coordinate them so that all the best projects get support. It's easy for a project to get underfunded because each donor assumed that other donors would support it, or for some projects to get collectively overfunded by a few donors, whilst another worthy project gets nothing. Typically, a foundation is more coordinated internally than it is with another external (even if aligned) foundation, so fewer foundations tend to make for better coordination.

---

[3] Timothy L. O'Brien, Stephanie Saul, "Buffett to Give Bulk of His Fortune to Gates Charity," NY Times, June 26, 2006, accessed Feb. 2023, https://www.nytimes.com/2006/06/26/business/26buffett.html

**Fewer choices to make:** Finally, by picking a foundation to fund, you only have to make one big decision instead of picking every individual grant. This means you can go much deeper and put considerably more thought into this decision, assuming you can access enough information on other foundations' operations.

The risks: There are a few large risks in supporting another foundation. The first one is implicit assumptions: Many things that might seem clear or objective from afar can contain far more judgment calls than expected. Two foundations might share the value that lives matter equally, but how does improving education get weighed against improving health? As you will see in this handbook, there are a lot of difficult decisions to be made in setting a foundation's scope and strategy and running its grantmaking process. Reasonable people can and do come to very different conclusions. By trusting someone else's decisions, your money could end up going to projects that are very far from what *you* would think is most impactful if you had looked at it yourself. Because these decisions are so difficult and often subjective, we think it is valuable for the worldviews of the donors in a given space to be diverse to reduce the chance that we put all our eggs in the wrong basket.

When it makes sense: Donating to a highly-capable existing foundation can be a good fit for someone who does not want to spend a lot of time on grantmaking (e.g. wants to use their time elsewhere but still have their funding deployed). However, with a bit more effort, someone in this position could launch a foundation and hire someone else to lead it (as discussed in Chapter 7.3.1).

Given this, we think the most appropriate scenarios for donating to another foundation are when:

- You want to spend as little time on decision-making as possible and for there to be no ongoing work
- You're more confident in your ability to pick an excellent existing foundation than in your ability to pick an excellent leader for a new one (after all, the latter decision is more difficult in general)
- The total amount of funds is too small to justify hiring someone to disburse it (e.g. their salary would be more than 10% of the funds)

## 2.2.2. Starting a new foundation

The case:

**Existing foundations don't meet all of the world's greatest needs:** The world is big - there are a lot of problems to solve, many potential solutions to consider funding, and a lot that needs to be learned to do this well. As a result, most foundations make the wise decision of limiting their scope by some combination of cause area, geography and recipient organization size/maturity (e.g. GiveWell focuses on mature global health organizations with direct-delivery interventions that can absorb many millions in funding). In aggregate, the scopes of these foundations do not sufficiently cover all of the most important areas. This results in gaps that are underfunded. To achieve better coverage of the world's problems, we need more organizations and more grantmakers working on figuring out what to fund.

**It is valuable to have many perspectives:** When deciding whether another foundation would add value in a given area, it is helpful to ask yourself what the ideal funding ecosystem would look like for that area. For example, maybe an ideal ecosystem for supporting mature charities in the global poverty cause area would look something like: One charity evaluator (that is supported by a large number of small donors), one funding circle (with 10 individual actors in it), and three large foundations that use their own methodology. This would result in at least five different decision-making processes and 14 different donors with different perspectives who could possibly support an impactful project. An ecosystem like this is unlikely to miss a good project, so supporting one of the existing actors in this ecosystem could make sense. On the other hand, if an ecosystem contains just one very large foundation and one small foundation, lots of strong charities will get missed. A new foundation bringing a fresh perspective would likely be far more impactful than doubling one of those foundations' assets.

**Promising grantmaking strategies are underutilized:** The field of grantmaking is just getting started in figuring out how to efficiently fund the best projects. There are many promising methodologies and strategies for disbursing funding with the potential for high impact that few, if any, existing foundations have tried yet. We discuss some of these in Chapter 8.6. of this handbook. We believe there is a need for more foundations to test out these approaches and fill functional niches within the grantmaking ecosystem.

The risks: It's easy to think you are a great decision-maker or are using a revolutionary method, but to ultimately underperform. Many are too humble when it comes to deciding whether they're capable of successfully launching an impactful foundation. But there is also the risk of being over-confident. Meanwhile, starting a foundation takes time and focus, so it's easy to get distracted and for progress to stall or for your efforts to fall short.

When it makes sense: If you're interested enough to read this handbook and ambitious enough in your altruism to continue to read more widely on the topic of effective grantmaking, there's a good chance you are dedicated enough to consider launching your own foundation.

Looking inwards, it might make sense to launch a foundation when:

- The amount of capital you have is particularly large, making it hard to find someone who can deploy for you in addition to their own existing funding (e.g. if you were to double The Gates Foundation's funds today, would they be able to deploy it in a reasonable time frame?).
- Your worldview or approach is particularly unique, meaning it's more likely to add a missing perspective to the funding ecosystem.

Meanwhile, looking outwards, it might make sense to launch a foundation when:

- Problems or solutions you consider important are not fully served by existing foundations (e.g. they aren't covered within any foundations' remit, or there are gaps at the size or geographic level.)[4]
- The funding ecosystem for a problem or solution you consider important only has a couple of major donors, so some great opportunities might be overlooked.

## 2.2.3. Join a funding circle – the best of both worlds?

In brief, a funding circle is a group of multiple funders that share a common interest (e.g. a cause area) and collectively source grant opportunities and discuss who should find them. It's best thought of not as an alternative to starting a foundation but rather as a way to minimize some of the risks of starting your own foundation while keeping many of the benefits. Funding circles can enjoy the coordination benefits of one large

---

[4] See Chapter 6.4. for a discussion of some specific funding gaps.

foundation, as well as the ability to attract more and better grant applicants due to there being a single point of contact to apply to. They also bring the viewpoint diversity benefits of having many separate donors. Funding circles are the best fit for an individual philanthropist or a foundation with a small number of staff (say three or less) who could benefit from more information, community, and a unified application process.

## 2.2.4. A note on deference

At its core, the question of whether to donate to another foundation or start your own is all about deference. Should you decide how to spend the money yourself or defer to someone else for all the decision-making? But the question of when and how much to defer is also relevant day to day if you decide to start your own foundation. In fact, it's relevant for everyone, so it's worth giving some thought to.

To function in modern society, we constantly defer to other people, from asking our doctor what medication to take to trusting a mechanic's advice about our car. It is impossible to be an expert in everything, and making hard decisions around doing good is no different. However, if a culture is too high in deference or defers using the wrong metrics, it can become homogenized and great opportunities can be missed.

Suppose you're an amateur motor enthusiast who has put thousands of hours into learning about cars. In that case, this puts you in a different position than someone who drives but has never looked under the hood in terms of deference to a mechanic. Often, advice about how much to defer in philanthropy amounts to 'defer more' or 'defer less.' But neither of these pieces of advice will be appropriate for everyone. One foundation might defer too little (like someone who has never opened up the hood of a car being confident that they can fix things themselves). At the same time, another might defer too much (like the enthusiast who trusts the local mechanic to fix a rare and tricky problem on their car that they have been fixing by themselves for years).

It's also important to know which questions are objectively answerable and which are based on personal values or unclear epistemic trade-offs. It makes more sense to defer to others on the former type of questions than the latter. For example, if you are an individual donor with little time and want to save the most lives possible with a high degree of confidence, deferring to GiveWell's well-researched recommendation of bednets to prevent malaria is a sensible choice. (Side note: We mention GiveWell many times throughout this handbook. This is because they are a field-leading grantmaking organization that embodies three principles we highly value: impartiality, transparency, and prioritizing counterfactual impact.) However, GiveWell is far less confident in the objective basis of their trade-offs between increased income and lives saved. Thus, it makes less sense to defer on that topic. Deferring to GiveWell when it comes to matters of personal values is like deferring to your mechanic on the best color for a car.

Let's consider some other examples in the context of philanthropy.

## High deference - New funder with little time

*Paul is new to grantmaking and has read a single book on the topic. Although he loves the concepts, he feels overwhelmed with all the new information and does not plan on engaging with it super deeply. He is already well into a solid career and does not imagine grantmaking becoming a big part of his life. Nonetheless, he wants his pretty sizable donations to make the maximum impact from the fairly standard view of saving more lives and reducing pain. He defers and ends up donating 10% to GiveWell-recommended charities, seeing it as a safe, impactful option that does not take a ton of time.*

Given the amount of time and energy he wants to put into the topic, we think that Paul has made the right decision. But let's imagine a much more knowledgeable funder using the same level of deference:

## High deference - Experienced funder

*Christina has been involved in grantmaking and the effective charity movement for six years. She led an 'ambitious altruism' society for a couple of years before joining a well-respected impact-focused organization full-time. She has spent several hundred hours engaging with the discourse on effective philanthropy and has a deep understanding of what the cruxes of disagreements are between different funders in the space. However, when it comes to donating, she still feels uncertain. She sees problems with the movement and its granting and has knowledge of some unique opportunities that most funders are unaware of. She puts in several dozen hours to investigate a couple of opportunities. However, she also knows that larger grantmakers are more experienced in this area and likely have access to more information. She thus decides to donate evenly between several expert-advised philanthropic funds, guessing that the experts will ultimately have better judgment than her own.*

This seems like a real loss. Christina fits the profile of someone who could be a good grantmaker and strengthen the entire grantmaking space. She would likely be able to have far more impact if she independently considered opportunities to find the best one - she is like the motor enthusiast in the mechanic example above. In addition to understanding the facts, Christina also understands the differences in opinion that are a matter of personal values in a way that Paul doesn't. She's in a better position to make different decisions to major funders on this basis, potentially funding opportunities missed by those other funders that do not conform to their moral values and avoiding donating to causes that do not align with hers.

The central claim here is that someone's deference should reduce as they become more knowledgeable in an area. Someone working full-time in grantmaking for years should probably take the time to thoroughly think through their cause prioritization. Someone who will pick a career primarily based on impact probably should do enough research to have a good sense of the options, not just pick something from the top of a published list.

Let's look at more concrete examples of when it makes more sense to defer vs. investigate and reach your own conclusion as your philanthropic knowledge and experience increase.[5]

| Experience level | Description | Example questions to defer | Example questions to investigate |
| --- | --- | --- | --- |
| Low | A grantmaker who has read one book and has put in ~1 hour or less a week for under a year | What are the best specific charities? | Is GiveWell the best charity evaluator to defer to? |
| Medium | A grantmaker who has read 3 books on the topic and been involved in the NGO space for 1-2 years | Which avante- garde cause areas are worth considering? | Given my values, beliefs, and epistemics, what is the best reputable cause area to focus on? |

[5] Note: The advice to defer or investigate will not apply to everyone who roughly meets these descriptions; there are more factors to consider, like the person's available time, how much money they are looking to give, and the counterfactuals of their time. These are just rough heuristics.

| High | A grantmaker who has led a foundation for 2+ years and worked at an effective charity for 1 year | What should a specific organization's plan be? | What are my ethical and epistemic tradeoffs in detail? |
| --- | --- | --- | --- |
| Very high | A funder who has been working full-time in grantmaking & has been considering the philanthropy ecosystem for years | Sub-comparison between charities doing similar work (e.g. AMF vs Malaria Consortium) | What are the biggest weaknesses of leading views on effective giving, and how should my actions change based on that? |

This table shows the evolution of how, as someone gains more expertise in an area, they should defer less and less, particularly on topics that might be value-sensitive or that relatively few others in their community are considering independently.

One factor that should influence how much you defer on a given topic is how much groupthink occurs within the discourse on that topic or the communities that think about that topic. Groupthink is where the desire for harmony and conformity leads people to reach a consensus without critically evaluating their position and its alternatives. It's dangerous, as it can lead whole groups of people to believe something false. Some ideas spread because they are well thought out and easy to validate. However, other ideas spread mainly because of a persuasive individual or strong social pressure to agree. Here are some potential warning signs to help you determine if an idea's prominence is due to groupthink or from actual merit:

| Red flags (likely groupthink) | Good signs (likely meritable) |
| --- | --- |
| • The idea is localized to a certain location or social group<br>• The idea can not be easily externally vetted<br>• The merits and weaknesses of the idea are not openly discussed (in a | • The idea was independently converged upon multiple times, using multiple methodologies.<br>• The idea is seen as strong outside of a single social movement |

| | |
|---|---|
| public way), and discussing weaknesses is frowned upon | • Critical thinking is encouraged around the idea |
| • People are *extremely* confident in the idea, even when it's highly counter-intuitive | • There are limited other incentives to support the idea (e.g. financial or status benefits) |
| • Ingroups and outgroups are formed around the idea | • The idea has changed or been improved on over time |
| | • The idea has feedback loops and has been tested by skeptical and critically-minded evaluators |

So before you decide on whether to donate to another foundation or start your own, or before you decide to defer to the views of another grantmaker about a specific grant, ask yourself: Am I really worse-equipped to make the decision? How likely is it that groupthink is guiding the judgment of the decision-makers I'm considering deferring to?

# 2.3. Why start a foundation with a relatively small amount of money?

A discouraging sentiment can often be found in philanthropy: 'Very large foundations have all the impact.' After all, what can a $1m a year donation do if an actor in the space gives 100 times that? Although facing harsh realities is important, we do not believe this is one of them. Foundations of different sizes have different natural strengths and weaknesses, and being big has some major negative trade-offs. Let's look at why small foundations can have an outsized impact:

**1. Small funders play an important role that large ones can't.**

The level of rigor that massive foundations like GiveWell put into vetting projects is hard to compete with. But because they invest so many resources into each grant decision, GiveWell can only consider mature organizations that can absorb tens of millions in additional funding.

But assessing smaller, less mature organizations is also very important because:

(a) If no one supports early-stage organizations, they will never become mature enough for large foundations, and (b) there are likely many extremely impactful opportunities that aren't scalable enough to ever be supported by the largest foundations.

In this way, small and large foundations are complementary parts of the nonprofit ecosystem.

## 2. Foundations can have an impact beyond their funding.

Any foundation has the opportunity to become a thought leader in the philanthropic community. They can put forward new grantmaking strategies that haven't been considered, promote better norms like requiring grant recipients to invest energy in monitoring and evaluation or bring attention to a neglected problem or intervention. This opportunity is available to small and large foundations alike, and foundations can often punch well above their weight. For example, the Mulago Foundation has been a prominent voice in the discourse on increasing the impact of the nonprofit sector, including writing a methodology and publishing free tools to assist charities in defining an explicit strategy to scale.

## 3. Being small comes with other comparative advantages.

a. Generalized staff: Large foundations tend to specialize their grantmaking staff, which has advantages. But the generalists at smaller foundations can better apply lessons from one field to another and fund things that fall through the cracks between specialities.

b. Ability to take risks: Big grantmakers have big reputations and must be careful that grantmaking in one field does not affect their grantmaking in others. This leads them to be more risk-averse than smaller foundations (and some high-risk projects have a very high potential for impact).

c. Ability to capture time-sensitive opportunities: Small foundations are more nimble and less bureaucratic. Hence, they are better able to respond quickly to time-sensitive opportunities, such as natural disasters, a pandemic outbreak, or a sudden policy window. They can also pivot much more quickly if evidence shows that the direction they are headed is not as impactful as previously thought.

Here's an example of when a smaller foundation has an advantage over a large one: Imagine two foundations that both finance microcredit interventions. Foundation A has four staff members, deploying $2m in funding each year. Foundation B employs 30 members of staff and deploys $50m per year. Now let's say a large meta-analysis is done on microcredit (p.s. this analysis really was done).[6] The data results are disappointing, showing far fewer effects than either had hoped for.

What does Foundation A do in this situation? Well, it's a relatively simple process; they gather their four staff together and talk about the findings. Although some of the staff have to update more than others, they each are working in multiple areas, and deprioritizing microcredit gives them more capacity to expand their work elsewhere. They do not have a large number of long-term commitments in the space, and the organizations they fund would survive without them. Relatively quickly, they come up with a transition plan to move away from the area over the next six months.

Over in the office of Foundation B, it's a different matter. 15 of the staff do not do any work in microcredit and thus did not even see the analysis. Of the five staff who read it, three of them are working full-time on microcredit and have been in the field for years. Deprioritizing the area would likely result in them quitting or being fired. In addition, they have made large and public commitments to the area. Moving out of the space would have major ramifications, not just on those they grant to but on the area as a whole. Several meetings later, the director of the foundation makes a call that they will fund their own two-year analysis of the area and re-evaluate at that point. Until then, they would maintain but not grow their grantmaking in the area. If they left the area, they would have a three-year transition period, allowing the field to stabilize without their presence.

These are very different outcomes, even though these two foundations share the same values and respond rationally to the same evidence; one foundation leaving the area fully in six months, and the other staying for at least five more years. This is similar to the advantage a new for-profit startup has over a large, established company.

---

## Making the call

There is a great need for more funders in the world, and there are many unexplored areas where a foundation can make a real difference, regardless of its size. When it comes to choosing how to spend your time and money to have an impact,

---

[6] Justin Sandefur, "The Final Word on Microcredit?" Center for Global Development, Jan. 22, 2015, accessed Feb. 20, 2023, https://www.cgdev.org/blog/final-word-microcredit

we can't prescribe one solution to you – it depends on your circumstances. But if you're in a position where spending your time or money on grantmaking is an option, we strongly encourage you to consider it.

# PART A
# Making Good Decisions

Making good decisions is arguably one of the greatest skills anyone could possess, and it's not difficult to see why. Consistently good or bad decisions add up, leading us to achieve our goals... or leave our desired results frustratingly out of reach. Some people may think they are just not good at making decisions, but the truth is that it is a *skill*. Skills can be learned, even if they do not come naturally. The way to learn how to make good decisions is to learn decision-making tools. Unfortunately, these are not generally taught in schools, but they are concrete life skills that are possible to learn and hone.

A craftsman can possibly make a few items using only a hammer, but to create something truly valuable, they need to expertly utilize a number of tools. To become a truly skilled craftsman, they need to practice and master these tools. In this section, we will discuss the tools your foundation will need to make good decisions consistently.

When your goal is to change the world for the better, there are three types of tools that we recommend adding to your decision-making toolkit:

1. **Forms of evidence** that will point towards the right decision
   *(e.g. the scientific method, rationality, independent experts)*
2. **Ways of aggregating evidence** to choose the best of many options
   *(e.g. weighted-factor models, cost-effectiveness analyses)*
3. **Best practice processes** from the philanthropic sector for decision-makers to use as they progress from idea to execution
   *(e.g. theory of change, monitoring and evaluation, benchmarking)*

We will explore tools from each of these types in detail, but first, let us lay out (a) the benefits of choosing the right tool for the job at hand, (b) why we should use multiple tools, (c) how to strike the right balance between investing in decision-making and execution, and (d) how to tell if we are making good decisions.

## Different tools have different comparative advantages

The comparative advantages of each tool can be broken down into speed, breadth of application, and accuracy.

**Speed** refers to how quickly we can use the tool. If two tools are otherwise equal, but one is faster, using the faster one is better. In many situations, we will only have the time to use quick tools, such as when comparing hundreds of options or making a time-limited decision. In this case, heuristics, discussed in Chapter 3.4, are particularly useful due to the speed with which they can be used.

Most decision-making tools can be used at varying speeds, but increasing speed can make the tool less rigorous. This can impact the tool's usefulness; for example, a five-hour cost-effectiveness analysis (CEA) might be considerably different in usefulness from a 50-hour CEA.

Almost every individual tool can be put on an optimal time curve (how much time will yield the most effective results). For example, spending five minutes speaking to experts will yield almost no information (as you generally will not even be able to contact them in that time). Alternatively, talking to the 51st expert is not likely to yield the same value you obtained when talking to the first three. Many tools will follow a similar trend: put too much time into a CEA, and the returns of a further hour are small; put in a sufficiently small amount of time, and marginal additional hours would make it more valuable.

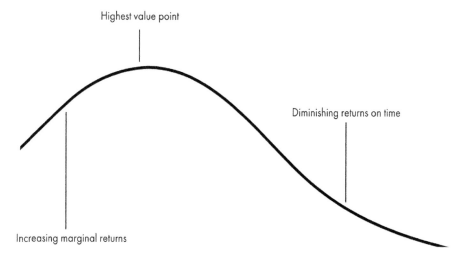

The optimal amount of time to spend using a tool is not easy to determine in the abstract and is likely to vary depending on the experience of the tool user and the complexity of the problem. A five-hour CEA might be overkill for comparing toasters but insufficient for comparing cause areas.

**The breadth of applicability.** The best tools can be efficiently used in multiple situations. For example, interviewing experts is a helpful way to make almost any decision more informed. On the other hand, CEAs aren't particularly helpful when trying to make a philosophical decision about how to trade off the welfare of humans and non-human animals. Tools do not need to be universally applicable. But the more broadly we can use them, the more value we can get from our proficiency in using that tool.

**Accuracy** is arguably the most important quality for a tool but also the most complex. An accurate tool provides a high degree of certainty that our decision is a good one and allows us to make significant updates to our predictions. For example, if we want to know if it will rain, a highly accurate tool might give us a lot of confidence in a prediction – "Oh, the weatherman says there is a 95% chance of rain." Walking to the window and looking to see if there are clouds is still fairly accurate; it's not enough to know for sure, but it does provide some data on the odds of it raining- "Oh, there are clouds, rain *might* happen."

The more accurate a tool is, the more weight we can give it when making decisions. However, it is harder to tell whether a tool is accurate than to tell if it's fast or widely applicable. This is particularly true for situations where the outcome is unknown or has never happened before. For example, if we cancel our picnic plans and it pours down that afternoon, we know our decision-making tool is accurate. On the other hand, we can utilize what we think are the most accurate tools to decide on a career, but we might never know if we chose the truly optimal path.

Trade-offs often have to be made between a very fast but semi-accurate tool and a slow but more accurate one. The trade-off will depend on the importance of the decision, how much time we have, and how many options we are comparing. However, this is not to say there is no overall "strength of tool." We can take into consideration the time taken vs. accuracy; this is shown in the figure below.

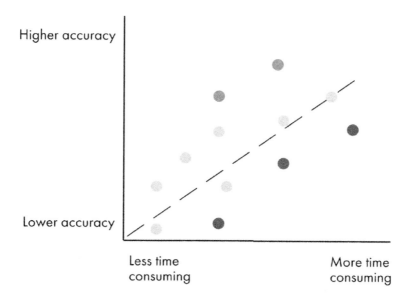

Tools that fall close to the line (light gray) might be considered average. Those above the line (medium gray) are particularly accurate considering how long they take and are highly useful. Tools further below the line (dark gray) are below average – they might take a long time and still not be that accurate. For the purposes of this graph, all tools are assumed to be equally cross-applicable to all decisions.

Determining the overall strength of a tool is impossible to do perfectly, but it's worth spending some time trying. Decision makers all too often rely on informal, unquantified, inconsistent, unconsidered tools. Even an imperfect prioritization based on a short amount of careful thought can point us in the direction of the strongest tools for the decision we face. We can know which to value, when to use them, how to deal with conflicting results, and how much to adjust our thinking after getting data from a tool. A quick sign of a useful tool is if it aligns with more detailed and time-consuming tools. Say, for example, you consistently find that one-hour chats with experts give very similar results to a 30-hour meta-analysis of the research, suggesting that expert chats are very high value considering time vs accuracy.

## Use re-evaluation points to be intentional about 'explore' vs. 'exploit.'

*Abhijeet's foundation was about to make a big decision: which cause area to focus on for the next year. They had done their homework, considered many options, and even made a few small 'learning grants' to test the waters, but pulling the trigger felt like a big step. Abhijeet was both smart and skeptical. Whenever he thought about making a final decision, he froze, unable to proceed. Finally, he made the call and sent the confirmation email, but his heart sank. Had he done enough research? Instead of fully throwing himself into the cause area, Abhijeet spent several months re-considering different options. He eventually decided to switch to something else, only to return to his original decision a month later.*

The world is complicated and always changing, so it makes sense to spend a significant amount of time exploring your options before making a decision. But when it comes to choosing the highest-impact activities or the most optimal projects, it can seem impossible to achieve the confidence needed to pull the trigger. Sometimes new information you gain over time or from further research can make plan A seem better than plan B, only for things to reverse the very next day. This can cause some people to get caught in analysis paralysis or to switch far too frequently between plans, making little progress on each one. To get anywhere, at a certain point, you need to stop exploring options and start exploiting the most promising one. On the other hand, some people can pick a direction and never update their reasoning again, constantly leaving potential impact on the table. So how do you find a balance between 'explore' and 'exploit?'

We can't offer any one-size-fits-all answer to the question of how much to explore vs. exploit. But one thing we can recommend is that you make sure to be intentional about which mode you're in. A solution to this problem is to set planned reevaluation points where you review your project and plan with fresh eyes, looking over all the data you can to see if it is still worth doing. Between reevaluation points, you stick to execution ('exploit') mode. You can set reevaluation points for specific strategic decisions as well as for your overall plan. The right frequency depends on how long you have already worked on one path. It might start as once every three months but double in length every reevaluation until it's once every couple of years. You can set reevaluation points for a specific moment when you expect to be better informed – for example, at the end of a study or program. These points can allow you a deeper level of focus without sliding into questioning the whole project every week. It also still ensures you update appropriately based on long-term trends and evidence.

On some days, ambitious projects will be going great, and you will feel positive. On other days, it will take all of your energy just to stay afloat, and everything will feel like it's falling apart. Days like this will come and go, and although it's great to think carefully about impact if you are constantly reevaluating a project, it will be tempting to abandon it on a hard day. The real trick to holding off from making drastic decisions between plan reevaluations is having strong confidence in your initial decision-making phase so you know you made a good call at the time. This system can save a lot of pain and increases your chances of staying on an impactful project long term, rather than pivoting when you hit the first speed bump.

| Foundation example of re-evaluation points | Re-evaluation points applied elsewhere |
|---|---|
| The project was going terribly, and the foundation staff felt like pulling the plug on funding. However, they had set a plan reevaluation for two months from that date, so they resolutely decided to hit the mark. After two weeks, a few things had changed for the better. By the end of the two months, the project had hit a big milestone that had previously seemed miles away. With clear heads at the reevaluation point, they decided to continue funding the project. | • A manager frustrated with an employee set a reevaluation point to revisit the issue. After reconsidering a few weeks later, they felt confident that letting the employee go would be the right call.<br>• The research team had gotten so caught up in their research that they had not improved or looked critically at their process. A planned reevaluation point gave them a chance to take a step back and correct course. |

## Use iterative depth to explore options efficiently.

When making a decision or evaluating options, hundreds of possibilities can often stretch as far as the eye can see. But we have limited time to explore these options. Iterative depth is a principle that can help us make the best decision possible within our time constraints. The basic idea is to perform a fast and shallow assessment of all the options, discard the worst-performing options, increase the depth, and repeat.

For example, at Charity Entrepreneurship, we face the challenge of narrowing thousands of charity ideas in a given area down to a reasonable number for deeper research. Our solution is to conduct multiple rounds (iterations) of research, sometimes using different techniques, at different levels of depth. As the list slowly narrows, the level of depth increases. We start with a 30-minute assessment of hundreds of ideas, then a longer two-hour prioritization of dozens of ideas, and finally, an 80-hour prioritization of the top five to 10. Each level of depth examines fewer ideas than the previous round but invests considerably more time into each one.

Iterative depth is particularly relevant for some of the common scenarios grantmaking foundations face, such as assessing hundreds of grant applications or candidates for a job at the foundation. In these contexts, we recommend looking for factors that are fast to assess and highly correlated with overall performance, such as a job applicant's performance on the application form. We discuss heuristics further in Chapter 3.4.

## Determining whether we're making good decisions

People are bad at judging how good they are at decision-making. Making a bad decision often feels the same as making a good decision. But there are ways to tell the difference.

**Making predictions** is one of the fastest ways to judge decision-making. Think you've found a way to beat the stock market? Try investing a small amount of money in that system and review the outcome of your prediction. You can also predict simple things, such as the odds of something happening, discussed informally with friends. Try estimating real numbers on these guesses and see how often you are right. If you win so often, your friends stop wanting to play—that's a good sign.

You can also make predictions without any other actors. If you think there are two possible outcomes to a given event, try writing down an explicit probability.

You'll likely find patterns that differ between reality and your predictions. Most people tend to be consistently optimistic or pessimistic in their predictions. Making predictions gives us a constant source of real-world data; just make sure to track them consistently so you notice both the hits and misses, e.g. in a spreadsheet or notebook.

**External reviews:** We might not feel different making a good decision rather than a bad one, but external actors sure will. Ask people you trust as good thinkers and decision-makers to review your process and conclusions. Many careful thinkers will recognize a solid reasoning process, even if they disagree with the conclusion.

Having a trusted external group of decision-makers also provides opportunities for feedback and growth. Keep in mind that our external reviewers won't always agree with all of our processes and conclusions, even the ones that are right. Even the best decision-makers can be biased, wrong, or under-informed. But on average, they'll be a better judge of where we have gone astray. This gives us feedback to improve our toolset and its application, and strongly heeding their advice for issues we cannot rapidly test is a wise idea.

Reviewing other people's work, talking to them, and getting a sense of their processes will also be well worth the time spent for the benefit it provides to our own.

**Results:** Ultimately, even good decision-makers will recognize a simple fact: they won't get every decision right. Luck, both good and bad, will affect them. However, like good poker players, they will do better with the cards they are given than others.

We will now delve into the various tools at our disposal to help us make good decisions. Some you might be very familiar with, while your grasp of others may be a little shaky. Feel free to focus on what is most useful to you personally.

# Decision-making tools explored in this handbook:

| | Tool | Description | Foundation use case examples |
|---|---|---|---|
| **Forms of evidence** | Scientific method | Empirical evidence, analysed with statistical methods as a means of testing falsifiable hypotheses | • Assessing the evidence base for competing interventions<br>• Funding a study to update your confidence in an intervention |
| | Rationality | Think through it from first principles to figure out what the decision hinges on, and what can be easily ruled out | • Systematizing your moral values<br>• Identifying crucial considerations<br>• Crafting a grantmaking strategy based on comparative advantages |
| | Independent experts | Reduce time spent digging into primary evidence by seeking the recommendation of experts whose views should be correlated with the truth. Use them to source new perspectives and test your thinking | • Building a broad view of the current state of resource distribution within a cause area, to identify gaps to fill<br>• Pressure testing a promising idea with a limited track record<br>• Sense-checking a plan/strategy & identifying risks you've missed |
| | Heuristics | Decision-making shortcuts to quickly arrive at a decent first assessment of an option, or to test for factors that rule some options out (e.g replaceability) | • Rapidly prioritizing many grant proposals, interventions or causes (e.g. using ITN & limiting factor)<br>• Using a back of the envelope calculation to sense check an alleged cost-effectiveness |
| **Ways to combine evidence** | Cost-effectiveness analysis (CEA) | Use a detailed, systematic model to estimate the cost per unit of impact | • Reviewing & editing a charity's CEA to assess their effectiveness<br>• Comparing the cost-effectiveness of different interventions |
| | Weighted-factor models | Compare options by scoring them on various uncorrelated metrics, using different forms of evidence, and summing scores such that no one variable dictates the decision | • Comparing cause areas<br>• Comparing grant opportunities<br>• Comparing job applicants<br>• Assessing the success of past grants |
| **Best practice processes** | Theory of change | Causal account of how an organization or project's activities will achieve their stated goal (analogous to a business model) | • Quickly pressure testing the plausibility of a project plan<br>• Identifying key assumptions or areas with weak evidence that would benefit from further M&E |
| | Monitoring & evaluation | Scientifically test the efficacy of an intervention; monitor metrics to measure impact & make ongoing improvements | • Setting minimum M&E standards for grant recipients<br>• Co-designing a RCT to measure a key step in a theory of change |
| | Benchmarking | Quality thresholds for grantmaking decisions | • Deciding if each grant application is good enough to fund<br>• Enabling disciplined grant-making with consistent standards |

# 3. Forms of Evidence

Imagine two charities: Stop AIDS (a made-up charity for illustration's sake) and Homeopaths Without Borders (a real charity, unfortunately). Stop AIDS provides antiretroviral drugs, which are clinically proven to dramatically improve the quality and quantity of life of HIV-positive patients. Homeopaths Without Borders provides "medicine" that has been proven ineffective.[7] Now, we chose an obviously ineffective charity to prove our point, but this isn't an unfair example to use. Sadly, it's the norm for charities to lack any concrete evidence of their impact.[8] Even when charities do use evidence to assess their effectiveness, they tend to rely on the weakest forms and fall victim to confirmation bias.[9] Even worse, there are a fair few charities out there that have been evaluated and deemed not only ineffective but *harmful*. Yet, they're still actively seeking and accepting funding.

Any money spent on an intervention that doesn't work is wasted – money that could have saved lives. This is why we've got to have a high level of confidence that the interventions we support are as well-evidenced as possible and have the highest impact in expectation. At a systemic level, funders also have an important role to play, setting the norms for the strength of evidence required for a charitable project to receive funding.

---

[7] NHMRC, "Homeopathy," Oct. 14, 2021, accessed Feb. 20, 2023, https://www.nhmrc.gov.au/about-us/resources/homeopathy.
[8] GiveWell, "Most Charities' Evidence," accessed Feb. 20, 2023, https://www.givewell.org/giving101/Most-Charities-Evidence
[9] Confirmation bias is the tendency to interpret new evidence as confirmation of one's existing beliefs or theories.

This chapter will explore the most useful forms of evidence for funders aiming to maximize their impact, but first, a brief look at three of the weaker and overused forms of evidence.

**Anecdotes and personal stories:** The weakest and most commonly used in the charity sector. Sometimes called 'case studies' to inflate their perceived credibility, they are almost always cherry-picked and unrepresentative of the norm. That's not to say that personal stories don't have a place in the charity sector. Good personal stories can be extremely compelling emotionally and can be a great way to attract donations for a cause that other evidence already supports. This sort of evidence is best used to understand or explain the narrative of why something (as proven by stronger methods) is happening.

**Case studies:** Whereas anecdotes and personal stories are narratives, case studies are analyses. At their best, they involve using a predetermined methodology to collect and analyze qualitative data (e.g. interviews, official records, news media). They can be useful for showing that something is possible (precedent) and for understanding a context (e.g. the perspectives of individual patients or healthcare providers or the politics or policies in a given country), which can then inform decisions about executing a program in that context. Together, a group of case studies can be useful to set a base rate for chances of success (e.g. for attempts to pass new animal welfare laws). Despite their strengths compared to personal stories, case studies have significant limitations (e.g. they can't prove causation) and should be used cautiously, given their susceptibility to bias.

**Historical evidence:** When used effectively, historical evidence can help identify promising interventions, which can then be subjected to further testing. Sadly, there are significant problems with most historical evidence. In practice, most charities' historical evidence is cherry-picked to support a predetermined conclusion.

Some general characteristics of good and bad historical evidence:

| Bad historical evidence | Good historical evidence |
| --- | --- |
| • Theory before evidence<br>• Non-systematic (researcher's time allocated based on personal interest)<br>• Anecdotal and cherry-picked<br>• Over-confident causal attribution<br>• Only looks at confirming evidence<br>• Example: "Protesting worked for the civil rights movement in the past, so it will work for our cause!" | • Evidence before theory<br>• Systematic (researcher follows a predetermined process)<br>• A large, representative sample<br>• Cautious causal attribution<br>• Looks at confirming and disconfirming evidence<br>• Example: Open Philanthropy's "History of Philanthropy" |

The rest of this chapter will be dedicated to the strongest forms of evidence for funders to add to their decision-making tool kit. Their strengths and weaknesses are summarized below:

| Evidence | Strengths | Weaknesses |
| --- | --- | --- |
| Rationality | • High speed (for making initial progress)<br>• Breadth (applicability, information capture)<br>• Makes intuitions/heuristics explicit<br>• Generates general insights that are broadly useful | • Susceptibility to cognitive biases because (a) it lacks a pre-committed methodology, (b) it overweights personal experience, (c) it's non- numerical<br>• Vulnerable to individual errors<br>• Risks wasting time on intractable issues<br>• Hard to adapt analysis for different values/epistemology |
| Scientific method | • Incredible track record (responsible for many of the largest advances in global well-being seen to date)<br>• Well defined methodology<br>• Auditable by third parties<br>• Causally proximate to the truth (unlike experts for example) | • Slow to make progress<br>• Scope limited to situations where empirical methods are possible and realistic<br>• Expensive to generate new research<br>• Bad incentives lead to bad practices (e.g. insufficient replication studies, p-hacking)<br>• Requires scientific literacy to avoid being misled |

| Experts | • Breadth (applicability, information capture) <br> • Allows for comparison of strategies <br> • Allows for specific plans to be pressure tested <br> • Robust against individual errors <br> • Great at determining the consensus in a given field <br> • Can provide info that's not publicly available <br> • Can direct your search | • Susceptibility to cognitive biases (but less so than rationality), in particular, confirmation bias and groupthink <br> • Lack of transparency of reasoning <br> • Inconsistent and unclear epistemology <br> • Limited specificity and decisiveness |
|---|---|---|
| Heuristics | • High speed (fastest tool to get to an approximate result) | • Limited accuracy <br> • Strong anchoring effect <br> • Potential to narrow one's thinking |

Finally, before looking at these forms of evidence in detail, a note on the importance of falsifiability and on handling extraordinary claims:

Falsifiability: A claim is "falsifiable" if evidence can prove it wrong. In other words, a claim is falsifiable if we can test a prediction, and it is possible for the prediction to be proven wrong/false. An example of a falsifiable claim is "all grapefruits taste bitter" – all it takes is one sweet grapefruit to falsify the claim. On the other hand, "faith can move mountains" is unfalsifiable: if you cannot move mountains, one can say that only shows that you don't have enough faith. Claims that aren't falsifiable are useless; whether they're true or false has no practical implications if they can't produce predictions. "A theory that explains everything explains nothing."[10] To be an excellent decision-maker, it's important that all of your beliefs are falsifiable.

In practice, cultivating technically falsifiable beliefs is the easy part – what's hard is being psychologically willing to let your beliefs *be* falsified when you come across disconfirming evidence. As a result, it's common to see 'unfalsifiable charities' (and foundations) who ignore any evidence against their effectiveness or explain it away with after-the-fact rationalizations.

---

[10] Attributed to Karl Popper.

For example, many studies have shown that microloans don't increase income, and it's better to give impoverished people money with no strings attached.[11] However, microloan charities still exist and either ignore this evidence or say that the real point of microloans is to empower women. When more evidence comes out casting doubt on whether they are even successful at that,[12] they say the point of their services is actually to smooth out income fluctuations. Microloans are technically falsifiable but apparently not psychologically falsifiable for their proponents. They did indeed make claims that were disproven. Nonetheless, the proponents either refused to see the evidence or moved the goalposts, making it unfalsifiable in practice.

Just as scientists had to accept that the world is round, charities and foundations must learn to admit when they realize their interventions aren't working and when their decisions are wrong. To improve the world, we need to acknowledge and learn from our mistakes. Some best practices to keep ourselves honest:

1. **Ensure the intervention has clearly defined success and failure conditions**, so you cannot sidestep confronting failure by later saying it was trying to accomplish something different anyway.
2. **Counter confirmation bias by actively trying to prove the intervention wrong.**
3. **Prepare for the possibility that the intervention doesn't work**. It helps to have a Plan B you're excited about so that you do not feel like the world will end if Plan A doesn't work out.
4. **Get an external review**. It's very hard to evaluate the evidence objectively, but an intelligent third party can be much more impartial than you. (GiveWell is a good example of this.)[13]

**Extraordinary claims:** The more shocking or extraordinary the claim, the stronger the evidence you need to believe it. If someone said they saw a red car outside their window, you would likely take them at their word. But if they said they had seen a red elephant, you would probably want to see a picture.

---

[11] Holden Karnofsky, "Cash transfers vs. microloans", The GiveWell Blog, modified April, 2013, accessed Feb. 20, 2023, https://blog.givewell.org/2013/01/04/cash-transfers-vs-microloans

[12] Sam Donald, "Why We (Still) Don't Recommend Microfinance," Giving What We Can, March 12, 2015, accessed Feb. 20, 2023, https://www.givingwhatwecan.org/post/2014/03/why-we-still-dont-recommend-microfinance.

[13] GiveDirectly, "Research at GiveDirectly," accessed Feb. 20, 2023, https://www.givedirectly.org/research-at-give-directly.

Moreover, if they claimed that seeing red elephants increases life expectancy, you would probably want to see a number of quality scientific studies and a rational causal explanation endorsed by independent experts. This principle is key to considering how strongly to weight a piece of evidence. Two studies may look equally good, but if one makes a far more extraordinary claim, you might believe it far less.

Now that you're psychologically willing to have falsifiable beliefs as well as set high evidence bars for extraordinary claims, you're ready to explore the main forms of evidence to use in grantmaking decisions.

# 3.1. Rationality

## 3.1.1. Role in your toolkit

Like the humble hammer, rationality (i.e. using reason and logic[14]) is a tool that most are familiar with and many will have used, although few are experts. It can be used to make quick progress and is a key tool in building new things. However, people often make the mistake of relying too heavily on it as their go-to tool – as the saying goes, "if all you have is a hammer, everything looks like a nail" – and hammers can cause a lot of damage if used improperly.

Becoming an expert practitioner of rationality is a lifelong undertaking (unlike becoming an expert hammer user). Fortunately though, it is possible to learn techniques that lead to better decisions and tips for avoiding common mistakes in something as short as this chapter.

Rationality has a pervasive role to play in our decision-making about improving the world, but three functions stand out in particular:

**1. Systematizing your moral values:** Moving from abstract moral values to practical decisions can be hard, and rationality has a key role to play. In areas like this, where scientific studies cannot be done, the only way to make progress is by reflecting on our moral intuitions and deducing the underlying principles that they come from.

---

[14] To elaborate, rationality is the cognitive ability that allows one to start with a set of assumptions, and to make deductions and inferences to arrive at new conclusions. It can be contrasted with other ways of knowing, like perception (seeing, hearing etc.) and intuition.

If well applied, rationality can make our value system clearer and more internally consistent. This is relevant for foundations because, as discussed in Chapter 6.1 on values, if you are to help others as much as possible, you will need to decide who it is important to help and what it means to help them- which in turn impacts your choice of cause areas and interventions.

**2. Generating crucial considerations:** Rationality allows us to think through problems and potential solutions and identify the considerations that matter most for the viability of those solutions. We can then dig deeper into these considerations using expert interviews or scientific studies. For example, suppose your goal is to convince people to consume less meat, and you want to assess how valuable it is to appeal to concerns about climate change. In that case, rationality allows you to identify the "small animal replacement problem." This refers to the fact that shifting consumption patterns from larger animals (e.g. cows) to smaller ones (e.g. chickens) can cause a greater number of animals to suffer due to the increase in lives lost for the same number of calories. This should make you think twice about using climate change as an argument against meat consumption; cows may be more emissions-intensive than pigs or chickens. If a person is convinced by the climate change argument, they may just switch from eating cows to numerous small animals. Particularly when you consider that the conditions for factory-farmed chickens and pigs are generally worse than for cows, appeals to climate change could do more harm than good for farmed animal suffering.

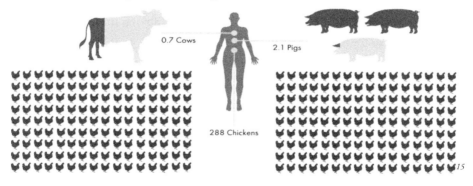

[15] BlitzResults, "Meat-Calculator to Evaluate the Environmental Impact of Meat Consump- tion," March 23, 2021, accessed Feb. 20, 2023, https://www.blitzresults.com/en/meat/ The image here has been altered and is licensed under the Creative Commons Attribution - ShareAlike 4.0 International License. To view a copy of the license, visit https://creativecommons.org/licenses/by-sa/4.0/.

**3. Crafting a winning strategy:** Rationality can be used to think through the current landscape of a given cause area and identify neglected gaps that best match your strengths and resources. This process can allow you to find your comparative advantage in doing good. Rationality is also helpful for thinking through how the various stakeholders in a given cause area are likely to behave in different scenarios, given their goals and incentives, so that you can identify a viable path to victory. For example, in the cause area of farmed animal welfare, you might identify and try to capitalize on the 'radical flank effect,' where the more radical faction of a movement (e.g. the animal advocacy movement) can help or hinder the moderate faction by either making its demands seem more reasonable or by tainting it by association.[16] Another example would be using rationality to identify the counter-intuitive tactic of campaigning for better work conditions for chicken farmers and providing ways for them to transition to farming plants, as this increases the cost of labor and reduces the amount of chicken (and suffering) produced.[17] Once you've crafted a winning strategy, you can use rationality to think through possible failure modes in order to avoid them.

## 3.1.2. Strengths and weaknesses

### Strengths

**High speed:** Rationality can be used to make quick progress when making decisions. One can get a broad topic overview by quickly reading and synthesizing information without a prespecified question list or methodology. We can use rational consideration to eliminate options that won't be viable or identify the crucial considerations that need to be explored more deeply. Rationality is a far faster tool than science and faster than independent experts when we need to come to an initial conclusion on a topic, but slower than experts to come to a comprehensive conclusion.

**Breadth:** Rationality has breadth in two senses; firstly, it can be put to use in some way on nearly any decision. Secondly, it captures a wide range of information

---

[16] Max Carpendale, "Pathways to victory: How can we end animal agriculture?", Effective Altruism Forum, Sep. 14, 2022, accessed Feb. 20, 2023

[17] Robert Wiblin et al., "Leah Garcés on Turning Adversaries into Allies to Change the Chicken Industry," 80,000 Hours, May 21, 2021, accessed Feb. 20, 2023,
https://80000hours.org/podcast/episodes/leah-garces-chicken-industry/.

that would otherwise be missed by other decision-making tools. For example, rational consideration can take into account information such as:

- The argument that lab-grown meat theoretically has a lower minimum cost than factory-farmed meat because you only have to grow the meat product you want instead of also having to grow non-productive parts of the animal (e.g. beaks)
- The "wisdom of the crowds" or Chesterton's fence[18] arguments in favor of an intervention
- The observation that some interventions, like family planning support, might not look like the most cost-effective option when solving for any one outcome (e.g. improved income) but may be extremely competitive when all positive outcomes are taken into consideration
- Informal conversations at a conference that influence our confidence in an intervention - we might not remember the exact combination of individuals who influenced us, but we have gained valuable information nonetheless

Often, formal methodologies and models do not offer a clear way to include this sort of information, even to a small degree. But this data is still important and can lead to differences in researcher-intuition vs. model-based results. Rational consideration gives both time and space to outline this sort of evidence.

**Makes the intuitions/heuristics that already guide our decisions more explicit:** Almost every important decision relies on intuitions, heuristics, or best guesses at key points, but often, they are not spelled out explicitly. Writing out a rational consideration of the options when making decisions is a good way to make these intuitions more explicit. This allows people to pressure-test those intuitions and understand whether and why they disagree. This is beneficial for the person making the decision as well as others seeking to understand it.

**Cross-domain knowledge is generated:** The hours spent in rational consideration, trying to answer a question for a specific purpose, can often end up generating knowledge that can be applied more broadly. For example, the ITN framework (importance, tractability, neglectedness) was the product of rational

---

[18] "Wisdom of the crowds" is the concept that large groups of people may have better sense than individual experts. "Chesterton's fence" refers to the saying, "Don't remove a fence until you know why it was put up in the first place." Essentially, there might be a good reason that things are done the way they are, you just don't know it yet.

consideration and is useful for assessing a diverse range of charity ideas, from improving public schools in England to chicken feed fortification.

## Weaknesses

### *Susceptibility to cognitive bias:*

**Lack of a pre-committed methodology:** It is best practice to have a pre-analysis plan when generating and reviewing scientific evidence.[19] It's far harder and less common to pre-commit to a methodology when it comes to rationality, at least without losing the speed and breadth benefits that make it useful to begin with. As a result, rationality is particularly susceptible to confirmation bias.

**Overweighting personal experience**: If someone has tried an idea or methodology in the past and it did not work for them, this is extremely likely to affect their judgment of similar ideas in the future- even when it should not. For example, imagine your odds of success at an activity are ten percent. Suppose you try once and don't succeed. In that case, this shouldn't significantly change how confident you are in that activity- the odds of success are still ten percent- but in practice, the change in your intuition will often be substantial.

**Non-numerical:** Evidence from rationality tends to be non-numerical. This can result in considerations being weighted inappropriately by those performing the rational analysis and those assessing it. For example, does "Factor A is far more important than Factor B" mean it's roughly twice as important or a hundred times more important? When we do attempt to assign numbers to factors as part of rational analysis, we tend to be scope insensitive,[20] which makes these numbers fairly inaccurate.

### *Structural weaknesses:*

**Often vulnerable to individual errors:** When decisions are made entirely on the basis of a single linear argument, one wrong step in the argument can cause the entire result to be wrong. This means that rationality can be more prone to errors

---

[19] See Rachel Glennerster,"Module 8.3, Pre-analysis plans, Plain," under "Resources," accessed Feb. 20, 2023,, https://rachel-glennerster.squarespace.com/lecture-notes, for a useful Powerpoint and further reading.

[20] Scope insensitivity refers to the cognitive bias where the weight people assign to problems of different sizes is not proportionate with those differences in size, particularly when it comes to very large or very small numbers (e.g. they might treat a problem that affects a billion people as only about twice as important as a problem that affects a million people)

than other forms of evidence. For instance, when consulting independent experts, usually no one expert drastically influences the decision.

**Risk of wasting large amounts of time on intractable issues:** Given this methodology's focus on theoretical issues, it's easy to spend a considerable amount of time on a question that cannot be resolved. Some issues will be important for decision-making but very difficult to progress on; for example, metaethics.

**Harder to adapt analysis for different values or epistemology:** With some decision-making tools, such as cost-effectiveness analyses, it's easy to set them up in such a way that someone with different values or epistemology can change a single input and understand how the results differ. But with rationality, you can't just change a variable in a quantitative model – you often have to start again from scratch.

## 3.1.3. Making decisions more rationally

### Avoiding Biases

Most books or courses on rationality start with a large section dedicated to the many biases and common mistakes the human brain makes. These biases are numerous and damning to our ability to make good decisions. Some are well known, such as loss aversion (the tendency to prefer avoiding losses to acquiring equivalent gains) and confirmation bias (the tendency to look for evidence that favors the conclusion we already have). Others are less familiar, such as the illusory truth (the tendency to believe something if it's said multiple times).

Knowing about cognitive biases is a far cry from escaping them. For every choice, dozens of biases push in every direction, and it's often fruitless to try to determine which option is more biased. The better path is to minimize biases by (a) cultivating attitudes and (b) creating systems that are less susceptible to them.

### *Cultivating less biased attitudes*

In her book *The Scout Mindset*, popular rationalist Julia Galef draws a distinction between two attitudes: the soldier mindset and the scout mindset.[21] When people are in the soldier mindset, they are motivated to defend their ideas against threatening evidence or arguments. When people are in the scout mindset, they are motivated to

---

[21] Julia Galef, *The Scout Mindset: Why Some People See Things Clearly and Others Don't*. Portfolio, 2021

go out and build an accurate map of reality, i.e. to see things as they are, not as they wish them to be. When presented with a piece of evidence that contradicts their current belief, the soldier asks, "*Must* I believe this?" (and if there is any way to justify disbelieving the evidence, they will). The scout, on the other hand, asks, "*Can* I believe this?" (they approach the evidence with intellectual honesty and curiosity about what is true). The soldier sees reasoning as a process of defensive combat, and the scout sees reasoning as a process of collaborative discovery.

To avoid biases, we should cultivate the scout mindset. There are a number of practices that can help with this, for example:

- Trying to notice what mindset we are in during each conversation, so we can change course if we find ourselves in the soldier mindset.
- Thinking about our views in terms of probabilities (e.g. "I am 85% confident that chickens are sentient") instead of binaries (e.g. "I believe chickens are sentient") so that we can make small, gradual (and so less difficult) changes to our views.
- Rather than letting our identities be attached to our beliefs (e.g. "I am a libertarian"), which makes us more likely to fight to defend those beliefs from disconfirming evidence, reframing our identities as being truth-seekers.
- Spending more time with people who practice using a scout mindset, social groups with norms and values of truth-seeking, and changing one's mind based on the evidence.

### Creating processes that reduce bias

We can also add steps to our decision-making processes to reduce bias. For example, we could set a rule that a minimum number of days must pass between first setting out to make an important decision and reaching a conclusion. This can help to reduce the influence of temporary biases on decisions. Galef suggests a number of thought experiments we can include in our decision-making process to reduce the risk of bias:[22]

- **The double standard test:** To avoid tribalistic bias towards our in-groups and against our out-groups, imagine that the person/group in question is a person/group we like a lot less instead. For example, we might imagine they are a member of a political party that we usually disagree with– would we

---

[22] Julia Galef, *The Scout Mindset: Why Some People See Things Clearly and Others Don't*. Portfolio, 2021

make the same decision, or would we judge the person/group by a different standard?

- **The outsider test:** To avoid the sunk cost fallacy[23] or concerns about being judged for changing our mind or admitting failure, we can imagine what an outsider with access to all the same information as us would decide if they took over our role in the decision.
- **The conformity test:** If we find ourselves wanting to make a decision that most people agree with, we may be making the mistake of following the crowd rather than following the truth. To avoid this, we can try to imagine what we would think if most people disagreed instead – would we make the same decision?
- **The selective skeptic test:** To avoid confirmation bias, when we find ourselves dismissing evidence that doesn't support our beliefs, we can ask ourselves – if the evidence supported my belief, would I still dismiss it?
- **The status quo bias test:** To avoid this bias, we consider our current situation and imagine that it is no longer the status quo – would we choose it as the best option?

## Steelmanning

Two common terms used when considering arguments are the "strawman" and the "steelman." Strawmanning an idea is when you consider a weak and often exaggerated version of it that is easy to refute, while steelmanning is when you consider the strongest version of it that is hardest to refute. For example, when one person says, "I think we should regulate the ownership of firearms to reduce accidental deaths and ...," a strawman interpretation might be, "They want to take away everyone's guns because they don't care about people's rights to protect their family." Meanwhile, the steelman interpretation might be, "They want to place some restrictions on the ownership of firearms because they think this will lead to a better balance between respecting people's rights to defend themselves and avoiding unnecessary injuries and death."

If our goal is to make good decisions, we should aim to steelman the arguments for each of our options in order to choose the one that is truly the strongest. Some questions to ask to encourage steelmanning:

---

[23] The sunk cost fallacy is the human tendency to double down on unsuccessful resource investments, even when investing more marginal resources doesn't make sense, e.g. choosing to spend time finishing a boring movie because you've already paid for the ticket.

- What is the strongest possible version of this argument?
- Can I paraphrase a person's argument to them so that they might respond, "That's even better than how I said it"?
- Am I confusing the strength of an argument with the strength of the arguer?

## Epistemic modesty

Epistemic modesty is about genuinely considering the possibility that someone else is right and we are wrong (no matter how correct we feel internally) and acting accordingly. It means being humble about our own viewpoints, particularly when compared to those of someone equally or more knowledgeable on a topic. If we assign an equal chance to our peers being correct as we do to ourselves, we should weight their views accordingly. This is common in some instances (e.g. if a doctor tells us what's causing our symptoms, we tend to defer to their judgment, not our own), but it is not practiced as widely as it should be.

Epistemic modesty is good practice because it ensures that we consider all the options before reaching a conclusion and that we don't place too much emphasis on our intuitions simply because they're ours. It also makes changing our minds less psychologically difficult. Some questions to ask to foster epistemic modesty include:

- Do I act (and not just speak) in a way that shows that I take seriously the possibility that I am wrong?
- When did I last go against my intuition and trust someone else? Is this situation meaningfully different from that one?
- Whose views on this topic (if anyone's) would I weight equally or more highly than my own?

## 3.1.4. Summary

- Evidence from rationality is particularly helpful for the following:
  - ○ Systematizing our moral values
  - ○ Generating crucial considerations
  - ○ Crafting a winning strategy
- Rationality's strengths are its (a) high speed, (b) breadth [both its usefulness across a range of domains and its ability to incorporate a broad range of information], (c) ability to make explicit the intuitions/heuristics that were already guiding our decisions, and (d) ability to generate insights that can be generalized across domains.
- Rationality's weaknesses fall into two categories:

  1. Factors that make it susceptible to cognitive biases, like (a) lack of pre-committed methodology, (b) it overweights personal experience, and (c) it's non-numerical.

  2. Structural weaknesses of rationality, like (a) vulnerability to individual errors, (b) the risk of wasting large amounts of time on intractable issues, and (c) it's hard to adapt analysis for different values or epistemology.

- To make more rational decisions:
  - ○ Avoid cognitive biases by cultivating a 'scout mindset' and creating processes to identify and reduce bias
  - ○ Steelman competing options
  - ○ Practice epistemic modesty

# 3.2. Scientific Evidence

## 3.2.1. Role in your toolkit

Science is the process of gaining knowledge by using empirical observations to test hypotheses about the world, with those observations often being analyzed using statistical methods to arrive at precise conclusions.

Science loves taking things apart and understanding how they work. Scientific progress is often slow and incremental, like tightening a screw. Similar to how there are hundreds of types of screwdrivers, the range of scientific techniques is huge, and they are useful in a wide range of different situations.

The scientific method is probably the most established and proven of the tools that we cover in this book. While you will not be able to learn it as quickly as other tools, e.g. heuristics, it can be used to build a much stronger foundation of evidence and confidence in how the world works.

For most foundations and grantmakers, using scientific evidence will involve interpreting the existing literature on a given intervention to understand its effectiveness. However, foundations have a unique opportunity to fund the creation of new scientific evidence, such as an RCT on an intervention. This can be highly valuable, even if there's already some strong evidence that the intervention has been effective in the past. For example, a new study could take into account metrics that other RCTs do not typically measure, such as subjective well-being, or look into any potentially important flow-through effects.

## 3.2.2. The hierarchy of scientific evidence

There is a hierarchy of different strengths of scientific evidence. When discussing science in the context of effective philanthropy, we are generally referring to the types of scientific evidence towards the top of this hierarchy, such as randomized controlled trials (RCTs) or meta-analyses.

**Meta-analyses and systematic reviews** identify all the studies that satisfy predefined criteria, such as a target population or level of statistical power. They then analyze the dataset and determine which conclusion is best supported by all the currently available studies. We recommend starting with this type of scientific evidence when first engaging with the literature on a given topic.

General standards for meta-analyses and systematic reviews make them more comprehensive and less prone to bias than simply perusing the existing literature according to interest and coming to a conclusion at an arbitrary point. The best charity evaluators, like GiveWell, are very valuable for the same reason. They look at large numbers of studies and put together important overviews that allow others to come to an informed opinion relatively quickly and easily.

**Individual scientific studies** are generally valuable sources of evidence. We recommend digging into this type of scientific evidence when quality meta-analyses are unavailable, when you want to build a more nuanced understanding of a topic, or when you want to pressure-test the evidence more rigorously.

However, different types of studies can vary widely in strength, from randomized controlled trials (the 'gold standard') to observational studies, which are much weaker. Similarly, within a given type of study, the strength can vary widely based on the sample size, the methodology's quality, and the researchers' scrupulousness. Since they vary in quality, do not take the results of individual studies at face value but rather evaluate each one based on its own merits.

## 3.2.3. Strengths and weaknesses

The scientific method is an incredibly powerful tool that propels entire fields forward. The amazing progress of medicine over the years is due in no small part to its utilization of scientific methodology. Breakthroughs like understanding how infectious disease spread used early scientific methods and hypothesis testing to uncover results that were surprising at the time (like cholera spreading through drinking water rather than air). However, like every tool, it has strengths and weaknesses.

### Strengths

**Track record:** Scientific tools have the most demonstrated ability to improve our decision-making. In fact, introducing the scientific method into different fields in the past has transformed many of them for the better – from medicine to psychology, economics, and policy. You can see this in the nonprofit world, too; fields like global health and poverty, which are among the most scientific, are making huge strides.

**Well-developed and well-defined method**: Scientific methodology has been painstakingly developed and documented for hundreds of years and has been a mainstay in key fields like medicine and biology for years. Although it's less common in the charity world, it has rapidly been gaining traction, with the 'randomista' movement[24] in global health leading the charge. Since scientific tools and methodologies have been used for so long, a wealth of information is available on how to use them well.

**Consistent and auditable:** Due to the amount of time and effort invested in developing science as a methodology, it is used relatively consistently (compared to tools like rationality or expert interviews). For example, although there are entire books about how statistical significance is misused, there is at least a high degree of consistency in the relevant terminology and formulae used. The scientific method is transparent and lends itself to third-party review, unlike other processes, such as using reason, which can be quite opaque.

## Weaknesses

While science might be the most reliable tool, it does have weaknesses that mean it cannot be used in every situation.

**Slow speed:** One of the biggest flaws of science is that it can be a very slow methodology, both to learn and to use. Typically, the best sorts of scientific evidence can take years to generate. If it goes through formal publishing channels, it can take years more to be peer-reviewed. The long timeframes involved also create short-term lock-in: A foundation that decides to run a large-scale scientific study to test a certain intervention has to commit to operating that intervention for quite some time without the ability to adapt or change the model during the study if the context changes or new information arises. This can mean that generating new scientific evidence is best suited for a foundation later in its life that can make and stick to longer-term plans. Meanwhile, for those who plan to only interpret existing scientific evidence without generating new evidence, this is still a very time-consuming process to do thoroughly.

**High cost:** Generating scientific evidence is often very expensive compared to other means of making decisions. A weighted-factor model (discussed in Chapter 4.2) can be done by a single staff member with a few months' training. The cost of running a quality study can be hundreds of thousands or even millions of dollars, depending on the context. Often, one study is not enough to make the full case for a

---

[24] Proponents of randomized controlled trials in development cooperation. See the Nobel prize-winning work of Esther Duflo, Abhijit Banerjee, and Michael Kremer; starting point at Ewen Callaway, "'Randomistas' who used controlled trials to fight poverty win economics Nobel," Nature News, Oct. 14, 2019, accessed Sept. 16, 2022,

given hypothesis, meaning this cost ends up being incurred multiple times over. Meanwhile, interpreting existing scientific evidence is still costly due to the amount of labor required to do it well.

**The narrow scope of applicability:** Science can sometimes be limited in the range of decisions it can be applied. Applying the scientific method can sometimes be hindered by high costs and low speed. It can only be used on subjects where it is *possible* to accurately measure and use 'gold standard' practices like randomization and controls for bias. Scientific tools also have little to say about creating hypotheses or comparing the value of different options. They are designed to guide "how" to test a given idea rather than the "what" of which idea should be tested.

Science is also vulnerable to measurability bias, where decision-makers focus on more measurable things, even though these may not be the most valuable or impactful options. Focusing on what can be measured well is helpful to understand our impact as close to objectively as possible. But the fact that something is difficult to measure does not mean it is not valuable. The main thing to keep in mind is that measurability bias can lead to a tendency to only try measuring what is *easy* to measure. We believe that trying to measure difficult things is important to advance our understanding of impact and cost-effectiveness - grantmakers shouldn't quickly accept "it's hard" as a reason for not trying to measure something important.

**Requires scientific literacy to avoid being misled:** As we will discuss below, science can be used to mislead people, particularly when they aren't well-versed in the best practices and common pitfalls.

## 3.2.4. Tips for interpreting science

Scientific evidence, like most other systems, can be gamed and made misleading. Entire books have been written on how to lie with statistics[25], and these are worth reading. In the interim, a few fast tips can help you sort the strong scientific evidence from the weak and apply scientific evidence correctly in your decision-making.

**Check measures of statistical significance:** The p-value (a number aiming to tell you how likely it is that a study's outcome occurred by random chance) is valuable to understand and is probably the most commonly reported measure of statistical significance. P-values of under 0.05 are often referred to as statistically significant,

---

[25] For example, see Huff, Darrell, How to Lie with Statistics, California, Penguin Group, 2009

but this is an arbitrary cut-off point used as a heuristic and should not be used as a binary. The lower the p-value, the more likely a study is to replicate. The more surprising the study's claim, the lower the p-value we need to see to be significantly swayed by it.

**Remember effect size:** When assessing the strength of scientific evidence, people tend to focus on measures of statistical significance and forget about the magnitude of the effect, despite the latter determining whether a scientific finding is actually important. For example, it could be statistically true that eating a certain food reduces the risk of cancer. However, changing your diet would likely not be worth it if the effect size is extremely small. With respect to charitable interventions, it might be true that clean water reduces diseases. But the really important question is how *much* does it reduce them – i.e. what is the effect size?

**Consider external validity:** External validity is the extent to which you can generalize the findings of a study to other situations, populations, or settings. Applying the lessons from a scientific study to the real world almost always involves making generalizations (often unconscious ones) because the real world is almost always different from the circumstances of the study. But not all generalizations will hold. Just as we can't simply assume that an effect observed in a study on mice would also apply to humans, we can't simply assume that an intervention proven effective in one country will be effective in another. The more relevant differences there are between the circumstances of the study and the application, the weaker the evidence that the effect will apply in practice. So when applying scientific evidence, first make all your generalizations explicit. Next, ask yourself: What relevant differences might exist between the context of the study and the context you're applying it to?[26]

**Beware abstracts:** An abstract is a short summary of scientific findings. It is a handy tool for quickly understanding a study. But in its brevity, it can often oversimplify or overstate what the evidence shows. For studies that are really important to your foundation's impact, you will have to dig a bit deeper.

**Beware the incentive for strong, oversimplified claims:** Popular science has a different goal than normal science; its primary goal is to be noticed, read, and remembered – accuracy comes second (or worse). This tends to lead popular science

---

[26] As a starting place for learning more about how assess external validity, see the following resource from the Stanford Social Innovation Review:
https://ssir.org/articles/entry/the_generalizability_puzzle

to make much stronger and less nuanced claims than a proper systematic evaluation because stronger claims are more interesting. A study claiming that "Chocolate is healthy" is far more attention-grabbing than one saying, "Some minor negative effects and some minor positive effects found in mice eating chocolate." This same incentive applies when charities talk about science on their websites.

**Remember 'regression to the mean:'** On face value, an extremely strong cost-effectiveness result in a scientific study looks like evidence of an extremely effective intervention. However, the result could just be an outlier caused by random variance. In general, extreme or very surprising initial measurements tend to become closer to average the next time they are studied. This statistical phenomenon is known as 'regression to the mean.' This should make you very cautious when an individual piece of evidence shows exceptional effects; the more you study the phenomenon, the less likely it will continue to look exceptional.

**Check and correct for biased sampling of multiple effects/studies:** Unrelated variables in data sets can appear to correlate by random chance.[27] Measures of statistical significance, like p-values, help us determine how likely an apparent correlation is to be caused by random chance instead of indicating a true effect. For example, it's common practice for researchers to disregard any apparent correlation with more than a 5% chance of being caused by random chance (i.e. p-value < 5%). However, the more variables you test for correlation, the higher the probability you find one that meets this threshold but is a false positive.

Let's say you are trying to determine the effect of jellybeans on cancer, and you measure and analyze a single variable. You will likely find that jellybeans have no statistically significant effect. However, if you break the jellybeans down into ten groups by color and test each one individually, or if you test the effect of jellybeans on ten different types of cancer, the chance that you find an apparent effect in the data with a p-value of < 5% becomes over 40%! The more effects you look at, the more likely you are to generate false positives. The same applies if you look at ten studies that test for the same effect and conclude that an effect exists based on just one study finding an effect.

---

[27] For some humorous examples, see Tyler Vigen's "Spurious Correlations", accessed Feb. 20, 2023, https://www.tylervigen.com/spurious-correlations

The takeaway: Beware of studies that test for multiple effects or literature reviews that look for one effect in many studies. There are also simple ways to correct this kind of bias, like with a Bonferroni correction.[28]

Some resources to help interpret scientific research (including some upskilling exercises and a cheat sheet) can be found in the online resources at *charityentrepreneurship.com/foundation- program-handbook*.

## 3.2.5. Lessons from science on the importance of replication

Many scientific fields have recently had a crisis, shaking the confidence in studies and the scientific methodology as a whole. It is known as the replication crisis. Hundreds of studies, including some very important ones, were found not to replicate – meaning the same effect was not found when they were tested again by a different scientist. This cast serious doubt on the validity of these studies' findings. It also led many to doubt the strength of the scientific method itself. This latter concern is understandable but mistaken. Rather than revealing a flaw with science as a methodology, the replication crisis serves as a reminder that science, as an institution, does not yet have the right incentives and safeguards in place to allow us to take the results of individual studies at face value. We still need to assess study methodologies carefully for bias, and we need to place a higher emphasis on findings that *have* been replicated.

This lesson on the importance of replication should be applied more broadly in decision-making. If you come across an important finding (scientific or otherwise), looking at it from another angle can be a great way to confirm it. This could be by having an independent third party assess or replicate it (as in peer reviews and replication studies) or by attempting to replicate it using a different approach or another form of evidence. Replication is a highly useful technique to distinguish surprising, true effects from methodological errors, random variance, or biased interpretations of the evidence.

---

[28] See Weisstein, Eric W. "Bonferroni Correction." MathWorld--A Wolfram Web Resource, accessed Feb. 20, 2023, https://mathworld.wolfram.com/BonferroniCorrection.html for a more detailed explanation of the mechanics and further resources

## 3.2.6. Summary

- Science's strengths are its (a) track record, (b) well-defined, consistent methodology, and (c) auditability.
- Science's weaknesses are its (a) slow speed, (b) high cost, (c) narrow scope of application, and (d) requirement of scientific literacy to avoid being misled.
- To gain an understanding of the scientific evidence on a topic, start at the top of the 'evidence pyramid' (with meta-analyses), using individual RCTs to dig into the details as needed.
- When interpreting science:
    o Check measures of statistical power
    o Remember effect size
    o Consider external validity
    o Beware of abstracts
    o Beware the incentive for strong, oversimplified claims
    o Remember 'regression to the mean'
    o Check and correct for biased sampling of multiple effects/studies
- Science teaches us the importance of replicating decision-relevant findings. There are three ways to do this: (a) have a third party replicate it, (b) replicate it using a different approach, and (c) replicate it with a different form of evidence.

# 3.3. Independent Experts

## 3.3.1. Role in your toolkit

No matter how talented we are, we will always need outside help. Great decision-makers know how and when to get expert advice, just as an excellent carpenter sometimes calls a colleague for a second opinion. But when it comes to consulting experts, it's important to choose contacts we can trust and to know which topics to take their advice on. On the flip side, one shouldn't rely on expert opinion alone when making decisions, so it should never be the sole tool used to make a decision. It's also worth considering that if an expert you speak to is the author of scientific papers you rely on, even though speaking to them may deepen your understanding of a topic, it can't be counted as an independent source of evidence.

Independent experts are helpful for decision-makers at charitable foundations for:

a. **Building a broad understanding:** Experts can synthesize a large amount of knowledge into layman's terms. Decision-makers can build an understanding of a topic without having to spend as much time engaging with the primary evidence.

b. **Sense-checking a plan or strategy:** By consulting experts, decision-makers can tap into a repository of professional experience to form a better-calibrated view of whether a plan or strategy is realistic and likely to succeed in the real world.

c. **Reducing the risk that one key mistake jeopardizes our impact:** When decision-makers run their thinking by a diverse group of experts, it's more likely that a key mistake or oversight they've made will be noticed than it is when decision-makers work alone.

Understanding the causal relationship between experts' beliefs and truth is important for understanding the role they should play in your toolkit. Experts are a form of secondary evidence in that their views are based on more primary evidence (e.g. studies they've read, experiences they've had, arguments they've heard), as well as other secondary evidence (e.g. conversations with other experts). The best experts on a topic will be particularly good at interpreting the primary evidence and forming accurate beliefs about it. So we should expect their views to be correlated with the truth. But the primary evidence itself is more fundamental.

Here are some situations where we will need to rely on the claims of authorities or experts:

1. **We can't access the primary evidence**, e.g. we know that the experts agree that global temperatures are rising, but we don't have their evidence on hand
2. **We don't understand the primary evidence**, i.e. it's too technical or subtle for us to follow
3. **Adequately reviewing the primary evidence would be too costly**, e.g. it would take six months to review the data ourselves and come to a conclusion

The first situation is very rare in the internet age. The second situation is relatively narrow. The third is by far the most common.

In practice, even if you've thoroughly reviewed the primary evidence, it is often still worth consulting the experts because you may have made a mistake when reviewing the evidence, which consulting the experts can help you identify.

## 3.3.2. Different types of experts

We can divide experts into three groups: Specialist, domain, and broad experts.

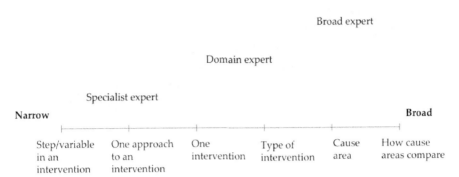

## Specialist experts

Specialist experts have deep knowledge in a very specific context, like a single step or variable in an intervention or one approach to an intervention. These could be factual specialists (who have 'knowledge-that') or practitioner specialists (who have 'knowledge-how'). These types of experts have insight into an element of the intervention but not the whole. They can provide a piece of the picture but not a broad comparison. For example, a specialist in postpartum depression would probably not be able to compare this issue to body dysmorphic disorder and may not even be willing to offer a guess on the relative burden. However, they would be able to provide highly specific information about a specific treatment style for postpartum depression that you have identified as promising.

## Domain experts

Domain experts have broader knowledge than specialists, often having deep knowledge about an entire intervention or type of intervention. They might know about cage-free campaigns for chickens or corporate campaigns for animals in general. But they likely wouldn't be able to compare chicken welfare interventions to fish welfare ones. They also might not be able to give you an overview of the biggest challenges and opportunities in the farmed animal welfare cause area more broadly. Domain experts can be highly useful to speak to after you have selected a cause area but before investing major funding into any one intervention.

## Broad experts

Broad experts can provide comparisons across different domains. For example, another funder who supports half a dozen different fish organizations might have a strong sense of how the issue of disease compares to problems caused by transportation, even if she does not have the same detailed sense of specific diseases as the specialist expert. An example of a broad expert might be a researcher at an evaluation organization, such as GiveWell or the Copenhagen Consensus, or an author on the Disease Control Priority reports. However, they could also be a large funder or cross-area researcher with a good sense of the space overall. These broad experts are the folks who might make a good fit for board members and will be key for both you and your staff to speak to, even pretty early on in your process.

––––––––––

All three kinds of experts can be very helpful but in very different situations. Consulting experts should almost always be one of the decision-making tools used but rarely should hold more than one-fifth to one-third weight in a final key choice. Taking notes on your conversations with experts will give you something to come back to and help you retain their insights. GiveWell has some of the best expert conversation notes in the charity field – it's worth taking a look at their archives.[29]

# 3.3.3. Strengths and weaknesses

## Strengths

**Breadth:** As with rationality, consulting experts is broad in terms of the range of scenarios it's applicable to and the breadth of information it captures. Experts have formed their views from a wide range of sources, ranging from studies to discussions with other experts and personal experience in the field. This reduces the chance that an important factor or perspective is missed. Also, experts sometimes have access to information that's not publicly available at the time, like (a) insights from studies that won't be released for years, (b) controversial opinions they aren't willing to share publicly, and (c) information on what research is in the pipeline.

---

[29] GiveWell, "Notes from Research Conversations," last updated Aug. 2022, accessed Feb. 20, 2023, https://www.givewell.org/research/conversations

**Can directly compare possible strategies**: We can present an expert with highly specific plans and have them compare different elements much more quickly than a more formal model, like a cost-effectiveness analysis, could. If we consider three interventions in three different countries, with three different partner organizations, the number of permutations quickly becomes overwhelming for a formal model. Experts can compare multiple iterations and suggest which combination is best.

**Pressure testing our specific plans:** Scientific studies will provide evidence on a similar scenario to our own and require some generalization to a different location, population, or approach; however, experts can provide guidance on our specific plans while considering the exact details. They can provide guidance on our plans grounded in first-hand experience more readily than rational consideration can.

**Robust against individual errors:** By aggregating a number of independent perspectives, conclusions informed by expert advice are a lot less vulnerable to individual errors than conclusions based entirely on rationality (which often involve a single linear argument) or a single cost-effectiveness model. Of course, for this to work, the perspectives do need to be truly independent (i.e. not all proponents of the same narrow school of thought or students of the same dogmatic teacher).

**Captures field-level convergence**: Speaking to experts can give a sense of whether individuals within a field have a fairly unified view (i.e. if all five experts you speak to agree on a topic) or if there is a lot of disagreement (i.e. five experts give five different answers). Provided the experts reached their conclusions independently, then a high level of convergence can justify higher confidence in their expert view. Divergence helps you identify the crucial considerations that warrant further investigation.

**Helps to direct and focus our search for evidence:** Experts can often provide insight on which experts we should speak to next and which resources we should read. They can also often connect us directly to these other experts and resources. This allows us to only spend time engaging with the most useful evidence. For this reason, speaking to an expert fairly early in our decision-making process can make sense, particularly those with whom we already have relationships.

## Weaknesses

Expert judgment has been found to have a significant number of weaknesses. Studies have shown that in some areas, such as predicting the future[30], "many of the experts did worse than random chance, and all of them did worse than simple algorithms."[31] These concerns limit experts' usefulness and make us confident that they should not be the only perspective used; deference to experts should be limited.

Not all of the following concerns apply to every expert, but they are generalized and will apply to a large number:

**Susceptibility to cognitive bias**: As discussed in the chapter on rationality, a number of cognitive biases affect all humans. Experts are, in the end, just better-informed humans, so they suffer from the same biases as the rest of us. They are distinguished by their particular experience or education on a given topic, not by their ability to assess evidence impartially and avoid motivated reasoning. One mitigating factor is that if multiple experts are spoken to, their biases will not necessarily overlap, and their average quality of judgment tends to be higher than that of a single expert. Still, cognitive biases weaken expert opinions as a form of evidence. In particular:

- **Confirmation bias, resulting in unequal application of rigor**: Experts are often far more rigorous in attempting to falsify claims that conflict with their current viewpoint than with claims that support it. In particular, experts are often anchored to the approaches they've used and the projects they've been involved with in the past and will be unduly skeptical of competing approaches.
- **Groupthink**: This bias, caused by the desire for harmony or conformity within a group, results in group members reaching a consensus conclusion without critically evaluating alternative options. Under the influence of groupthink, group members ignore or suppress dissenting viewpoints. For

---

[30] Here we're making a distinction between subject matter experts, who don't have a great track record at making predictions about their areas of expertise, and 'Superforecasters' (see Philip Tetlock's book about them) who are skilled at prediction in general and have strong track records making predictions across domains.

[31] Daniel Kokotajlo, Katja Grace, "Evidence on good forecasting practices from the Good Judgment Project: an accompanying blog post,"AI Impacts, accessed Feb. 20, 2022, https://aiimpacts.org/evidence-on-good- forecasting-practices-from-the-good-judgment-project-an-accompanying-blog-post/

example, in the case of charity ideas, if an idea has not been previously tested or considered by other experts in their field, experts will often be more inclined to dismiss the idea than they would if the same concept was presented by someone connected to their in-group. Although this is a useful heuristic for experts to use, it can make them underweight new ideas relative to more established ones.

**Lack of transparency of reasoning**: Experts have formed their views using a considerable number of sources and experiences A byproduct of this is that it's often difficult to pinpoint the exact basis for a given viewpoint. This can make it very challenging to confirm or disprove a given idea or to know how much weight it should be given.

**Inconsistent and unclear epistemology:** All experts have had to apply weights to different types of evidence when forming their beliefs, but few have thought explicitly about what their weights should be. Even fewer have made their epistemology public. So while experts are highly likely to have engaged deeply with the relevant evidence, they are less likely to have integrated it carefully or consistently to form a viewpoint.

**Limited specificity and decisiveness**: Our research team has conducted hundreds of expert interviews and found that many experts are unwilling to give specific estimates, such as a percentage-based chance of success. They are also often unwilling to make claims that could be used in other methodologies, such as CEAs, particularly if those claims cannot be anonymized. In fact, experts will often be unwilling to make general evaluations at all – for example, they might be willing to list the advantages and disadvantages of a given intervention but not actually recommend whether or not to implement it.

## 3.3.4. How to know which experts to trust

When wheeled into a hospital with a broken arm, you place your trust in multiple people and establishments. You trust that the nurses are giving you the right medication and that the doctor will make the right call on how to fix your arm.

We defer to people all the time on different issues, whether it's the doctor at a hospital, the weather presenter for the forecast, or a chef on how to cook a new recipe. Even in our own domains of expertise, we often trust others to tell us what the data says because it would be unnecessarily time-consuming to always pore over the data ourselves.

Knowing whom to trust is a difficult and important skill. Trust the wrong person; they can fill our heads with the wrong information. But trust no one, and we have to fix every broken bone ourselves. So how can we determine who is credible and who is not?

There are five main ways to test whether a source or person is worth putting our trust in. In descending order of how good an indicator it is, we can:

1. **Test against reality**
2. **Test against other sources of evidence**
3. **Test expertise on adjacent topics**
4. **Assess their incentives/motivations**
5. **Check for references**
6. **Check traditional signals of credibility**

Each of these is more of a spot check than perfectly predictive, and not all can be done in every case. Over time, as sources become highly reliable, we can use them to check other sources: For example, if we check Cochrane[32] a dozen times and it dovetails with further research, we could eventually start to use it as a reliable source to check others against.

## Test against reality

The best way to test if we can trust a person or source is to test their statements against reality. Say there are two weather forecasters; we are unsure whom to trust. In this case, a reality check is easy. We could compare each of their historical predictions with the historical weather to see who has been accurate more often. This does not guarantee who will be a better source in the future, but it's strongly suggestive. Similarly, suppose a source predicts a certain reality, particularly in an easily falsifiable manner. In that case, this evidence can be used to support or create skepticism for its credibility.

Reality checks can also be used for groups of sources. For example, lots of people go to the hospital with broken arms and generally come out with a cast and an

---

[32] A global independent network of researchers, professionals, patients, carers, and people interested in health.

improved state. Thus, we might generally trust hospitals to fix broken arms, even if we have not checked the specific doctor.

Reality is the ultimate arbiter. It does not matter if one weather forecaster speaks more confidently on TV, wears a better suit, or has a PhD – the one whose predictions more closely correlate with reality is the better source. And if someone systematically makes predictions that cannot be tested against reality - that should urge us to be cautious about taking their claims or predictions at face value, as they are operating without feedback loops.

In the context of a charitable foundation, 'testing against reality' looks like assessing their track record of public predictions and claims and monitoring whether the advice they give leads us in the direction that makes the most sense once we have all the facts. For example, we have checked over a dozen sections of GiveWell's work, often putting several dozen hours of research into a specific claim. Again and again, from our best assessment, it looks like they are correct. Over time, this builds trust, so we can now use GiveWell as a reliable source to check other claims against, thus building a network of trusted sources.

## Test against other sources of evidence

Not all claims can be easily tested against reality, but a large number can be tested against other sources of evidence. For example, suppose we were deciding whether to trust the advice of an expert with no public track record of claims or predictions and who is providing us advice for the first time. Suppose they predicted something we initially find counter-intuitive, like that the population of China will halve in the next 50 years. If, after looking into it, the empirical evidence suggests rapidly declining population growth and the best rational arguments suggest that we should expect such a decline, we might be more inclined to trust the expert.

## Test expertise on adjacent topics

Trustworthy in one domain does not always mean trustworthy in another. Despite the hospital fixing a broken arm, we would be wary of their ability to predict the weather. However, we probably would place quite a bit of trust in their ability to treat a pet dog with a bacterial infection because this is sufficiently similar to their area of expertise. If GiveWell (a trustworthy global health charity evaluator) started recommending charities in an area that is more difficult to measure, like policy or animal welfare, we would be more inclined to trust them – even if we could not yet test their recommendation against reality or other sources of evidence.

## Assess their incentives/motivations

Try to imagine reasons an expert might bend or distort the truth; establish if they have any motive or incentives to advise you in a certain direction that may not be the most impactful. For example, an expert could have the incentive to give advice that points you towards giving more grants to one intervention or fewer grants to a competing intervention if it makes it easier for them to secure ongoing support for their research into that intervention. The most trustworthy experts will be those who have nothing to lose or gain from your decisions.

Often the incentive at play will be subtle, and the experts may not even be conscious of it themselves. For example, a common form of bias that experts fall victim to is to over-prescribe the method they specialize in, far beyond the contexts it's best suited to – in line with the saying, "If all you have is a hammer, everything looks like a nail." The incentive here may simply be the desire to justify the decision to specialize in a given method by concluding that it's the most useful option. Many readers will have experienced this in the context of medicine, where surgeons (to name just one example) often seem biased towards a surgical solution to a problem that could be better solved another way.

## Check for references

It is always worthwhile to ask around for reviews of an expert whose work you plan on using. If other experts who have earned your trust endorse their work, they are more likely to be trustworthy.

## Check for signs of credibility signaling

The last way we can try to get a sense of whom to trust is by looking at generally accepted forms of credibility signaling (e.g. an individual's qualifications, the reputation of the institutions they belong to). This is the most common approach but the weakest single indicator. It has the advantage of being quick, but it's also fairly unreliable compared to the other methodologies. A flashy website with lots of long-form content is a strong signal that a source has invested significant resources in it (funding or labor) but a pretty weak signal in terms of them being trustworthy. Credibility signaling is often where people go wrong with trusting a source – by giving a certain signal far too much weight compared to its actual correlation with reality.

## 3.3.5. How to speak to experts

Experts are, ultimately, just people like anyone else, so most standard conversational rules apply to them. A few elements to highlight are:

- **Be humble:** Often, when talking to experts, they will know a lot about a field but might be pretty worried about saying anything you, as a funder, might disagree with. Come in humble and open-minded, and you will be more likely to get useful responses.
- **Be prepared**: It's important to be prepared when consulting an expert to show that we value their time. If they have written a whole book on a given topic, we should, at the very least, review a summary before talking to them about it. The same goes for website content they have created. In addition to reading content beforehand, you should come prepared with questions and a view on which ones to prioritize or skip if we're running out of time.
- **Ask comparative questions**: Few experts will have a great sense of the probability of something happening or a clear expected value for a given intervention, but they often give excellent answers to more comparative questions. For example, you're more likely to get an answer to "Does X seem like it would cost more per person than Y?" than you are to get an exact number for either.
- **Keep an eye out for potential mentors/connections**: When speaking to experts, keep in mind that we might come across someone who could be a good fit as a potential mentor, particularly if they are very excited about the project and give great advice.

### Note-taking and summarizing

Although recording the interview would be ideal, some experts will be less open if they are being recorded, particularly if it's a sensitive topic. This can be mitigated in part by specifying that the recording will be for internal note-taking purposes only and that we will ask the expert for permission before attributing any claims to them. However, you may ultimately decide that the best way to get the information we need is to not record the meeting and to give the expert the option of keeping certain statements off the record. If you are recording the interview, you can save time taking notes by using an AI-enabled automatic transcription software.

Whether we record the interview or not, we recommend spending 10 minutes after the conversation summarizing the key points into a single page while they're fresh in our minds. You may wish to send a copy to the expert so they can comment if they feel we misunderstood anything. Later, we can synthesize the summaries of each expert interview into a concise summary of the collective expert view. This can include a narrative explanation of the most commonly held views, the most controversial ones, the apparent crux of any disagreements, and a table with a rough quantification of expert opinions.

## 3.3.6. Summary

- Evidence from experts is particularly helpful for:
    - Building a broad understanding
    - Sense-checking a plan or strategy
    - Reducing the risk that one mistake jeopardizes our impact.
- The strengths of consulting independent experts are (a) breadth [both its usefulness across a range of domains and its ability to incorporate a broad range of information], (b) ability to directly compare possible strategies, (c) ability to pressure test our specific plans, (d) robustness against individual errors, (e) gives a sense of field-level convergence, and (f) helps to direct and focus our search for evidence.
- The weaknesses of consulting independent experts are (a) susceptibility to cognitive biases, in particular confirmation bias and groupthink, (b) lack of transparency of reasoning, (c) inconsistent and unclear epistemology, and (e) limited specificity and decisiveness.
- We should determine which experts to trust by testing them. Five types of tests, in decreasing order of predictive power, are:
    - Test against reality *(preferred option)*
    - Test against other sources of evidence *(second best option)*
    - Test expertise on adjacent topics *(third best option)*
    - Assess their incentives/motivations *(always important)*
    - Check for references *(good practice generally, but weaker test than the options above)*
    - Check traditional signals of credibility *(fastest option, but least predictive – beware)*
- When speaking to experts, remember to:
    - Be humble
    - Be prepared
    - Ask comparative questions (to get more concrete when an expert is unable or unwilling to provide a specific number or prediction)
    - Keep an eye out for potential mentors/connections

    Consider whether recording the interview or using an automatic transcription service is likely to affect an expert's candor. If it is, we may be best off taking notes in real time.

# 3.4. Heuristics

## 3.4.1. Role in your toolkit

Sometimes we don't have time to use our most rigorous and accurate tools, but we still need to get to an outcome that is 'good enough.' In such cases, our metaphorical craftsman might reach for a chisel. She can use it to make quick progress, carving down a marble slab to a rough but passable version of the final design. Later, if needed, she can pull out the more precise tools and refine this first version into something more accurate and robust. In the context of decision-making, heuristics are our chisel.

Heuristics are mental shortcuts; simple rules or frameworks, based on past experience, are applied to new problems to reach passable solutions, despite time constraints. For example, at Charity Entrepreneurship, we have a heuristic for being frugal without investing too much time comparing options: "Buy the best product in the lowest cost tier." This heuristic is based on our experience that the very cheapest products have often cut too many corners, and the products beyond the low-cost tiers generally don't have enough extra value to justify the extra cost. Even though the heuristics are not always correct, they will be correct more often than any other decision-making method could be under the same time constraints.

Heuristics are helpful for decision-makers at charitable foundations for:

a. **Rapidly screening many grant proposals, interventions, or cause areas:** There are many options of cause areas to focus on, and the number of interventions or grants to fund is vast. It's not practical to consider every possible option in depth. The heuristics discussed in this chapter help decision-makers figure out which options can probably be discarded and which look attractive and should be prioritized for further investigation.

b. **Sense-checking numbers:** When encountering a surprising number in a scientific study or a charity's impact estimates, the 'back of the envelope calculation' heuristic can be used to quickly indicate whether the number is suspicious and requires extra scrutiny.

c. **Managing some risks to impact:** Certain heuristics, like considering counterfactuals and checking for negative side effects, help to catch risks that threaten a foundation's impact and can be applied to almost every decision a foundation makes without slowing things down significantly.

A craftsman who doesn't have a chisel in their toolkit will produce very little and miss deadlines, but a craftsman who *only* has a chisel will produce many defective products- and none that are truly excellent.

Many useful heuristics can be incorporated into your decision-making; this chapter will focus on some of the heuristics that are particularly important for grantmakers.

## 3.4.2. Strengths and weaknesses

### Strengths

**High speed:** The primary strength of heuristics, which justifies their use, is their ability to make fast evaluations.

**Able to embed a principle:** Heuristics are a great way to make a complicated principle clear and memorable for everyone in an organization, which helps with the challenge of keeping a large organization moving in one direction.

**Can build up over time:** Like collecting methodologies, over time, we can collect specific heuristics from many different disciplines to be used in new and novel situations. Reading a book like Ray Dalio's *Principles* can distill a lifetime of heuristics from finance, many of which can be directly applied to grantmaking.

## Weaknesses

**Limited accuracy:** Heuristics' speed comes with a trade-off in accuracy. Even if we combine heuristics with other tools to compensate for this, because those tools will only be applied to the most promising options, some great options will already have been discarded.

**Anchoring effect:** When evaluating options, decision-makers have a tendency to become overly anchored to the results they get from using heuristics. They can be resistant to updating their views when further evidence pushes in a different direction to the heuristic.

**Can narrow one's thinking:** The use of heuristics can lead decision-makers to spend less time looking for other considerations or considering other perspectives when assessing options.

# 3.4.3. ITN framework

The ITN framework (Importance, Tractability, Neglectedness) is an example of a very useful heuristic to compare different issues or causes. Looking into these three traits specifically can help you quickly ascertain the likelihood of cost-effective funding opportunities in this area:

| Trait | Definition | Correlation with cost-effectiveness |
|---|---|---|
| IMPORTANCE | How many beings are affected, and how significant is the effect? *(e.g. while depression inflicts intense suffering on ~5% of adults, psoriasis inflicts relatively mild discomfort on 0.2%)* | There are often economies of scale in addressing large-scale or densely concentrated problems. Also, for two interventions with a similar cost per person, the one that solves a bigger problem for those people will do more good per dollar. |

| | | |
|---|---|---|
| **TRACIBILITY** | How easy is it to make progress in the area?<br><br>*(i.e. do effective interventions exist? are they easy to execute successfully?)* | If the best ways to solve a problem are resource intensive or have a high chance of failure, the problem itself is less likely to be cost-effective to solve |
| **NEGLECTEDNES** | How much attention is paid to the issue?<br><br>*(i.e. how much money is being spent on it, and how many organizations and staff are working on it?)*[33] | Overlooked areas are likely to have more low-hanging fruit in terms of cost-effective ways to do good. |

This framework has the benefit of being fairly intuitive. It is also useful for making a first comparison of a wide range of disparate problems (from lead pollution to violence against women). We support the use of this framework as part of an early assessment of problems or cause areas, but only in combination with other considerations (like limiting factors– discussed below – which reduce the addressable scale of the problem).

We'd also caution against misuse of this framework, in particular the common mistake of using ITN to assess solutions (rather than problems for which it was designed) and continuing to use ITN assessments when more precise evidence is available (e.g. once we have a strong scientific study on the cost-effectiveness of bednets to prevent malaria, our early heuristic judgment is far less relevant).

ITN is very useful, but it has some limitations to be aware of:

**Decreasing marginal returns aren't consistent across the cost curve:** Neglectedness is included as an indicator of cost-effectiveness because of the following logic: If each marginal dollar spent on a problem is used on the most cost-effective option available, then the pool of remaining options will become less cost-effective with each marginal dollar. Whilst this is accurate enough in most cases, it

---

[33] It's important to keep in mind that even if massive organizations are spending billions on a problem, if they're not effectiveness-focused (i.e. trying to do as much good as possible based on the best evidence available) then the problem should still be considered neglected, as the low-hanging fruit remain to be picked by effectiveness-focused actors.

ignores the fact that the most neglected issues may require spending on enabling infrastructure before the low-hanging fruit can be picked. Sometimes spending also removes bottlenecks to greater efficiency, and sometimes payoffs only occur towards the end of solving a problem.

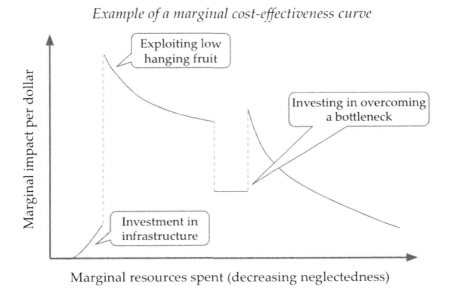

*Example of a marginal cost-effectiveness curve*

**Neglected problems may be neglected for a good reason:** Sometimes, a problem is neglected because there is a high risk of causing harm by working on it or because it is too controversial. As such, neglectedness may not always be a good thing.

**Small scale might not need to be a dealbreaker:** A small problem would score poorly on 'importance' and may score poorly on ITN. But often, there are relatively small-scale problems where good can be done very cheaply (e.g. eradicating an infectious disease in a small island nation or outlawing the sale of foie gras). It's understandable why ambitious altruists want to prioritize big issues; they allow for economies of scale, and piecing together hundreds of small, cost-effective problems to absorb a very large amount of funding is impractical. However, these opportunities may be worthy of consideration for a foundation with a relatively small amount of funding.

**The three factors are interdependent, causing a risk of double counting:** An issue may be neglected because it's intractable. It may be intractable because it's so neglected that there's no expertise or infrastructure to use to work on it. It may be important because it's so neglected that the problem has become particularly acute.

This dependence can lead to double-counting of reasons to work on a given problem or not.

## 3.4.4. Limiting factor

Some cause areas and interventions can look very important due to the very large scale of the problems at hand, such as the far future or wild animal suffering. There is no doubt that the magnitude of an issue can suggest that it would be very promising to fund: a larger problem suggests a potential for a large impact. But there are often other factors that will limit the amount of possible impact to a fraction of the issue's total scale. For example, the issue of existential risk from artificial intelligence is arguably massive in scale. But the limiting factor is the number of people with the right technical skills to work on it. Funneling large amounts of additional funding into this issue because of the large scale may then be a mistake if it does not take into consideration the limiting factor of talent.

To be clear: For some organizations, the limiting factor might be the scale of the issue. An organization working on a nearly-eradicated disease might find its limiting factor to be just how much more of the problem is left to deal with. However, this is generally not the case. The limiting factor is more often something else, like funding, talent, or infrastructure.

- **Funding:** Giving a seed grant to a charity working on a very large issue may not be a wise investment if they won't be able to garner enough funding in the future from governments, private foundations, or donors to reach the scale where they become highly cost-effective.
- **Talent:** The size and quality of the pool of willing workers with the appropriate skills (e.g. technical skills, management, entrepreneurial skills, research skills) can limit how much of an issue can be addressed.
- **Infrastructure:** For a charity that distributes bed nets to prevent malaria, do adequate roads exist to reach those in need? For an organization researching how to increase the effectiveness of mass social movements, do the right forums exist to disseminate their findings and influence actors?
- **Proven interventions:** Issues like wild animal suffering or risks from supervolcanoes might be large, but do we know of any effective measures that can be taken to address them?

- **Technology:** Does the solution require technical solutions that don't exist yet? (e.g. cultured meat may be limited by tissue engineering technology.)
- **Policy windows:** Will an upcoming change of political party in power render an intervention untenable?

Let's consider the example of surgery in low-and middle-income countries, as analyzed by GiveWell.[34] Thinking purely about scale, one might reason that since a ton of surgeries remain to be done, this is a worthwhile issue to focus on. A limiting factor model would suggest that an attempt to address this issue would be quickly capped by the number of surgeons. Below is a very simplified comparison of vaccinations and surgeries using a limiting factor model.[35]

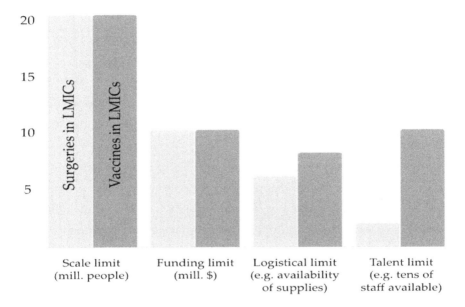

A scale model would only take into account the leftmost column in the bar chart – the size of the problem. The limiting factor model shows that although the scale is similar, surgeries are limited by the talent pool far sooner than vaccinations hit their limiting factor. And both are limited several times before their problem's scale limit. In this case, scale does not matter if a new charity will be stopped by talent, logistics, and funding before they can help even a fraction of the people affected. The

---

[34] GiveWell, "Developing-world corrective surgery," 2010, accessed Feb. 20, 2023.
[35] These numbers are estimates based on our work and research in these areas. The magnitudes of the categories are set to be more cross-comparable (e.g. 1 million compared to 10 full-time staff).

importance of a charity getting funded in this area is not directly connected to the scale of the problem.

As this example shows, considering scale alone will lead to poor decisions when deciding which issues are the top priorities to work on. What really matters is how much impact can be achieved by addressing the limiting factor and at what cost. Suppose the limiting factor in a given field is talent. If we were to address that limitation (e.g. by funding training in that field), how much of the issue would then be able to be addressed before hitting the next limiting factor? What would the next limiting factor be, and how difficult would it be to overcome?

## 3.4.5. Counterfactuals (aka Replaceability)

Counterfactuals are connected to, but distinct from, 'neglectedness' – one of three factors in the ITN framework.[36] If we funded a project bringing chlorine to a village in rural Kenya with no safe water source, we would probably feel like we'd accomplished some good in the world. If, on the other hand, we funded a project bringing the same gift to the average Swedish city, they'd probably give us a funny look – they already have chlorinated water.

This heuristic is widely applicable; when deciding to take any action, it's *always* valuable to consider what would happen if we do nothing. Sometimes figuring this out is easy, but sometimes things are more complicated. For example, when considering corporate cage-free campaigns as an intervention,[37] the counterfactuals aren't as simple as "were it not for these campaigns, Corporation X would have continued to use eggs from battery cages forever." They might have made the change anyway due to growing consumer concern for animal welfare or due to government regulation. Maybe they would have transitioned away from using eggs altogether because of a change to their menu. Perhaps they would have gone out of business.

---

[36] The distinction between neglectedness and counterfactuals is that the former is abouthe tendency to see diminishing returns as more resources are invested into an area and the low-hanging fruit opportunities are picked, while the latter is about the possibility that investing resources into a specific opportunity won't have any impact at all, because that opportunity will receive resources from someone whether you are involved or not.

[37] This is a popular intervention in the animal welfare cause area, where advocacy groups pressure corporations that use eggs in their supply chain to pledge to transition to cage free (higher welfare) eggs by a certain date.

Perhaps chicken farmers are on the verge of a technological breakthrough, meaning battery cages aren't the most cost-effective option anymore.

For this reason, it often makes the most sense to think about counterfactuals in terms of a number of scenarios that each have probabilities assigned to them. We don't need to consider every possible scenario; the granularity of our scenario analysis can scale with the complexity of the situation and how high the stakes are. Of course, the scenarios where the problem goes away don't mean that cage-free campaigns have no impact – they still have the impact of speeding up the solution by years, preventing a lot of suffering.

## 3.4.6. Back-of-the-envelope calculations (BOTECs)

Back-of-the-envelope calculations (also known as Fermi estimates) are rough calculations used to make quick quantitative estimates, aiming to be accurate to the nearest multiple of 10. They can be used by foundations to get a quick sense of the relative scale of different issues and to sense-check numbers put forward by other organizations, experts, and scientific studies or by members of their own teams.

The steps for BOTECs are as follows:

1. **Identify the quantity that we want to estimate.** For example, this could be the number of people affected by a problem, the cost-effectiveness of an intervention, or the impact (in dollars equivalent) of publishing a piece of research.
2. **Break the problem into smaller parts** that can be more easily estimated based on your knowledge and quick desk research. For example, suppose we are trying to estimate the addressable population for a mental health app in Brazil. In that case, we might break it down into the population of Brazil, the percentage with access to smartphones and the internet, and the percentage with relevant mental health issues.
3. **Estimate each of the smaller parts** using any relevant information at our disposal.
4. **Use simple math to combine our estimates** for the smaller parts to get an estimate for the target quantity.

This process is simple and intuitive, but breaking the problem down into parts that are easier to estimate is a skill that takes practice. When relevant data is particularly scarce and hard to estimate, we may need to use a bottom-up method instead, starting with the numbers we have and seeing if we can combine them to estimate the target quantity.

For particularly uncertain variables, it's helpful to run the calculation with a confidence interval, e.g. suppose we're ~90% confident that the population of London is between 5 million and 15 million. Putting that range into a model can give a sense of the possible outcomes.[38]

---

[38] If you need a specific value, rather than a range, you shouldn't take the mid-point, because this isn't conducive to the goal of estimating to the nearest order of magnitude. For example, the midpoint of 2 and 500 is 251, which is within an order of magnitude of the upper bound, but more than two orders of magnitude larger than the lower bound. Instead, you should take the geometric mean , which is ~31.6 and is roughly one order of magnitude from either bound. See the post on 'Fermi Estimates' by 'lukeprog' on the forum LessWrong for more tips on BOTECs.

## 3.4.7. Summary

- Heuristics are particularly helpful for:
    - o Rapidly screening many grant proposals, interventions, or cause areas
    - o Sense-checking numbers
    - o Accounting for certain risks (like replaceability and unintended downsides)
    - o Embedding a decision-making principle throughout your organization
- The key strength of heuristics is their high speed. The weaknesses are (a) limited accuracy, (b) their strong anchoring effect, and (c) their potential to narrow one's thinking.
- The limiting factor heuristic is useful for adjusting our view on the scale of a problem or intervention to account for factors that will limit how much of the total problem can be addressed before hitting a bottleneck, like (a) funding, (b) talent, (c) infrastructure, (d) proven interventions, (e) technology, or (e) policy windows.
- The ITN (importance, tractability, neglectedness) heuristic is a useful framework for estimating the relative cost-effectiveness of spending resources on a given problem.
    - o It should be used for an early assessment of problems, but it's important to consider limiting factors (either under 'importance' or 'tractability')
    - o Once we've started comparing solutions to problems or have firmer cost-effectiveness estimates, ITN is far less relevant.
- Back-of-the-envelope calculations are useful for sense-checking numbers or forming our own views of a roughly estimated quantity, like a cost, a population size, or the impact of an intervention.

# 4. Ways of Aggregating Evidence

So far, we've discussed four forms of evidence, their relative strengths and weaknesses, and how to use them. But important decisions should draw on multiple types of evidence and lots of it, so we need to know how to aggregate it.

**Look for a convergence of evidence.** It's extremely rare to find a piece of evidence that we can be 100% confident in. Therefore, to reduce the chances of making the wrong decision, we recommend looking at multiple pieces of evidence and seeing whether they converge on a given decision being sound. If they do, the chances are far lower that this is the wrong decision. The value of convergent data is partly why replication studies are done.

It's all the more powerful if these pieces of evidence come from different *types* of evidence. This can help compensate for weaknesses, blindspots, and potential groupthink within each type of evidence. For example, suppose experts, rational arguments and a scientific study all suggest that a certain charity is likely to be high-impact. In that case, we can be more confident in that conclusion than if a single rational argument were used.

**Be aware of diminishing returns.** Looking at a decision from more angles and using different forms of evidence improves our chances of finding the truth. But it's also likely that the benefit of convergence between different angles also hits diminishing returns at some point.

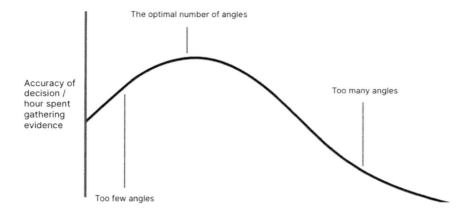

**Be systematic – i.e. use a tool.** When it comes to aggregating different pieces of evidence to make a decision, several tools for the job will ensure that we are being systematic in our approach. In this section, we will discuss two such tools: cost-effectiveness analyses and weighted-factor models.

# 4.1. Cost-effectiveness analysis

## 4.1.1. Role in your toolkit

When we want to produce a single numerical output from all the information we have about something, the tool we reach for is a calculator. Cost-effectiveness analyses (CEAs) are the grantmaker's calculator. Commonly used in economics, health policymaking, and charity evaluation, CEAs calculate the ratio of the cost of a given action or intervention relative to its modeled impact. Cost is usually measured in dollars, with impact measured in concrete terms (e.g. lives saved) or more abstract ones (like Disability-Adjusted Life Years).

Imagine two charities that have been modeled with a CEA. One can train one guide dog to assist one blind person for each additional $1,000 donated. The other can perform one vision-restoring cataract surgery for each additional $35 donated. While these are two very different interventions because they are both fundamentally aimed at alleviating blindness, we can use cost-effectiveness analyses to decide that funding cataract surgeries is a far more efficient way to achieve that goal.[39]

CEAs are a particularly useful item in a grantmaker's toolkit because they can aggregate all of the information you have about an intervention, such as the results of scientific studies, probabilities and scenarios from experts, and heuristics, like replaceability, into a single number. This allows you to easily compare interventions with each other. But like a calculator, the single numerical output of the CEA tends

---

[39] Boris Yakubchik, "It is Effectiveness, not Overhead that Matters," The 80,000 Hours Blog, Nov. 4, 2011, accessed Feb 20, 2023

to inspire a greater sense of trust than can be justified. After all, a calculator's outputs are only as good as the quality of its inputs, and its calculations are very sensitive to user error. Therefore you should check your own and others' calculations twice and sense-check the results against trusted data points.

**Cost-effectiveness estimates should play an important but limited role in grantmaking decisions.** It is important to distinguish between the true cost-effectiveness of an action and the modeled cost-effectiveness. The true cost-effectiveness of an action – if known – could be weighted very heavily when making a decision. However, we generally lack important data about the world and have various uncertainties. The closest we can usually get to the true cost-effectiveness of an intervention is through constructing a model – an imperfect estimate. It's important to remember the saying, "all models are wrong, but some are useful".

Sadly, low-evidence CEAs are almost always overly-optimistic and regress to the mean when further depth is put into them. This is part of why both GiveWell and CE are far less excited about a highly-speculative CEA that looks promising than one that's been conducted more deeply. Given their limitations, it is important to only use CEAs in conjunction with other methodologies, looking for options that look strong from multiple perspectives. We expect CEAs to be more useful in areas where quantitative differences can be very large, where analysis based on our other evaluative criteria is less reliable, and where objective data and strong evidence are available.

# 4.1.2. Strengths and weaknesses

## Strengths

**Enables comparison of options in terms of impact; our fundamental goal**: Ultimately, the question ambitious foundations need to answer is how to have the most impact possible with finite financial resources. A CEA may be an imperfect model, but it speaks directly to our key question by quantifying the impact-per-dollar of each option so that we can choose the best one. Out of all of our decision-making tools, it has the clearest theoretical correlation with good done, even if model errors weaken it in practice.

**Enables formal sensitivity analysis**: A sensitivity analysis can locate the most important assumptions, variables, and considerations affecting the endline conclusion – the factors that could most radically change the amount of good achieved. Formal sensitivity analysis can be done quickly and easily on a CEA, showing the key parameters most important to get right.[40]

**Transparency**: With all the variables and formulae on display, an outsider can tell what factors are reflected in the output and how. Meanwhile, with each variable clearly quantified and sources attributed, an outsider can understand the evidence the decision is based on and where assumptions are made. This makes it easier for them to sense-check the decision and to understand why it might deviate from their own.

**Scope sensitive**: Humans are notoriously bad at properly understanding scope,[41] so it's a major concern that many non-CEA models don't explicitly reflect it. An expert may tell us that one intervention is "far, far better" in one dimension than another, but unless we explicitly quantify that in a model, we're unlikely to capture the significant difference between being 100x better or 1000x better in that dimension.

## Weaknesses

## Vulnerable and prone to single errors:

- **Individual CEAs are vulnerable to errors:** Most CEAs are structured as linear calculations, such that a single error can massively distort the outcome. For example, GiveWell once found five separate errors in a Disease Control Priorities DALY figure for deworming that contributed to an overestimation of the intervention's cost-effectiveness by one hundred times.[42]
- **Individual CEAs are error-prone:** Single errors are common, even among the most rigorous modelers (see the example above). In fact, because rigorous modelers tend to produce more thorough and complex models, their models have a greater number of variables and formulae in which to make errors, and it is more difficult to find these errors.
- **Aggregating CEAs is particularly vulnerable to errors:** Perhaps even more concerning than the risk that individual CEAs have errors is the risk that those CEAs are the ones that end up guiding decisions. When decision-makers optimizing for cost-effectiveness review the outcomes of many CEAs,

---

[40]Ozzie Gooen, "Visual Sensitivity Analysis in Guesstimate," The Guesstimate Blog, May 17, 2016, accessed Feb. 20, 2023

[41]Wikipedia, "Scope neglect," last modified Jan. 29, 2023, accessed Feb. 20, 2023

[42]Alexander Berger, "Errors in DCP2 cost-effectiveness estimate for deworming," The GiveWell Blog, Feb. 3, 2014, accessed Feb. 20, 2023

they select outliers in the option set. But outliers can be caused both by outlier cost-effectiveness and modeling errors. Depending on the underlying distributions, this can result in optimizers systematically selecting for results with errors (this formally proven phenomenon is called the 'optimizer's curse')[43]

Overweighting CEAs in our decision-making could lead you to neglect good opportunities that did not have as many favorable errors.

**Slow**: Properly creating or reviewing a CEA is very time-consuming, especially compared with weighted-factor models (another method for aggregating evidence discussed in this section).

**Can depend heavily on subjective value judgements**: It is surprising how much value judgments can differ. For example, GiveWell assumes that the "value of averting the death of an individual under five [years of age]" is 50 times larger than the value of "doubling consumption for one person for one year."[44] Reasonable estimates could vary by a factor of ten in both directions. The best CEAs make these value judgements explicit and allow users to edit them to match their own values. But nonetheless, it means that the results of many CEAs can't be generalized – they need to be understood with reference to the underlying values of the modeler. This makes comparisons between the results of CEAs from different organizations particularly fraught.

**Inefficient at capturing multiple effects, so often neglect indirect effects**: CEAs work well when the majority of an intervention's costs and benefits come from a single direct effect. Unfortunately, effort scales roughly linearly with the number of additional effects we model. Meanwhile, indirect effects are often more complicated to model and numerous than direct ones. As a result, CEAs are less efficient at modeling interventions that are effective via a number of effects (like family planning, which likely influences maternal health, children's health, family economic outcomes, animal welfare, and environmental outcomes). Ultimately, these more complicated interventions end up having a smaller percentage of their cost and

---

[43] James A Smith, Robert Winkler, "The Optimizer's Curse: Skepticism and Postdecision Surprise in Decision Analysis," Management Science 52, no. 3 (March 1, 2006): 311–22, accessed Feb. 20, 2023, https://doi.org/10.1287/mnsc.1050.0451.

[44] GiveWell, "Research on Moral Weights - 2019," 2019, accessed Feb. 20, 2023

benefit included in the model, leading to unfair comparisons with interventions with simpler effects.

————————

Concerns with reliance on CEAs in charity evaluation have been discussed in depth elsewhere. For further reading, we recommend GiveWell's discussion of the theoretical concerns[45] and Saulius Šimčikas's exposition of practical concerns.[46]

## 4.1.3. Creating CEAs vs. reviewing others'

It's best practice for most foundations to incorporate formal cost-effectiveness analysis into grantmaking decisions, especially those involving large amounts of funding. But should you do the cost-effectiveness analysis yourselves or review the work of others? There are significant trade-offs involved in this decision.

### Trade-offs

There are a number of clear costs associated with creating CEAs yourself:

- **Slower speed:** Whilst reviewing a CEA properly is time-consuming in its own right, creating one from scratch is generally far slower. This can be a problem when you have a time-sensitive funding decision to make.
- **Higher cost:** The amount of labor required to create a CEA means high costs. Even if your organization is willing to devote the capacity to creating a CEA, you may not actually have the capability in-house, in which case you'll need to develop it, hire it, or pay an independent third party to create it on your behalf. This last option carries with it many of the costs of reviewing the existing CEAs of others.
- **Less access to information** (sometimes): As an outsider, you'll typically have poorer access to primary data on an intervention than those conducting the intervention themselves. To the extent that you rely on others to provide you with that data, you are exposed to the risk that they cherry-pick data that will lead you to judge them favorably. Of course, this only applies to

---

[45] Holden Karnofsky, "Why we can't take expected value estimates literally (even when they're unbiased)," The GiveWell Blog, July 25, 2016, accessed Feb. 20, 2023

[46] Saulius Šimčikas, "List of ways in which cost-effectiveness estimates can be misleading," Effective Altruism Forum, Aug. 20, 2019, accessed Feb. 20, 2023

interventions already being implemented – if it's a new idea, you may be in just as good of a position as the implementing organization.

But there are also clear benefits:

- **Better incentives**: Organizations seeking funding have an incentive to arrive at positive conclusions when analyzing their own cost-effectiveness. Even well-meaning organizations that seem to have impact as their primary goal are susceptible to bias. This applies less when using the CEA of an independent organization, like GiveWell or an academic institution, but you should still be mindful of their incentives as well.
- **Avoids adopting others' implicit assumptions:** High-quality CEAs will make their assumptions as explicit as possible, but no CEA is perfect. As a result, using the CEAs of others often means adopting their implicit assumptions unless you're able to catch them during the review process. These assumptions can be about the facts; for example, an independent reviewer of GiveWell's CEA of unconditional cash transfers found that they were implicitly assuming that the portion of cash transfers that isn't invested is consumed in one year.[47] These assumptions can also be moral, like assigning no value to changes in the number of people who will be born, or epistemological ones, like how to account for uncertainty about future outcomes. When creating the CEA yourself, you may forget to make all your assumptions explicit. But at least the result will reflect your assumptions, not that of another organization. It is also important to remember that everyone in your organization will have different implicit assumptions, and even if you hire people with similar beliefs, there will be differences you need to be aware of.
- **Contributes to a greater diversity of perspectives:** Cost-effectiveness analysis is hard, and as a result, there are relatively few analyses of any given intervention and even fewer high-quality analyses. This makes the philanthropic sector more vulnerable to poor resource allocation decisions caused by a single error in one influential CEA. Creating new CEAs not only

---

[47] Hazelfire, "Type Checking GiveWell's GiveDirectly Cost Effective Analysis", Effective Altruism Forum, Jun. 23, 2021, accessed Feb. 20, 2023

increases the likelihood that errors in existing CEAs are found but also helps the philanthropic sector be more robust against those individual errors.

So should you create or review? As with most things, no one answer makes sense for everyone. However, one piece of universal guidance we can give is not to prematurely rule out creating your own. We have observed that people tend to underestimate how much work is involved in properly reviewing others' CEAs, leading them to choose this option more often than they should. In reality, properly reviewing others' CEAs isn't much less costly than creating a CEA yourself, so you should consider this a real option. You can also use others' CEAs to save time coming up with potential structures and data sources.

## Best practices for creating CEAs

When creating a CEA, the key is to start really simple; a small number of very well-cited variables is the best way to start. Factors like the cost of an organization and the number of beneficiaries helped are often easy numbers to find good evidence on. The size of the benefit per beneficiary (e.g. how much using a bednet helps people) will be much harder, but can start to be drawn from academic literature. Creating a good CEA is beyond the scope of this book, but we have some detailed resources on it at *charityentrepreneurship.com/foundation-program-handbook*.

## Best practices for reviewing CEAs

### Vetting CEAs

One way to review third-party CEAs is to vet them for accuracy and then use their results as is without significantly building upon the CEA ourselves. Some best practices for how to do this, which we can do to varying degrees of rigor:

**Check whether you agree with the assumptions:** You may need to adjust them to reflect your organization's views. Ensure that when comparing the results of two different CEAs, they use compatible assumptions.

**Conduct an evidence audit:** Look at the references for each value in the analysis. Do the values in the model actually match the underlying literature? There may have been a mistake in interpretation or even in transcribing the values. Is the literature generalizable to the CEA context, or are there relevant differences between the populations, geographies, interventions, etc.? When conducting this evidence audit, you should prioritize the variables to which the model's results are most sensitive.

**Conduct a formula audit:** Simple formula errors are common, even among the best CEAs[48], and are a greater risk the more complicated the model is. A quick way to do this is to change a variable and see if the model moves in the direction it should (e.g. if you raise the cost, does the cost-effectiveness, in fact, go down). You would be shocked how often this turns up an error.

**Question whether the results hold up at scale:** Instead of taking it as a given that the cost-effectiveness would remain constant if the intervention was conducted at a larger or smaller scale, consider first: Should you expect diminishing returns? Should you expect economies of scale? Are there limiting factors that would constrain the scale that this cost-effectiveness applies to, e.g. limited talent who can do the job?

**Make sure we know what is and isn't included:** Almost no CEA will be fully exhaustive in terms of the costs and benefits included. This is fine; as long as we know what is and isn't included, we can make fair comparisons of different interventions. In general, the more rigorous a CEA is, the less cost-effective it will find the intervention to be, as additional factors tend to mean more costs or discounted benefits. Inclusions/exclusions to look for:[49]

**Missing costs:**

- Does the analysis include the cost of fundraising? There can be vast differences in how much time and money different cause areas/interventions need to spend on fundraising. Some spend a lot of time applying for small grants, while others only solicit one big grant, for instance.

- Does the analysis include the cost of evaluation? Funders for different cause areas hold charities to very different M&E standards. The actual cost of conducting M&E varies dramatically for different interventions.

- Does the analysis include past and future costs? A homeless charity may have already spent huge amounts on housing but only counts its future costs in its cost-effectiveness analysis. Its cost-effectiveness would therefore be greatly exaggerated. A charity that conducts corporate cage-free egg campaigns may only count the cost of achieving the cage-free commitments and fail to

---

[48] See for example this critique of a GiveWell CEA: Joel McGuire, Samuel Dupret & Michael Plant, "Deworming and decay: replicating GiveWell's cost-effectiveness analysis", Effective Altruism Forum, Jul. 25, 2022, accessed Feb. 20, 2023

[49] Saulius Šimčikas, "List of ways in which cost-effectiveness estimates can be misleading," Effective Altruism Forum, Aug. 20, 2019, accessed Feb. 20, 2023

mention the future cost of enforcing those commitments. This would also greatly influence how cost-effective their intervention appears.

**Missing indirect effects:**

- What indirect benefits are included? Suppose you compare malaria bednet distribution to a family planning intervention. In that case, the former looks better when considering impact on human health alone. But family planning may come out on top if you also consider the impact on animal welfare and the climate.
- Are there indirect costs that aren't being included? If you distribute a certain product or offer a service, what does that do to local markets? What do cash transfers do to local inflation?

**Missing counterfactuals:**

- Most CEAs fail to consider the counterfactual cost of inputs. For example, if those involved in the intervention would have been doing something impactful if the intervention didn't exist, then the opportunity cost should be included for maximum accuracy. If the intervention's likely funders would otherwise be funding something else impactful, then that lost impact is an additional cost. If other actors bear some costs for the intervention (e.g. if the government has to spend money enforcing a policy), then you need to include what those resources would have otherwise been used for.
- You also need to consider counterfactuals on the benefits side: If a charity hadn't done the intervention, would things have eventually improved, or would nothing have changed? e.g. if LEEP hadn't convinced the government of Malawi to pass and enforce regulations against leaded paint, they probably would have done so of their own accord eventually; the benefit only comes from speeding it up.

### *Improving CEAs*

Another way to use third-party CEAs is to build on them to create something better, or at least better suited to your needs.[50] Some best practices for how to do this:

---

[50] This is similar to building your own CEA, using the work of others for inspiration. As a result, it may be more accurate to think of a spectrum: from building the CEA entirely by yourself without looking at the work of any others, to using the output of someone else's CEA as is, with no scrutiny at all. Both extremes are problematic.

**Do your own thinking before looking at the model:** When you receive someone else's CEA, opening it and seeing the juicy results immediately will be tempting. But seeing someone else's model tends to anchor your thinking about how the model ought to be structured, what variables are likely to be important, and what kind of assumptions and outcomes might be reasonable. For this reason, we recommend thinking through these factors before even opening the model. Then, suppose the model looks very different from what you had imagined. In that case, you can dig deeper to understand the better approach.

**Recreate the model in a new document:** It's easy to fail to spot errors in a model when you are just building on it. Despite the inconvenience, we recommend recreating it in a new document. Hence, you're less likely to reproduce the original author's errors. You may make errors of your own, but if you do, your results will deviate from the original (unless you make the same mistakes), prompting you to check your work to understand why. Recreating the model in a new document will also allow us to use a structure consistent with models we have for other interventions or organizations, allowing for easier cross-comparison.

**Focus on the most sensitive, least evidenced variables:** Prioritize efforts where they are likely to make the biggest adjustments to the model's output – on the variables that have the poorest evidence base and to which the result is most sensitive.

**Model missing factors that may change the outcome:** If any of the factors listed on the previous pages are missing from the model but seem likely to significantly impact the outcome, consider adding them.

**Consider removing extraneous factors:** All else equal, simple models are better. They're more readable and have fewer points of failure. If a model includes factors that significantly complicate the model but make a negligible difference to the outcome (e.g. if a CEA for mosquito nets included the effect of solar eclipses on mosquito reproductive patterns), you should consider removing them. You could summarize their negligible impact somewhere, in case the question of why those factors aren't included is likely to arise, or you could save a version of the model that still includes those factors.

## 4.1.4. Choosing your output metrics

### Use two types of output metric

Straddling the border between a question about tools and ethics is the question of what output metric to build our CEA around. CEAs should have two types of output metrics that serve two purposes: concrete impact and abstract (i.e. general) impact.

Concrete impact metrics are things like "cost to prevent a case of malaria," "cost to save the life of a child under the age of five," or "cost to avert a year of hen confinement in cages." These are comprehensible and intuitive, which makes them more useful for communicating to a broad audience, more motivating for those working on the intervention, and easier to sense-check (e.g. anyone can tell that if the CEA says it costs two cents to save a life, it's probably incorrect).

Abstract impact metrics are things like "cost per QALY (quality-adjusted life-year)" and "cost per DALY (disability-adjusted life-year)," which attempt to convert all sorts of different impacts into a common metric to make comparisons between different interventions. These metrics are unintuitive, harder to sense-check (is saving a DALY for $20 plausible?), and fraught with weaknesses (see below). However, enabling comparisons between interventions makes them an important part of a CEA.

Expressing cost-effectiveness with both metric types is a great way to avoid alienating anyone who disagrees with your way of distilling impact into an abstract metric. Some people might take issue with DALYs but agree that curing a person of blindness is a meaningful measurement, for example. By using both concrete and abstract, we reap the benefits of both while ensuring common ground on how to measure impact. This way, the most important conversations don't get cut short by distracting disagreements. Meanwhile, third parties have the option of converting the concrete metric to their abstract metric of choice.

### Choosing your abstract metric

Which abstract impact metric should we use when making comparisons? Different fields and cause areas use different metrics, which have unique strengths and weaknesses.

| Metric | Strengths | Weaknesses |
|---|---|---|
| DALY | • Widely used (more results to compare with), including by WHO and World Bank<br>• Captures many different types of ailments and risks<br>• Already used in studies and research | • Doesn't capture non-health costs and benefits<br>• Doesn't allow for a comparison of benefits to humans & animals<br>• Disability weights reflect uninformed judgements<br>• Doesn't allow for states of being that are worse than death<br>• Can't compare the outputs of analyses that use different age weights or time discounting |
| QALY | • Widely used (more results to compare with), including by USA and UK governments<br>• Allows for states of being that are worse than death (theoretically) | • Mostly per above, plus:<br>• No standard methodology for determining disability weights |
| WELLBY | • Includes wider costs and benefits outside of health (e.g. income, empowerment)<br>• Based on self-reports of those with first-hand experience (vs. flawed, misinformed guesses)<br>• Allows for states of being that are worse than death | • Doesn't allow for a comparison of benefits to humans & animals<br>• Few CEAs use them, so there are fewer analyses to compare with<br>• Unclear where the neutral point is on the 1-10 scale, below which is worse than death (is it 2? 3? 5?)<br>• Treats an improvement from 7 to 8 out of 10 as equal to from 2 to 3, which many find unintuitive |
| Welfare points | • Allow for cross-species comparison, including (theoretically) with humans<br>• Allows for measurements of small changes (short-lived suffering in the order of days or months is often rounded to zero with other metrics)<br>• Not many alternatives in the animal space | • Invented by Charity Entrepreneurship (few analyses to compare with; insufficient guidance on how to apply it consistently with CE)<br>• Subjective components are based on the judgments of a small, unrepresentative group of people (CE staff) who disagree<br>• Particularly abstract |

| Income | <ul><li>Used in many economic analyses and educational impacts evaluations</li><li>Is fairly concrete, despite being your 'abstract' metric</li><li>Can proxy things like enjoyment and freedom more than hard health metrics can</li></ul> | <ul><li>Benefits to happiness/health do not scale linearly with income, and it's an open debate exactly how they do scale</li><li>Surveys suggest that income gains are less important to people than the health gains captured by other metrics</li></ul> |
|---|---|---|

These metrics are outlined in more detail below.

**Disability-adjusted life years (DALYs)** represent the loss of the equivalent of one year of human life at full health. The metric captures the potential years of life lost (YLL) due to premature death and the equivalent years of healthy life lost due to living with a disability or illness (YLD).

- **Disability weights:** YLD is calculated by multiplying the length of time one experiences the disability or illness by a 'disability weight,' which attempts to capture how much the disability or illness affects the person. Disability weights are typically calculated using a method known as pairwise comparisons, where members of the public are given descriptions of two people's health status and asked who is healthier. Despite relying on subjective judgements, these judgements are quite convergent ($r \geq 0.9$ in all countries tested except one), even across countries on different continents and with vastly different income levels.[51] However, even if people's judgements are consistent, they risk being consistently mistaken because they are based on what people imagine certain ailments to be like and fail to consider that people seem to adapt psychologically to some conditions (e.g. blindness) far more than others (e.g. depression).[52]

- **Age weighting:** Once standard practice, it is now an optional extra step to assign different weights to DALYs lost at different ages. This step aims to capture the intuition that we value years lived as a young adult more so than

---

[51] Joshua A. Salomon et al., "Common Values in Assessing Health Outcomes from Disease and Injury: Disability Weights Measurement Study for the Global Burden of Disease Study 2010," The Lancet 380, no. 9859 (December 15, 2012): 2129–43, accessed Feb. 20, 2023, https://doi.org/10.1016/s0140-6736(12)61680-8.

[52] Daniel Gilbert et al., "Immune Neglect: A Source of Durability Bias in Affective Forecasting.," Journal of Personality and Social Psychology 75, no. 3 (January 1, 1998): 617–38, accessed Feb.20, 2023, https://doi.org/10.1037/0022-3514.75.3.617.

years lived as a newborn or elderly person. GiveWell uses an age-weighting curve generated by taking a weighted average of the results from a survey of donors (60% weight), a survey of low-income people in Ghana and Kenya (30% weight), and the views of GiveWell staff (10% weight).[53] A challenge with using DALYs is that there is no way of comparing results calculated using age weights to those calculated without or with different weights.

- **Time discounting:** Another optional feature of DALYs is to discount future benefits using a discount rate (e.g. 3%).

**Quality-adjusted life years (QALYs)** represent the gain of the equivalent of one year of human life at full health. They are the predecessor of DALYs and are often used interchangeably, despite having relevant differences:[54]

1. **Opposite direction:** A positive number of QALYs represents health- years gained, while a positive number of DALYs represents health- years lost
2. **Allow for negative states:** QALYs allow for states worse than death (e.g. extreme pain); however, this capability isn't commonly or consistently used
3. **Range of disability weight methodologies:** Unlike DALYs, which have converged on pairwise comparisons as the primary method for generating disability weights, QALYs use a range of methods, including the time tradeoff, standard gamble, discrete choice experiments, visual analog scale, and person tradeoff methods.
4. **Lack of central authority:** The Institute for Health Metrics and Evaluation (IHME) has applied DALYs to a wide range of scenarios in a sane and consistent way, which serves as a common source to inform different practitioners' analyses. Unfortunately, there is no real equivalent for QALYs.

---

[53] GiveWell, "Approaches to Moral Weights: How GiveWell Compares to Other Actors" 2020, accessed Feb. 20, 2023
[54] Derek, "Health and happiness research topics—Part 1: Background on QALYs and DALYs", Effective Altruism Forum, Dec. 9, 2020, accessed Feb. 20, 2023

**Well-being-adjusted life years (WELLBYs)** represent increasing the life satisfaction of one person by one point on a 10-point scale for one year.[55] They are a far newer and less widespread measure than QALYs or DALYs, which came into existence to address the complaints that existing metrics (a) focus only on health, which isn't all that matters to our welfare, (b) rely on the naive assessments of people who mostly haven't experienced the illnesses, and (c) generally don't account for the fact that certain outcomes can be worse than death.[56]

**Welfare points,** an invention of Charity Entrepreneurship, compare the well-being of different animals in a common unit.[57] This enables a comparison of different animal interventions and, theoretically, a comparison of interventions that benefit humans vs. animals. We say 'theoretically' because Charity Entrepreneurship has not used welfare points this way; we conduct our research rounds by cause area such that we don't need to compare interventions that benefit animals and humans. However, welfare points could be used to make such comparisons and could even be converted to DALYs. Each welfare point represents a difference of 1 on a scale from +100 (an ideal life) to -100 (a completely unpleasant life), with 0 representing uncertainty about the life being net positive or negative. A human or animal life is assigned a welfare score[58] through a weighted average of eight criteria:

- Death rate/reason (20% weight)
- Human preference from behind the veil of ignorance (20% weight)
- Disease/injury/functional impairment (17% weight)
- Thirst/hunger/malnutrition (15% weight)
- Anxiety/fear/pain/distress (15% weight)
- Environmental challenge (5% weight)
- Index of biological markers, like cortisol and dopamine (4% weight)

---

[55] Michael Plant, "The Measurement of Wellbeing", Happier Lives Institute, accessed Feb. 20, 2023, https://www.happierlivesinstitute.org/report/the-measurement-of-wellbeing/

[56] Joel McGuire, Samuel Dupret & Michael Plant, "To WELLBY or not to WELLBY? Measuring non-health, non-pecuniary benefits using subjective wellbeing", Effective Altruism Forum, Aug. 12, 2022, accessed Feb. 20, 2023

[57] Charity Entrepreneurship, "Is it better to be a wild rat or a factory farmed cow? A systematic method for comparing animal welfare," Sep. 16, 2018, accessed Feb. 20, 2023

[58] This welfare score reflects quality of life, but it doesn't incorporate the probability that different species are sentient in the first place, or how intensely they are capable of suffering or experiencing pleasure of suffering (which you might call their 'welfare range'). These variables have been explored by other organizations (e.g. Rethink Priorities' work on sentience probabilities) which can be combined with welfare points to allow for better cross-species comparisons.

- Behavioural/interactive restriction (4% weight)

We haven't yet published resources to enable other organizations to use our welfare point system for decision-making in a way that would be consistent with how we use it internally. However, we include it here as an example of how your foundation might be able to formulate its own metric to compare otherwise incomparable outcomes. Of course, the downside of using internal metrics is that it means your cost-effectiveness analyses aren't interoperable with the work of others.

**Income** is one of the most common metrics for impact and has some major benefits going for it. It is well-understood and easy to calculate and measure. However, there have been many critical arguments that income or GDP have been overly focused on and are easily gamed.[59] Income is most helpful when looking at multiple interventions that work on increasing long-term prosperity and where hard data is available on income but not on softer metrics like subjective well-being.

As this chapter has hopefully made clear, there is no obvious winner in the debate about abstract impact metrics. Any of the four we've discussed could be a sensible choice for you, depending on the main types of costs and benefits you need to quantify and the types of CEAs you need to make comparisons with.

# 4.1.5. Common mistakes

## Creating CEAs

**Overcomplicating things:** The more moving parts your CEA has, the greater the chances that an error is made and the lower the chances that you find it. You shouldn't shy away from accounting for complexity. But in most cases, a small number of variables and assumptions can get you ~90% of the way to the result that the most thorough model possible would.

*Naive adjustments for conservatism:*

- **Committing the 1% fallacy:** The 1% fallacy is a phenomenon in which entrepreneurs pitch investors on a big, speculative idea and then claim that even if they could only capture 1% of the market share or have a 1% probability of success, it would still be a good investment. Astute investors know not to fall for this pitch because "to capture 1% of the market share" is

---

[59] David Pilling, *The Growth Delusion: Wealth, Poverty, and the Well-Being of Nations.* Crown, 2019

actually an ambitiously large claim. "1%" is often much less conservative or reasonable than it might initially seem. Humans are not very good at accurately assessing small probabilities – 1% and 0.1% tend to be interpreted as the same generally small chance. Discounting and incorporating probabilities must be done separately for every assumption in your process, not just tacked on to the end of your analysis. Suppose your intervention relies on 10 separate assumptions to be true, and each of those assumptions comes with a 50% discount. In that case, the cumulative discount is actually 0.098% – an order of magnitude less than 1%.

- **Taking worst-case scenarios:** When a CEA rests on several difficult-to-estimate quantities (e.g. the efficacy of an untested antidepressant, the number of crustaceans that exist, or the externalities of an unprecedented policy change), a common tactic is to model a worst-case scenario for these unknown values, so that you can assume that the actual cost-effectiveness will be at least as good as the modeled result. For example, perhaps for each unknown value, you assume a number that you feel ~95% confident will be less favorable than reality. This approach is less conservative than it seems! The more assumptions you add, the more hopelessly optimistic your so-called 'worst-case scenario' becomes. If you make five assumptions like this, there's actually a $1 - 95\%^5 = 23\%$ chance that one of the factors is worse than you thought it was – that's hardly a worst-case!

**Double counting impact:** When an organization is estimating the impact of their work, they will generally take total credit for the impact that their work appears to have caused. At first glance, this looks perfectly reasonable. However, this approach becomes problematic when other organizations also play a crucial role in achieving the impact. This can occur when two organizations do similar, synergistic work, like two advocacy groups that collectively achieve an important policy change. It can also occur with organizations that do different work towards the same goal. For example, if the Lead Exposure Elimination Project (LEEP) didn't exist, the governments of Malawi and Madagascar probably wouldn't have made progress on reducing lead levels in paint so quickly. But if Charity Entrepreneurship didn't exist, an organization like LEEP probably wouldn't have come into existence for a while. But if it weren't for our funders, Charity Entrepreneurship wouldn't have been able to operate. Suppose all three of these groups model their counterfactual impact. In that case, you end up triple counting the one set of actual benefits in the world. This results in every organization having inflated cost-effectiveness analyses because they counted all of the impact but only a fraction of the total costs required to achieve it. Without accounting for these considerations, you can get strange outcomes like more lives saved in a location than the total population.

**Assuming your impact continues indefinitely:** Generally, anything you build will eventually fall apart due to failure or the world changing and moving on. Just because an intervention got a farm to pledge to fortify their chicken feed now doesn't mean they will keep fortifying it for decades. Just because you passed a government policy change, that doesn't mean that the policy won't be reversed in the future. On a similar note, it is often the case that someone else might have eventually implemented your intervention had you not done so. So it's often best to model your impact as speeding up the arrival of an intervention and to model impacts for a limited time into the future.[60]

**Incorrect assumptions about trends and distributions:** Not every distribution is normal.[61] Many statistical techniques will go wrong if you assume something has a normal distribution when it doesn't. Trends that seem linear will often hit diminishing returns eventually. Trends that seem exponential will often turn out to be sigmoid (S-shaped) curves.

## Interpreting CEAs

**Taking CEAs literally:** As discussed, cost-effectiveness analyses involve many judgment calls- not only in philosophical matters regarding morality and epistemology but also in much more arbitrary decisions about how to count or weigh things and which particular equation to use in a given scenario. In reading about this, we hope you've developed a bit more of an intuition for why you can't take expected value estimates literally (even when they're unbiased).

**Comparing dissimilar CEAs:** Because of all the aforementioned semi-arbitrary decisions and subjective judgment calls involved in creating a CEA, the precise

---

[60] Practitioners do this either through time discounting, through modeling a fixed number of years only (e.g. 20) or both. We recommend using a consistent approach in all your CEAs so that you are comparing like with like. In GiveWell's 2023 CEAs, they apply a time discount to benefits (4% annually) and also model the different benefits of different interventions for a fixed number of years, based on the research (e.g. for AMF they model income benefits as lasting 40 years; for GiveDirectly they model incomes benefits from investing cash transfers as accruing for 10 years).

[61] A normal distribution assumes the highest concentration of values around one average, with tails leading off either end.

numbers you get are heavily contingent on who did the modeling. Suppose one were to compare two completely different CEAs that were constructed under completely different methodologies. In that case, it's quite likely that the differences in the final numbers are mostly a result of methodological artefacts, not real differences in the impact of the interventions on the real world. To overcome this, you may need to make adjustments to the CEAs so they can be compared on a level playing field.

**Not catching the common mistakes in creating CEAs:** The mistakes discussed here are common enough that you can't just trust that others have not made them. You need to look out for common mistakes and not fall for poor reasoning.

## 4.1.6. Summary

- CEAs should play an important but limited role in grantmaking decision-making.
- The strengths of CEAs are (a) enabling direct comparison in terms of impact, (b) enabling formal sensitivity analysis, (c) transparency, and (d) score sensitivity.
- The weaknesses of CEAs are that they're (a) vulnerable and prone to single errors, (b) slow, (c) often heavily dependent on subjective value judgements, (d) inefficient at capturing multiple effects, and so often neglect indirect effects.
- When it comes to output metrics, it's important to use both a concrete impact metric (e.g. lives saved) and an abstract one (e.g. DALYs or WELLBYs) to enable comparison between different types of interventions.
- There are trade-offs when deciding whether to review existing CEAs or create your own.
  - Costs of creating your own CEA:
    - Slower speed
    - Higher cost
    - Less access to information
  - Benefits of creating your own CEA:
    - Better incentives
    - Avoids adopting others' implicit assumptions
    - Contributes to a greater diversity of perspectives
- Best practices when vetting CEAs:
  - Check whether you agree with the assumptions
  - Conduct an evidence audit
  - Conduct a formula audit
  - Question whether the results hold up at scale
  - Make sure you know what is and isn't included, checking for missing costs (e.g. past or future costs; fundraising), missing indirect effects (e.g. on animals or the environment), and missing counterfactuals (e.g. opportunity cost of labor)

- Best practices when improving CEAs:
  - Do your own thinking before looking at the model
  - Recreate the model in a new document
  - Focus on the most sensitive, least evidenced variables
  - Model missing factors that may change the outcome
  - Consider removing extraneous factors
- Common CEA mistakes to look out for:
  - Overcomplicating things
  - Naive adjustments for conservatism (like the 1% fallacy and 'worst-case scenarios')
  - Double counting impact
  - Assuming your impact continues indefinitely
  - Taking CEAs literally
  - Comparing dissimilar CEAs

# 4.2. Weighted-factor models

## 4.2.1. Role in our toolkit

If we were only allowed one tool, the Swiss Army knife would likely be our choice. With multiple smaller tools attached, it can be useful in a large number of situations. However, although it is broadly helpful, it would pale compared to using the right specialized tool for a given job or a full toolkit.

The Swiss Army knife of decision-making is the weighted-factor model (WFM). It involves generating a set of criteria – often between three and twelve – and assigning a weight to each. The options you're deciding between are then scored on each of the criteria. The final score incorporates the option's performance on each criterion and the weighting of each criterion, often by multiplying the two together.

WFMs are a useful tool for any decision with multiple important considerations. This includes professional decisions; like what career to pursue or which projects to prioritize, and personal ones; like which city to live in. WFMs allow decision-makers to combine:

Disparate types of evidence (e.g. both rational arguments and scientific papers about family planning interventions)

Objective and subjective factors (e.g. both the cost of living in a city and personal excitement about the lifestyle)

'Hard' and 'soft' quantitative inputs (e.g. cost-effectiveness given as '$/life saved' or a score out of ten).

*A simple example of a WFM*

| Option | Total score | Addressable population | Modeled cost-effectiveness | Scientific evidence | Expert opinions |
|---|---|---|---|---|---|
| *Weighting* | | *20%* | *40%* | *25%* | *15%* |
| Vaccine A | 8.0 | 50M | $80/DALY | 9 | 8 |
| Vaccine B | 6.6 | 36M | $100/DALY | 7 | 6 |
| Vaccine C | 4.8 | 200M | $180/DALY | 5 | 2 |
| Vaccine D | 4.4 | 1.2M | $300/DALY | 10 | 6 |

As with a Swiss Army knife, some of the functionality of each tool is lost as we compress it to fit in the one device. For weighted-factor models, what's lost is some of the detail and nuance of each included factor. For example, capturing all the nuance in a series of expert interviews is hard when we're boiling it down to one or two numbers.

Grantmaking foundations are likely to use something like a WFM whenever we need to make a high-stakes choice between a number of options, like which interventions to prioritize, which grant applications to fund, or which candidate to hire. They serve as a summary of the information we have on each option, including the results of any cost-effectiveness analyses.

# 4.2.2. Strengths and weaknesses

## Strengths

**Systematic comparison**: WFMs force us to compare options on the basis of a consistent set of criteria, which are given consistent importance. This makes for a more valid comparison between options than other tools, like cost-effectiveness analyses or consulting experts, which don't use a consistent structure or capture the exact same considerations across different options. When using other tools, it's easy to miss an important consideration when assessing an option, leading to an incomplete picture and an unfair comparison. WFMs make this impossible to miss, reducing the chance of gaps in our analysis. WFMs also force a more equal application of rigor to each option, making a fairer comparison.

**Robust against errors and uncertainty in individual values**: A large difference between CEAs and WFMs lies in the total weight that a single factor can hold. In a CEA, an outlier value for one variable can dominate the result relative to many slightly above/below average numbers for other variables. For example, suppose an intervention could potentially affect a huge number of beings but has a very low chance of working. In that case, this initial huge number can still make all the other numbers in the CEA trivial. In contrast, one large factor can affect a WFM far less, as each factor has a maximum weight. This means there are limits to how much an error can throw off the result, or how worried we need to be that an area we are highly uncertain about could determine the result.

**Clear and efficient communication:** WFMs efficiently communicate which factors went into a decision, their relative importance, and the performance of each option on those factors. This makes it easy to understand what led decision-makers to choose one option over another. Color coding can be used to draw attention to areas of strength and weakness across a large number of options and factors. Compare this with how long it would take to read a summary of expert interviews to understand the relative strengths of two options.

**Builds in emphasis on convergence:** Unlike CEAs, where individual outlier values can dictate the results, WFMs structurally favor options that look good according to a range of factors. This places an emphasis on the convergence of evidence, which, as we explained in the introduction to ways of aggregating evidence, is important for making robust decisions.

**Allows hard and soft inputs to be combined:** Some important factors are easy to get a single hard number on (e.g. "total population affected by measles"); for others, it's impossible (e.g. "the tractability of founding a new charity in India"). In a WFM, both types of factors can be combined by converting hard inputs to soft ones based on their Z-scores.[62]

## Weaknesses

**The weighting of factors is arbitrary and subjective:** There is no accepted methodology for arriving at the 'correct' weightings of factors for a given decision.

**The rationale behind scores is often opaque:** In some cases, the number given for a factor is supposed to summarize a lot of different information (e.g. the strength of support for an intervention among a hundred experts with very diverse viewpoints). This can make it hard to communicate why that score was given, and

---

[62] A Z-score represents, roughly, a statistical measurement of how far from the mean a data point is.

there will be some variance in the scores that different people would boil that information down to.

**Makes nonnumerical data look numerical:** A concern with the WFM is that it assigns numerical ratings to nonnumerical data (e.g. the relative moral consideration given to different animals). This can confuse and mislead people as to the objectivity of the system if not explained clearly.

**Hard to capture inconsistently-important factors:** The downside of the systematic nature of WFMs is that they don't naturally incorporate considerations that are very important for some options but completely irrelevant for others.

## 4.2.3. How to create a good WFM

There are eight steps for creating a good WFM:

| | |
|---|---|
| 1 | Choose a benchmark |
| 2 | Generate a list of options |
| 3 | Choose factors (that are relevant, cross-applicable & practical) |
| 4 | Pick tools for scoring each factor |
| 5 | Choose weightings |
| 6 | Determine any minimum thresholds |
| 7 | Score options (using iterative depth where appropriate) |
| 8 | Normalize inputs using z-scores (as needed) |

**Step 1 - Choose a benchmark:** When making a decision, it's helpful to be able to compare each option to a baseline or 'do-nothing' case, which can serve as a benchmark. For example, if you were creating a WFM comparing organizations to give a grant to within the global health cause area, perhaps you'd use GiveDirectly or The Against Malaria Foundation as your benchmark (see Chapter 5.3 on benchmarking). If you were choosing what city to live in, the baseline would be the city you currently live in. If deciding who to hire, the baseline might be 'no hire' or a previous staff member who just meets the acceptability bar.

**Step 2 - Generate a list of options:** In some cases, there's a clear set of options (e.g. countries to start a charity in). In other cases, you'll need to come up with the list (e.g. career options or global health interventions). In this case, you should:

MAKING GOOD DECISIONS 117

- Try to generate at least twice as many as you think are likely to be decent contenders
- Get ideas from brainstorming, desktop research, or asking experts/advisors
- Make sure you include a couple of options that you know are bad to test out your model design, and make it clear just how good the best options are (e.g. for career options, you could include 'become the president')
- Make sure you include your benchmark

**Step 3 - Choose factors:** Factors in the model can include anything from hard data, like CEA results, to very soft judgment calls, such as a general sense of logistical difficulty. Brainstorm more factors than needed and then narrow down based on the following criteria:

- **Relevance:** The first and most obvious, the factor has to be relevant. If you are trying to determine what charity to fund, the number of letters in the intervention name could, in theory, be a column. But it would not correlate with your endline goal. A much more relevant criterion might be how many studies have been conducted on the intervention.
- **Cross-applicability:** As discussed previously, tools must cross-apply. A column like "estimated lives saved from malaria" would work if you were only considering malaria interventions. But it would only apply to some of the options if you were considering many different global health interventions. Another thing to watch out for is columns that do not differentiate between options. If a factor is scored as "medium" for all options, it does not add value to the decision-making process.
- **Practicality:** Can you get data on it? A column that would take 10 years to fill out is not helpful for making a decision you must make in a month. Is it more objective or subjective? Can others understand what the column indicates? These sorts of factors can allow your model to be interpreted and criticized by outsiders.
- **Minimal overlap:** You want mutually exclusive factors to avoid double-counting certain considerations.

Finally, choose a set of 5-10 factors and group them by theme.

*The output of Step 3 for a career path WFM:*

| Theme | Short term impact | | | Long-term impact | | | Happiness | |
|---|---|---|---|---|---|---|---|---|
| Factor | CEA modelled | Outside view | Comparative advantage | Flexible skill building | Avoiding value drift | Learning what you're good at | Fun | Pay |

**Step 4 - Pick tools for scoring each factor:** For each factor, decide what evidence to use to score it (either a type of evidence or a specific source).

**Step 5 - Choose weightings:** Start by ranking the themes in importance. Next, divide 100% evenly between the themes and begin moving weight from less important themes to more important ones and asking, 'Does this make sense?' until happy with the weightings. Next, repeat this process for the factors within each theme. It's important to choose weights before assessing options and generating results. Otherwise, you're more likely to tweak the weights after the fact so that the results better match your assumptions (i.e. using motivated reasoning).

*The output of Steps 3-5 for a career path WFM:*

| Theme | Short term impact | | | Long-term impact | | | Happiness | |
|---|---|---|---|---|---|---|---|---|
| Importance | 2 | | | 1 | | | 3 | |
| Weight | 35% | | | 45% | | | 20% | |
| Factor | CEA modelled | Outside view | Comparative advantage | Flexible skill building | Avoiding value drift | Learning what you're good at | Fun | Pay |
| Tool | CEA | Experts | Rationality | Experts | Rationality | Rationality | Ratio nality | Statista |
| Importance | 1 | 3 | 2 | 1 | 2 | 3 | 1 | 2 |
| Weight | 15% | 7.5% | 12.5% | 20% | 15% | 10% | 15% | 5% |

**Step 6 - Determine any minimum thresholds:** Think through whether any factors ought to have minimum thresholds below which an option is rejected. For example, there might be a minimum level of happiness below which a career path is unsustainable.

In the context of grantmaking, you might have a minimum threshold on 'transparency.' For example, imagine you did a CEA for a charity that made it look really strong, but you spoke to others about the charity and learned it has a well-documented history of falsification of numbers and misleading donors. You would likely give the organization a 1/10 on 'transparency' and rightfully decide not to support them, no matter how strong the CEA is or how well they performed on factors in the model.

You might also set a minimum threshold on the strength of evidence. CEAs do not do a great job of capturing significant differences in evidence. And so many wise actors (including GiveWell) have a bar that the evidence needs to meet before treating an intervention as plausible. This could mean not funding an intervention that does not have an RCT conducted on it, no matter how exciting it sounds in theory. The more skeptical you are, the higher this threshold for evidence will be.

Relative (instead of absolute) thresholds are also valuable, particularly when it comes to cost-effectiveness. For example, suppose GiveDirectly is a strong charity in almost every way but has low cost-effectiveness compared to many of the options you are considering. In that case, you might set a threshold to not deeply evaluate anything less cost-effective than GiveDirectly. This can be a way of using your grantmaking benchmark (discussed in Chapter 5.3) to save time assessing options.

**Step 7 - Begin scoring options:** Next, it's time to use the pre-selected tools to score each option. For 'soft' inputs (where we score from 1-10), you may wish to start by scoring the option you know the most about or your benchmark option – you can then score other ideas in comparison to this. Once you've scored a column, you can sense check the scores to see if their implied ranking of options by that score is sensible.

*The output of Step 7 for a career path WFM:*

| Theme | Short term impact | | | Long-term impact | | | Happiness | |
|---|---|---|---|---|---|---|---|---|
| Factor | CEA modelled | Outside view | Comparative advantage | Flexible skill building | Avoiding value drift | Learning what you're good at | Fun | Pay |
| Weight | 15% | 7.5% | 12.5% | 20% | 15% | 10% | 15% | 5% |
| Option 1 | $80k | 8 | 6 | 10 | 4 | 7 | 9 | $30k |
| Option 2 | $200k | 5 | 9 | 2 | 4 | 8 | 6 | $90k |
| Option 3 | $90k | 7 | 7 | 7 | 8 | 7 | 5 | $45k |
| ... | ... | ... | ... | ... | ... | ... | ... | ... |
| Option 15 | $50k | 2 | 8 | 9 | 1 | 3 | 9 | $200k |

When you have many options to score (e.g. suppose you're vetting hundreds of grant applications), you may be able to save a lot of time by using the process of iterative depth, discussed earlier in this book. This is where you first assess all the options using the fastest method available (heuristic evidence is particularly helpful) so you can rule out the least promising options before vetting the remaining options more rigorously (e.g. assessing the scientific evidence). However, ruling out options using one factor is only sensible if that factor is closely correlated with overall performance. Otherwise, you could rule out the best option simply because it performs poorly on a certain factor, despite performing very well overall. Another example of when this approach is appropriate is when vetting job applicants. You can first assess all applicants on how well they did on the application form and only continue to assess those who pass a certain quality threshold.

**Step 8 - Normalize inputs using z-scores (as needed):** Sometimes, you'll be able to finish at Step 7, using the 'sum-product' formula in your spreadsheet software to calculate the weighted total scores for each option. But there are two common scenarios where you'll need to do some normalization first:

- **You have some 'hard' inputs:** Whenever using hard inputs (like population size) in a WFM, it's important to normalize these values somehow. Otherwise, factors with big scores, like population size (expressed in millions), will dominate the total score when combined with subjective scores like tractability (scored between one and ten) or lower-magnitude hard inputs, like disease rate (expressed as a %).

- **When the 'soft' scores for a factor don't reflect how significant the variance in performance actually is:** For example, perhaps you're scoring a group of people on value alignment, and you find yourself feeling bad about giving anyone worse than a 6 out of 10. In this case, the difference between a 6 and a 10 is bigger than it may seem, so you may wish to use z-scores to reflect this. On the other hand, perhaps there's a certain factor where your scores have been very polarized, but you think the actual difference in performance is less large than this suggests – you may wish to use z-scores.

The trick for normalizing these factors to combine them is to use z-scores. Z-scores are a statistical measure of how many standard deviations a data point is away from the mean. In layman's terms, the z-score is a measure of how much of an outlier a data point is. The closer to zero the z-score is, the less of an outlier (i.e. the more typical) it is.

For example, if a charity is considering rolling out an intervention in one of the five cities in the table below, it is hard to tell, based on the raw numbers, what is more of an outlier; City B's high population or City D's high incidence of disease. Looking at their z-scores, we can see that the answer is City B (its population is 1.22 standard deviations from the mean). An example of the formula for calculating z-scores based on average and standard deviation is provided in the shaded cell:

|  | Population (mill) | Incidence of disease | Z-score (population) | Z-score (disease) |
|---|---|---|---|---|
| City A | 1.8 | 76% | = (1.8 - 9.6) / 7.3 | 0.19 |
| City B | 18.5 | 76% | 1.22 | 0.19 |
| City C | 3.6 | 77% | -0.82 | 0.51 |
| City D | 15.6 | 78% | 0.82 | 0.83 |
| City E | 8.5 | 70% | -0.15 | -1.72 |

| Average | 9.6 | 75.0% |
|---|---|---|
| Standard dev. | 7.3 | 3.2% |

Don't worry too much about the nitty-gritty. The point of this is that there is a helpful way to compare very different data sets using a standard unit. In our career path example, both modeled cost-effectiveness and salary are given in absolute values and will require normalization. **If any one factor requires normalization, you will need to normalize them all so that they can be combined**.

*The output of Step 8 for a career path WFM:*

| Theme | | Short term impact | | | Long-term impact | | | Happiness | |
|---|---|---|---|---|---|---|---|---|---|
| Factor | Total | CEA modelled (z-score) | Outside view (z-score) | Comparative advantage (z-score) | Flexible skill building (z-score) | Avoiding value drift (z-score) | Learning what you're good at (z-score) | Fun (z-score) | Pay (z-score) |
| Weight | 100% | 15% | 7.5% | 12.5% | 20% | 15% | 10% | 15% | 5% |
| Option 1 | 0.33 | -0.35 | 0.58 | 0.07 | 1.01 | -0.05 | 0.20 | 1.34 | -1.83 |
| Option 2 | 0.14 | 1.12 | -0.43 | 1.16 | -1.14 | -0.05 | 0.68 | 0.13 | 0.07 |
| Option 3 | 0.17 | -0.23 | 0.25 | 0.44 | 0.20 | 1.18 | 0.20 | -0.27 | -1.35 |
| ... | ... | ... | ... | ... | ... | ... | ... | ... | ... |
| Option 15 | 0.09 | -0.72 | -1.44 | 0.80 | 0.74 | -0.97 | -1.72 | 1.34 | 3.54 |

Finally, you can use the weighted average z-score to determine which option looks the best (in this case, Option 1).

# 4.2.4. Using WFMs and CEAs together

Both these models are extremely useful when trying to assess how impactful something is. However, like all models, they don't perfectly reflect reality. As the saying goes: "All models are wrong, but some are useful." The key is to understand what each is good for and where each can mislead you so that they reliably improve the accuracy of your decision-making.

Because modeled cost-effectiveness is not the same as real cost-effectiveness, a CEA can look great despite the actual charity not being cost-effective at all.

Something can look great in all aspects of a weighted-factor model and still fail to have an impact. Meanwhile, some great projects will inevitably be ruled out using one of these models. Overall, we strongly suggest using both types of model (and possibly others) to come to far more robust answers than leaning exclusively on one of them or not using any formal modeling at all.

In our experience, it's more common for grantmaking decision-makers to rely on CEAs alone than on WFMs alone, so below, we'll make a more thorough case for the importance of not relying entirely on CEAs in your grantmaking decisions.

## The case for sandboxing

The concept of sandboxing is that certain variables are contained (confined to a metaphorical 'sandbox') such that they do not affect or dominate the entire model. This can mean bounding or otherwise limiting the strength a certain variable can have. WFMs involve sandboxing in that no single factor can cause one option to look best. If you'd like, an individual factor can rule options out by using minimum thresholds (e.g. in a model of different career options, you might decide to rule out any option that scores below 3/10 on enjoyment). CEAs don't involve sandboxing in this way; if cost-effectiveness is calculated by multiplying three variables together, e.g. AxBxC, and if an option's value 'A' is 1000x higher than other options, then the variable 'A' will likely dominate the calculation.

### 1. Sandboxed models are more holistic and lower risk

The 'deworming'[63] charities recommended by GiveWell score extremely well on models without sandboxing. They are very low-cost interventions, and the best available evidence suggests they improve beneficiaries' income many years later. When modeled in a CEA, even when discounted by over 90% for the low-quality evidence, they look unusually cost-effective.

GiveWell also recommends insecticide-treated bednets for preventing malaria. According to GiveWell's CEAs, bednets are not as cost-effective as deworming. However, when splitting the evidence into different variables, bednets look considerably stronger holistically; the evidence base is far stronger, with a wide-ranging set of studies with strong results across the board. The transparency is higher, and the mechanism by which they have impact is better understood and more easily

---

[63] These charities provide children with tablets that treat parasitic worms that cause diseases like schistosomiasis and helminthiasis.

measurable (allowing for better ongoing monitoring). Bednets also have more room to scale. These factors generally aren't captured in a CEA but stand out clearly in a WFM. Factors like the quality of each charity's leadership and organizational track record can also be considered in the WFM. Going all-in on a low-evidence cost-effectiveness estimate is far riskier than sandboxing modeled cost-effectiveness and considering other factors in our decisions.

GiveWell is clear that its recommendations are not solely based on cost-effectiveness and recently-removed deworming from its list of top charities, despite its highly modeled cost-effectiveness. Although these two models are useful, they can come to different conclusions and recommend different charities. Despite GiveWell being a highly numerical charity evaluator, it views CEAs as necessary but insufficient for making final recommendations.

### 2. Sandboxed models are more robust to user error

This point has been made already, but it is worth emphasizing. Without sandboxing, models are vulnerable to being massively thrown off by user errors, and user errors are easy to make! For example, a simple error, such as dividing the population by the percentage of people affected instead of multiplying it, can invalidate an entire CEA. For this reason, it's bad practice to rely entirely on models without sandboxing.

### 3. Massive differences between values that dominate CEAs are often less significant than they appear

One might push back against sandboxing by saying that some options perform hundreds of times better on one variable than others, and sometimes this should dominate the outcome. Sandboxing, they might argue, is not sufficiently 'scope sensitive.' This most commonly comes up with two factors: scale and cost-effectiveness. These factors can vary by 100x more clearly than the quality of evidence or leadership team can.

We don't deny this fact, and it's why CEAs should absolutely be a part of our decision-making. However, we also think this point on scope sensitivity is overblown and that we should use sandboxing anyway – and so does GiveWell, one of the most rigorous practitioners of the CEA. They state, "We often take approaches that effectively limit the weight carried by any one criterion, even though, in theory, strong enough performance on an important enough dimension ought to be able to offset any amount of weakness on other dimensions".[64] Let's walk through why a huge apparent difference in scale or cost-effectiveness might not be as important or large when carefully considered.

**Scale:** Scale is a factor that can swamp almost every other factor in a CEA, with order of magnitude differences being common in both population and prevalence of an issue.[65] For example, Laos's population of ~8 million is more than 10x smaller than its neighboring Vietnam's ~100 million and more than 100x smaller than India's ~1.4 billion. It's easy to see how differences like this can make India look like the best place to execute an intervention, even if we discount it by 75% for poor evidence. However, once we consider limiting factors (discussed in Chapter 3.4.4), the relevant extent of this difference in scale may become far smaller. For example, India has 28 very diverse states, such that many interventions need to be implemented at the state level while other countries would roll them out nationally. So perhaps it makes more sense to model India by state or just model the most promising state? This one decision can change the population from 1.4 billion to 50 million (over 20x difference). Perhaps population isn't a limiting factor for the intervention, but funding or talent is instead. If so, the population might not even be relevant. If it's only possible to deliver 10 million treatments, any difference in the number of sick people beyond this is unimportant.

**Cost-effectiveness:** Sometimes, a charity might look 1000s of times more cost-effective than another, and we don't deny that this is sometimes the case in reality. However, just as often, this apparent difference is the result of an over-simplified CEA model. As we previously discussed, simple CEAs often exclude many costs (e.g. costs paid by other actors like governments or costs incurred in the past or the future), naively over-estimate benefits (e.g. assuming the effect of an education intervention

---

[64] Holden, "Sequence Thinking vs. Cluster Thinking," The GiveWell Blog, July 26, 2016, accessed Feb. 20, 2023

[65] To clarify why scale might matter in a CEA: Scale may influence modeled cost-effectiveness because when the prevalence of an issue (e.g. % of people contracting malaria) is 10x higher, delivering the same intervention (e.g. a bednet) can have a far larger impact for the same cost. Similarly, when the total scale of the issue is higher, a charity can fractionalise its fixed costs (like HQ office costs and accounting) over a larger total impact, increasing cost-effectiveness. Another reason that modeled scale might be important, independently of charity cost-effectiveness, is that it takes a lot more resources for a grantmaker to deploy $10 million dollars by finding 100 projects to fund than it does to find 1 project to fund at the same cost-effectiveness; i.e. large scale projects can allow us to deploy funding faster and at lower costs to grantmakers. This will be of particular interest to grantmakers aiming to deploy very large amounts per year.

lasts forever), miss important indirect effects (e.g. on beneficiaries' families or communities, on animals, or on the environment) and ignore counterfactuals (e.g. assuming a problem would have lasted forever instead of being eventually solved without your intervention). In general, the more quality data that is acquired, the more these super-high cost-effectiveness estimates are lowered and brought in line with others.[66]

This is part of why Charity Entrepreneurship and GiveWell have stopped trying to find the single most cost-effective option and instead try to separate out "Tier A" options from lower tiers, knowing that these differences will be more robust than the difference between an outlier and other Tier As.

## Appropriately factoring CEAs into your assessments.

Here's a useful analogy when thinking about how to factor CEAs into your assessments: If one Amazon product is rated 5/5 by three people, and another product is rated 4.6 by 3000 people, which product would you buy? Most people would choose the 4.6, reasoning that three reviews is not very representative (and they could just be reviews from employees, friends or paid reviewers – in fact, we might be more inclined to trust a lower rating with so few reviewers!) A weak CEA is like the 5-star review from three reviewers, while a GiveWell CEA is more like the 3000 reviewer rating.

Using the Amazon analogy a bit differently, imagine three scenarios:

a.  There is a product with a 1.8-star review from 10 reviewers
b.  The product has a 1.8-star review from 1000 reviewers
c.  The product has a 3.8-star review from 1000 reviews

Suppose a new review comes in from a friend of yours, giving the product 5 stars, with a bunch of photos and details explaining why the product is excellent. In Scenario A, your friend's glowing review will have a far more significant impact on your assessment of the product than in Scenario B. This is because your opinion will be less strongly held in A than in B.

Even when your initial opinions have been informed by the same amount of evidence, like in Scenarios B and C, and so are equally strongly held, your friend's review won't lead you to update your assessment to the same score. You would update your score closer to 5 stars in Scenario C than in Scenario B because the new

---

[66] This is due to the statistical phenomenon of 'regression to the mean', discussed in Chapter 3.2.4.

evidence points towards a more surprising conclusion, and extraordinary claims require extraordinary evidence. It would take particularly strong evidence, like getting to try the product yourself, for you to update your score from 1.8 to close to 5 stars. These scenarios show that when considering the results of a CEA on a charity, the strength of the previous evidence on that charity and how surprising the CEA's results are, given this evidence, should impact how much you update your assessment of that charity.

Let's apply this to the previous GiveWell example: GiveWell might have a prior opinion that it's quite hard to affect income many years in the future with a minor health intervention (indeed, it's pretty unintuitive that deworming would do this). A CEA showing that deworming is amazing will need to be exceptionally strong to significantly change their assessment of deworming charities. A fairly uncertain CEA based on weaker evidence will not overly influence their prior opinion.

## Getting the benefits of both models

If all types of models have significant flaws, and using no model is even worse, how can you make the best possible choice? The answer is just like with methods of gathering information: layering one model on top of another makes up for gaps in each. A CEA might help to establish a broad area as highly effective (say, micronutrients). But you will have to take into account the strength of the team and many other factors when making the final call on a charity within that space. One way of bringing CEAs and WFMs together is to include the cost-effectiveness result as a factor in your weighted-factor model. This way, you can give the CEA significant weight (based on its strength) and can apply a minimum threshold to it (e.g. based on your benchmark – see Chapter 5.3). You can also sandbox its impact on your ultimate decision.

## 4.2.5. Summary

- Weighted-factor models are useful for systematically comparing options, e.g. of interventions, grant proposals, experts, potential advisors, or candidates when hiring.
- The strengths of WFMs are (a) systematic comparison with equal application of rigour, (b) limiting the maximum damage caused by error or uncertainty in individual values, (c) clear and efficient communication, (d) builds in an emphasis on the convergence of evidence, and (e) allows hard and soft inputs to be combined.
- The weaknesses of WFMs are (a) the weighting of factors is arbitrary and subjective, (b) the rationale behind scores is often opaque, (c) they make nonnumerical data look numerical, and (d) difficulty capturing factors that are very important for some options and irrelevant for others.
- WFMs involve sandboxing, while CEAs do not. Using both avoids some of the risks of non-sandboxed models. It allows you to use each type of model to compensate for the limitations of the other.
- The steps for creating a WFM are as follows:
  1. Choose a benchmark
  2. Generate a list of options
  3. Choose factors (that are relevant, cross-applicable & practical)
  4. Pick decision-making tools for scoring each factor
  5. Choose weightings (by ranking factors in importance and then adjusting weightings accordingly)
  6. Determine any minimum thresholds (which may help eliminate options)
  7. Score options (using iterative depth where appropriate)
  8. Normalize inputs using z-scores (as needed)

# 5. Best Practice Charity Decision-Making Processes

As the nonprofit sector has matured and some organizations have become more impact-focused, some decision-making best practices have emerged. If foundations understand them well, these best practices can serve three important functions:

1. **A filter for selecting who to fund:** Checking *if* grant applicants are using these best practices and how well they are doing so will help separate the best from the rest.
2. **An incentive for better decision-making norms in the nonprofit sector:** By promoting the use of these best practices among grantees or even insisting that they employ them, foundations can contribute to high standards for decision-making standards in the nonprofit sector.
3. **A system for continuous improvement of foundation effectiveness:** If grantmaking foundations employ these best practices themselves, they will operate with a clearer strategy, will have greater visibility of their grantmaking performance, and will hold their grantmaking to a consistent, high (and increasing) standard.

It should come as no surprise that we consider it best practice for nonprofit decision-makers to engage with the different forms of evidence and ways of aggregating evidence we've discussed in this book so far. Foundations should expect to see the following from an excellent charity:

| Tool | How excellent charities engage with the tool |
| --- | --- |
| **Scientific method** | They should have a basic understanding of what the science says on whether, how much, & why their intervention works. |
| **Rationality** | Charities should have considered the best arguments against their approach. |
| **Experts** | They should have engaged with experts to understand whether their plan will likely work and how to make it as effective as possible. |
| **Heuristics** | They should be able to answer questions about their replaceability and the limiting factors they expect to face on the path to scale. |
| **Cost-effectiveness analyses** | They should have attempted some explicit cost-effectiveness estimates. |
| **Weighted-factor models** | They need not use WFMs specifically, but it's a red flag if they don't use a systematic method for comparing options for key decisions, like which country to operate in. |

Beyond these, some specific decision-making processes are best practices. Two apply to both charities and foundations and one applies mostly to foundations:

1. **Theory of change:** The simple account of how the charity or foundation will convert inputs into impact and what evidence and assumptions that account is based on.

2. **Monitoring and evaluation (M&E):** The use of empirical measurement to validate the theory of change and check ongoing performance so that actual cost-effectiveness can be estimated and continuously improved.

3. **Benchmarking:** The explicit use of a quality threshold for all grantmaking decisions.

This chapter will explore these best-practice decision-making processes.

# 5.1. Theory of Change

Building something complicated without an explicit plan is risky. From skyscrapers to software, ambitious projects need detailed blueprints. When building an effective nonprofit organization, the theory of change is that blueprint.

In the same way that you wouldn't hire a builder who intends to build you a home without a blueprint, you shouldn't fund a leader who intends to build an organization or launch a project without a theory of change. Suppose the builder planned to create something particularly cutting-edge, like a home made entirely out of recycled cardboard that doesn't need heating or cooling. In that case, you'd be particularly adamant that the builder explains exactly how this is possible and what evidence or assumptions it depends on. The same applies when it comes to funding an ambitious project that aims to improve the world.

## 5.1.1. The 'what' and 'why' of a theory of change

A theory of change explicitly articulates the logical steps of a plan to achieve a specific goal. It is generally represented in the form of a cause-and-effect diagram. A well-designed theory of change allows an organization to clearly communicate its activities and how they lead to the desired outcomes and then to impact.[67]

---

[67] Practitioners disagree on the exact distinction between 'outputs' and 'outcomes'. In our experience, the distinction is unimportant. We recommend focusing on the 'cause-and-effect mapping' concepts and not the terminology used to describe it.

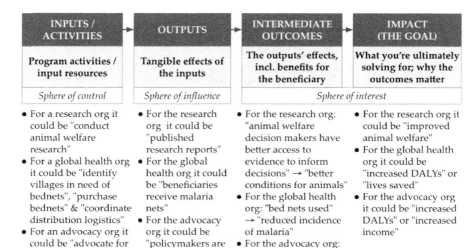

In fact, theories of change are more important for charities than business models are for businesses because businesses have better feedback loops. If a for-profit is based on a bad idea or is badly executed, it will see poor revenue and soon go out of business. On the other hand, if a charity is ineffective, it may limp along for years without having any impact, squandering limited funding and talent in the process.

Foundations deciding which opportunities to fund should expect a clear theory of change as table-stakes for potential grantees. In addition to spelling out how the potential grantee intends to convert your funding into impact, theories of change will allow you to determine how confident you can be that impact will be achieved. Is the causal chain tight or convoluted? Are the steps well substantiated by evidence or based on tenuous assumptions? Can any assumptions be easily tested? What is the crux that the project's success depends on? A smart nonprofit will use its theory of change to identify its priorities for measurement and evaluation and as the blueprint for its first cost-effectiveness analysis,[68] which foundations can then use to inform funding decisions.

---

[68] A clear theory of change can serve as the blueprint for a program's first cost-effectiveness analysis by laying out the activities that make up the costs, and the various causal steps towards impact, each of which have an effect size and/or probability of success based on the evidence and assumptions for those steps.

## Real-world examples

### Example 1: A research organization

Imagine an organization that wants to use research to make a difference. Without an explicit theory of change, their implicit mental model of how they might make an impact may look something like this:

*Review literature → Find insights that seem useful → Publish them*

This is not a good theory of change. It doesn't properly outline the goal, it doesn't explain how the actions will lead to that goal, and it doesn't explain how they will measure what they are doing. Presumably, the final goal is to impact living beings positively, not just publish papers. Even if the organization works very hard and publishes many widely cited papers, it may not make any difference.

Compare this implicit model to an explicit theory of change published by the Happier Lives Institute after they went through Charity Entrepreneurship's curriculum:[69]

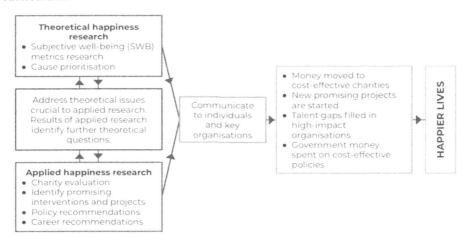

---

[69] Happier Lives Institute, "HLI Has Hatched: Strategy Update after the Charity Entrepreneurship Incubation Program," Oct. 29, 2019, accessed Feb. 20, 2023, https://www.happierlivesinstitute.org/2019/10/29/hli-has-hatched-strategy-update-after-the-charity-entrepreneurship-incubation-program/.

On the left, you can see the core research agenda of the Happier Lives Institute at a glance (the inputs/activities). On the right, you can see some measurable metrics such as money moved, new projects, and hires made (intermediate outcomes), which lead to the final impact – happier lives.

This is definitely an improvement on the implicit mental model:

- It connects activities all the way to impact (more complete)
- It gives a clearer depiction of what the activities actually look like (more concrete)
- It makes it easy to spot that "communicating to individuals and key organizations" is a crux of this process, which needs extra care and attention when it comes to execution (more action-guiding)

Having developed this theory of change, the Happier Lives Institute will be more likely to give adequate focus to ensuring that they don't just publish research, but that the right people read it and change their actions (e.g. fund more impactful organizations, start more impactful projects, or measure impact more appropriately).

That being said, this theory of change has significant room for improvement. In particular, the intermediate steps between communicating the research and organizations changing their actions ought to be spelled out: After receiving the evidence, organizations need to understand it, value it, and use it to change policies or ways of thinking. There are many ways that this could go wrong, resulting in little or no impact. Leaving this out of the picture risks these crucial details being neglected.

## Example 2: A conditional cash transfer program

Below is a theory of change for a program that uses cash transfers to increase child immunization rates in India.[70] The program has two "input" actions: providing resources to keep immunization camps reliably open and providing cash incentives to people who get vaccinated.

---

[70] J-PAL, "Theory of Change," Course lecture, J-PAL/CLEAR South Asia at IFMR, Delhi, July 2017, accessed Feb. 20, 2023, https://www.povertyactionlab.org/sites/default/files/Lecture%202-THEORY%20OF%20CHANGE.pdf

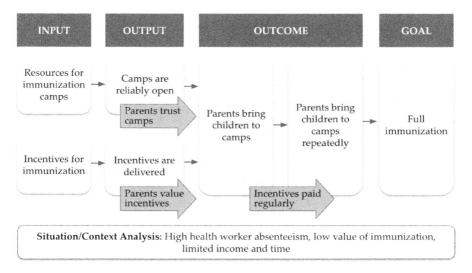

What's particularly attractive about this theory of change is how measurable each step is. For example, we can send someone to check and see if a camp is reliably open. We can create a verification system to check if incentives are delivered. We can count how many children come to the camps and how often they return for booster shots. If something is going wrong, we can check the explicitly listed assumptions (e.g. surveying parents to see if they trust the camps).

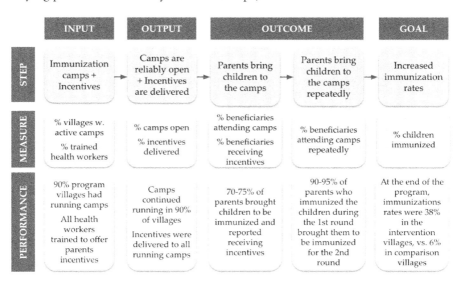

As a result of the clear, measurable theory of change, J-PAL (The Abdul Latif Jameel Poverty Action Lab) was able to evaluate the performance of the program to come to a view on its cost-effectiveness.[71]

# 5.1.2. The 'how' of theory of change

Creating a theory of change involves linking up a number of cause-effect relationships (based on scientific evidence, expert advice, or well-reasoned assumptions) to form a path from inputs to impact. It is the type of skill that is hard to teach in the form of a list of explicit instructions. Rather, it is best learned by doing and by looking at real examples and noticing what it is about them that is effective or ineffective.

However, as a starting point, we have provided some dos and don'ts to consider below and a theory of change template at *charity entrepreneurship.com/foundation-program-handbook.*[72]

### Tips for crafting a theory of change (Do's)

1.  **Invest sufficiently in understanding the context of the problem:** As anyone who works in the nonprofit sector will confirm, solving the world's problems isn't easy. Things might seem simple (e.g. 'vaccinations save lives, so all we need to do is produce enough vaccines, and we'll save lots of lives!'), but the world is complicated, and the devil is in the details (consider all the ways that the theory of change in Example 2 could go wrong). To craft a theory of change that works in reality, it's crucial that you sufficiently understand reality. This means you need to understand exactly who the people you intend to serve are and what their wants, needs, and views are (e.g. who has the most control over whether a child is vaccinated – the child, their parents, or public institutions like schools?). You also need to understand the barriers that have prevented people from resolving the problems they face. You need to understand who the stakeholders are and

---

[71] Abhijit Banerjee et. al., "Improving Immunization Rates Through Regular Camps and Incentives in India," J-PAL, 2007, accessed Feb. 20, 2023, https://www.povertyactionlab.org/evaluation/improving-immunization-rates-through-regular-camps-and-incentives-india

[72] Some further helpful writing on the topic of theories of change can be found at https://www.thinknpc.org/resource-hub/ten-steps/ (last accessed 11th July 2023)

their incentives and sufficiently understand the broader political and economic context. People who have spent time on the ground understanding the context tend to design the most realistic theories of change.

2. **Map the causal pathway backwards from impact to activities:** Programs should be defined by starting with the problem and looking for the best solution rather than by starting with a set of activities in mind and trying to find a plausible story for how those activities could solve the problem. Working backwards reduces your susceptibility to confirmation bias because instead of asking, 'What evidence can I find that this activity causes the desired effect?' you're forced to ask, 'What activity does the evidence say is most effective at causing the desired effect?'

3. **Question every causal step:** Given how easy it is for a charitable program to have minimal impact and given the stakes, we recommend approaching each theory of change with healthy scepticism. For each causal step, ask yourself, is it clear why A would cause B? How might this step fail? Can we justify how confident we are in this step?

## Hallmarks of an excellent theory of change (Some more Dos)

1. **A focused suite of activities:** A common way charities become inefficient is through mission creep. The reasoning goes something like, 'If we're already providing mosquito nets to prevent malaria, why not also provide vitamin supplements or distribute essential medicines?' Sometimes adding more activities is efficient, squeezing more impact out of a similar fixed-cost base. But most of the time, it isn't. This is the case for several reasons; for example, more activities mean an organization's focus is split between competing priorities. More activities mean more coordination costs at the organization. Adding additional activities that are less cost-effective than the first ones will often hurt average cost-effectiveness more than the synergies help it. Meanwhile, there is an incentive for organizations to add more activities to their theory of change because individuals, donors and undiscerning funders often think it is more impressive to have a larger, more holistic suite of programs. As a result, we have a heuristic that theories of change with a tight suite of activities tend to be stronger than those with a long list of activities that span a number of distinct interventions.

2. **Explicitly naming the evidence or assumptions behind each step:** One practice we'd like to see in more theories of change is an indication of the evidence, or the assumptions, behind each step. This makes it easier for outsiders to vet the theory of change: They can review the evidence and check whether they agree with the assumptions. It also makes it clear which steps most need measurement to validate assumptions.
3. **Communicating relative confidence in each step:** The most transparent theories of change clarify which steps are the most tenuous or liable to fail so that both those reviewing the plan and those implementing it can focus on those steps. This can be done by color-coding the arrows or boxes. Ideally, it can be accompanied by explicit probability estimates.
4. **Making it clear who the actor is in each step:** The clearest theories of change explain who should take action in each intermediate step (e.g. instead of 'children are brought to immunization camps,' it should be '*parents* bring children to immunization camps'). This makes the mechanics of the intervention clearer to outside readers and makes it easier to think about and prepare for how the step could go wrong ('why might the parents not bring their children?').

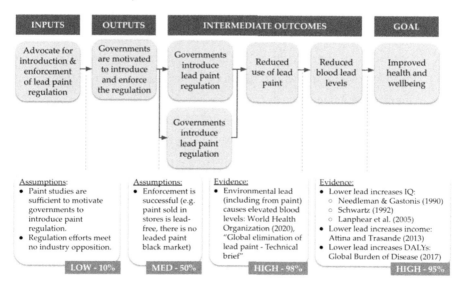

MAKING GOOD DECISIONS     139

## Common mistakes to watch out for (Don'ts)

1. **Not making fundamental impact the goal:** The conditional cash transfer example is a good theory of change, but can it be improved? Immunization isn't the end goal – saving lives and improving quality of life is. This may seem obvious, but it is very important to note it explicitly so that we remember to model how much disease is prevented and how many lives are saved by increasing immunization.

   If we skip this step, we might (for instance) end up choosing a location that maximizes the number of people who can be immunized (e.g. an area that has a good network of vaccination clinics) rather than one that maximizes the number of lives we can counterfactually save (e.g. by picking a location with a high disease burden).

2. **Insufficiently detailed:** Many theories of change make the mistake of leaving out important details in two ways:

   (a) Making large leaps between each step. For example:

   > *Publish research → lives are saved.*
   > *Raise awareness → less suffering.*

   By breaking these steps down into the main sub-steps, each of which depends on assumptions we can't be certain about, it becomes clear that these theories of change are much less likely to work than they initially appear.

   (b) Combining multiple major outcomes in one step. The best theories of change break out significant, independent outcomes like 'government introduces regulation' and 'government enforces regulation' into separate steps, making the important risk that something goes wrong in between salient. By contrast, 'government introduces and enforces regulation' makes it easy to forget that regulation can be introduced but not enforced.

3. **Set and forget:** Many organizations design a theory of change very early on, then put it in a drawer and never look at it again. Theories of change should be treated as living documents that are constantly revised as the charity tests things and gains new information.

4. **Not building your theory of change into a measurement plan:** One of the key purposes of articulating a theory of change is to determine what to measure so that you can validate whether and how much impact an intervention is having. A good theory of change makes it clear what steps are

the most uncertain and most in need of measurement. Despite this, it's common for charities to have no measurement plan at all, and when they do, for it to not be designed with reference to the theory of change. We will discuss this further in Chapter 5.2 on monitoring and evaluation.

# 5.1.3. Theory of change for foundations

There are two places where theories of change play a major role in grantmaking foundations' decision-making:

1. Assessing grantees
2. Defining a theory of change for the foundation itself

## Assessing grantees

The most obvious place for theories of change to play a role is that grantmakers should expect all potential grantees to have a theory of change for their organization or project, or at least they can produce one when asked. Funders in the nonprofit space need to hold grantee partners accountable for implementing an explicit, realistic and well-evidenced plan for turning funding into impact.

Better yet, grantmakers should expect that recipient organizations use their theory of change to identify priorities for their monitoring and evaluation plan and that they build a cost-effectiveness analysis based on the theory of change's structure (quantifying the costs of their inputs and the size and probability of the desired outputs, outcomes and impact).

## Theory of change for the foundation

It may be a little less intuitive, but theories of change also have a place in a foundation's decision-making, articulating the strategy for how the foundation itself will have impact.

### *The direct impact of grantmaking:*

At first thought, it might seem like there would be one theory of change for how all foundations have impact: 'We fund impactful activities.' In this sense, a foundation's theory of change is the sum of each of its grantees,' with an additional input at the beginning:

MAKING GOOD DECISIONS 141

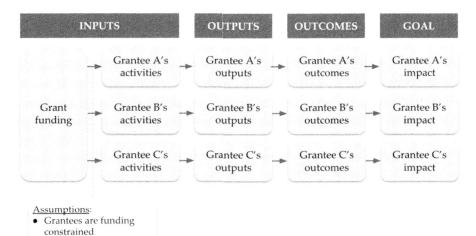

In some cases, foundations can define their theory of change in terms of a specific problem (e.g. inhumane chicken farming) or a specific type of solution (e.g. plant-based alternatives) that they have decided to focus on, where the theory of change reflects their view of the best strategy for how to improve the world within this focus area:

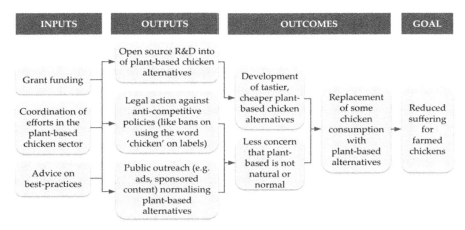

Armed with this kind of strategically-framed theory of change, foundations can seek grantees who can make a contribution and can publicly communicate how other organizations can play a role in realizing their vision. The downside of this type of theory of change for a foundation is that it forces you to have a clear and narrow view of the problem you will focus on and how it can best be solved. As a result, this approach isn't suitable for all foundations. When foundations take this approach, they should be mindful not to become anchored to one narrow view of improving the world.

### *Indirect foundation impact:*

In addition to the direct impact of providing funding, a foundation can also have broader impact through **thought leadership**. For example, you might publish research (like Open Philanthropy's reports on different cause areas), write blog posts (like the Mulago Foundation), develop impact metrics (like CE's Welfare Points) or create public cost-effectiveness analyses of charities and interventions (like GiveWell).

Foundations can also have impact by **influencing their network** (which may include other high net-worth individuals or even other foundations) to give more or give more effectively. There are many other ways foundations can create **leverage**, effectively multiplying their spending, such as by accessing government funding. Strategies for creating leverage are discussed in Chapter 8.4.

Another way of having an impact is by **setting good norms in the nonprofit sector**, making it a public policy to only fund organizations that follow certain best practices (e.g. pre-committing to shut down if the M&E doesn't show a predetermined threshold of cost-effectiveness).

Meanwhile, it is too narrow to only think about the impact of grant dollars in terms of the inputs those dollars fund. For example, sometimes, when a foundation gives a grant to an early-stage organization, it makes the difference between them going insolvent and them surviving long enough to scale into a massively impactful charity (like the Against Malaria Foundation). By **ensuring the longevity of a highly impactful charity,** the impact of the grant is not just the immediate activities covered by that money but some percentage of all of the good that the organization goes on to do in the long term. Similarly, as discussed in Chapter 8.2, foundations can be active in their grantmaking, **influencing how many and what type of**

**projects come into existence.** They then are partially responsible for those projects' lifetime impact beyond the activities they fund directly.

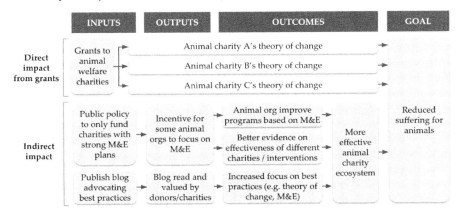

In some cases, these other forms of impact end up being much larger than the direct impact of the grants themselves! But the chances of this being the case accidentally are low – it takes thought and effort. For this reason, we encourage foundations to define their own theory of change so that they consciously decide which of these other forms of impact they will work to cultivate.

# 5.1.4. Summary

- Theories of change are the business models of the nonprofit world: You shouldn't provide funding to a project that doesn't have a strong one (let alone a project that doesn't have one at all!)
- A theory of change explicitly articulates the cause-and-effect steps for how a project or organization can turn inputs into a desired impact on the world (i.e. it's their theory of how they'll make a change). They generally include the following sections:
  - o Inputs/activities: What the project or organization does to create change (e.g. "distribute bednets")
  - o Outputs: The tangible effects generated by the inputs (e.g. "beneficiaries have access to malaria nets")
  - o Intermediate outcomes: The outputs' effects, including benefits for the beneficiary (e.g. "malaria nets are used" and "reduced incidence of malaria")
  - o Impact: What we're ultimately solving, and why the intermediate outcomes matter (e.g. "lives saved")
- Best practices when crafting a theory of change (i.e. for creators):
  1. Invest sufficiently in understanding the problem context (i.e. understanding the needs and incentives of the beneficiaries and other stakeholders, as well as barriers to change and the economic & political context)
  2. Map the causal pathway backwards from impact to activities
  3. Question every causal step (is it clear why A should cause B? How might it fail?)
- Hallmarks of an excellent theory of change (i.e. for reviewers):
  1. A focused suite of activities (because of the heuristic that more programs tend to signal lower cost-effectiveness)
  2. The evidence or assumptions behind each step are explicitly named
  3. The relative confidence of each step is clear
  4. It is clear who the actor is in each step
- Common mistakes to avoid in theories of change are:
  1. Not making fundamental impact the goal (e.g. stopping at 'increased immunizations' instead of 'improved health')

2. Being insufficiently detailed: (a) making large leaps between each step, (b) combining multiple major outcomes into one step (e.g. 'government introduces and enforces regulation')
3. Setting and forgetting (instead of regularly iterating on it)
4. Not building your theory of change into a measurement plan

# 5.2. Monitoring and Evaluation

"Measure twice and cut once" is a phrase commonly used when working on carpentry projects. It is equally applicable to running a charity or a foundation. Without taking rigorous and frequent measurements, a charitable project can be off by over a few inches – it can fail to have an impact altogether!

Monitoring and evaluation (or 'M&E') is the nonprofit world's tape measure. It allows charitable organizations to measure just how effective their implementation projects or grantmaking programs really are. A chef is unlikely to produce a delicious meal if they don't taste and make adjustments to the seasoning as they cook the soup. And an organization that doesn't conduct appropriate M&E as it goes along is unlikely to have the high impact it hopes for. But what do the terms "monitoring" and "evaluation" mean? They each refer to different ways of using empirical measurement to improve our understanding of how effective a charitable operation is.

**Evaluation** refers to the process of generating and/or analyzing empirical evidence to make an assessment of whether a program has achieved its pre-defined goals. Based on these assessments, decision-makers can decide which programs to continue (and perhaps scale up) and which should be overhauled or discontinued. Evaluation allows you to validate whether a hypothesized theory of change plays out as hoped when put into practice in reality. It can be used to validate specific causal steps in a theory of change and to quantify the change. For example, an organization might conduct an RCT to validate the assumption that distributing bednets reduces malaria incidence and determine the strength and confidence of this effect (e.g. 98% confident that distributing nets reduces malarial load by at least 28%). Evaluation is a time-bound exercise (as opposed to an ongoing process) which is conducted periodically.

**Monitoring** refers to the ongoing, systematic process of taking measurements at various steps across the theory of change to (a) track and improve the efficiency of the implementation and (b) estimate impact on an ongoing basis. Typically, monitoring uses metrics closer to the 'inputs' side of the theory of change because it would be too expensive or impractical to measure impact directly (e.g. with an RCT) on an ongoing basis.

For example, having validated and quantified the relationship between distributing bednets and reducing malaria, an organization might estimate its impact by monitoring the number of bednets distributed and multiplying by the known effect size. One might also monitor the number of bednets loaded into trucks, the number of bednets loaded out of trucks, the number still in use one year later, etc. This monitoring data can then be used to continuously improve operational performance. For example, they could then identify a problem with theft and introduce measures to combat it. You want as many useful data points as far to the right of a theory of change as is practical and affordable.

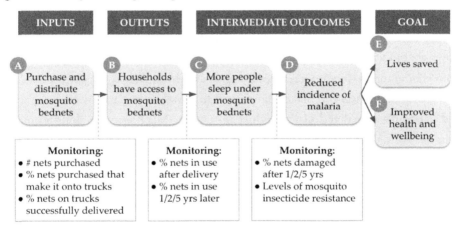

## 5.2.1. Setting expectations: M&E is hard!

### Figuring out <u>how</u> to measure is hard.

Many in the nonprofit sector experience a rude awakening when they discover how difficult M&E tends to be in practice. The challenge comes from the fact that most nonprofit interventions aren't data-rich by default.

Many of the services we interact with in our day-to-day lives generate huge amounts of data. We use websites and apps which can capture thousands of data points about how users engage with them. Even when we use a service in the physical world, like buying a product from a grocery store using cash (how old school!), there will almost always be a digital inventory management system tracking what is purchased, when, and in what quantities. The amount of digital technology, and therefore data capture, involved in delivering charitable interventions to the world's most needy is far lower.[73]

Nonprofits lack an inherent, objective measure such as revenue, which is readily available to the for-profit sector as an indicator of performance. Measurement must be intentionally incorporated into nonprofit systems, which can be a challenging and costly endeavor.

M&E is particularly difficult in interventions involving influencing people, like policy advocacy, training, or advice. How can you determine why somebody took the actions they took, and to what extent the advocate's influence was a necessary factor? In policy advocacy, in particular, it may take five or more years of work to see significant results- but can you wait five years for any signal that you're having an impact? Policy change often hinges on the decisions of a handful of specific people; how can you objectively measure your influence on their actions?

Though M&E is particularly hard for more indirect interventions, it's also hard for direct-delivery charities. Take Fortify Health, for example, a CE-incubated charity that partners with flour mills in India to prevent malnutrition by adding nutrients to the food staple. Yes, there is strong existing evidence base on the relationship between people consuming these nutrients and reduced malnutrition and between reduced malnutrition and improved life outcomes. Yes, they can verify that the nutrients are being added to the flour. But in the middle of the theory of change, things are harder to measure. For example, it's hard to track who ends up using the flour from the particular mills Fortify Health is partnered with to ensure it's being consumed (at least proportionately) by those with malnutrition. Perhaps the flour is being disproportionately exported or sold in wealthy neighborhoods? Or, as another example, perhaps the flour is being stored or cooked in such a way that

---

[73] As a side note, one of our co-authors worked at a large tech company and saw first hand how web and app-based services can be used to rapidly run experiments, test hypotheses on what features and settings lead to the best outcomes, and drive continuous, evidence-based improvement. We see a massive opportunity for a web or app-based charity idea to achieve huge scale and cost-effectiveness on the back of this, and so we recommend keeping an eye out for promising web or app based charities. In particular, we could see a use case for this technology in the delivery of mental health or health education interventions.

significantly degrades the nutrient content before it's ever consumed? Perhaps the flour has been contaminated by parasites, such that eating it does more nutritional harm than good?

## Figuring out <u>how much</u> to measure is hard too.

Figuring out how to monitor and evaluate a program is only half the battle – the other half is choosing the right amount of M&E to perform. Resources spent on M&E can't be spent on the program itself, so there's a trade-off between doing the work and ensuring it's impactful. Too little M&E is a problem, but so is too much. This balancing act is explored in detail in the book *The Goldilocks Challenge: Right-Fit Evidence for the Social Sector*[74], which we recommend as further reading on M&E.

One way for charities to navigate the Goldilocks Challenge is to aim to spend a percentage of the total time and money they deploy on validating that they're spending it effectively – somewhere in the ballpark of 10%. This means that an early-stage, low-scale charity will be willing and able to spend less on measurement than a more mature, large-scale charity. Suppose a charity can significantly increase its confidence in its effectiveness at a very low cost. In that case, it should do this early. But suppose their theory of change is already fairly well-evidenced, and the cost of measuring thoroughly enough is very high. In that case, it may make sense to wait until the charity is large enough for the cost of measurement to be an acceptable percentage of total costs.

## But measurement *is* possible & you cannot afford to neglect it

M&E is difficult but also crucial, and **some form of M&E is always possible**. In our experience, charities are too quick to use the difficulty of M&E in their particular case as an excuse to label it as 'impossible.' When talented people give the challenge some deep thought and get creative, they generally find a way.

It's also important to remember that **measuring your impact doesn't have to be complicated or expensive**. Even a small amount of data can be extremely informative. For example, if you randomly select five data points from a population, there is a 94% chance that the population median lies in between the lowest and the

---

[74] Gugerty, Mary Kay, and Dean Karlan, The Goldilocks Challenge: Right-Fit Evidence for the Social Sector (New York, 2018; online edn, Oxford Academic, 24 May 2018), https://doi.org/10.1093/oso/9780199366088.001.0001, accessed 3 Apr. 2023.

highest value you selected.[75] Generally, the less information you have in an area, the easier it is to rapidly get a somewhat informed view; an imperfect sense of things is good enough, particularly in the early days. You can find these and other tips in *How to Measure Anything*,[76] a book by Douglas Hubbard about finding creative ways to get figures without spending a ton of money or effort.

This chapter will first explore M&E best practices for charities to employ (and foundations to check for), then a consideration of how much M&E foundations should expect from grantees, and finally a discussion of how foundations can use M&E to understand and maximize their impact.

## 5.2.2. M&E for charities

This sub-chapter outlines the best practice process and key design principles charities should employ when creating an M&E plan. It's crucial for foundations to understand these principles to evaluate the quality of their grantees' M&E efforts or plans. Additionally, we provide a basic checklist for grantmakers to assess the quality of an M&E plan.

### The process of setting up M&E for a charity

**Phase 1:** Start with your theory of change, and build towards indicators

In Chapter 5.1, we discussed the importance of having a well-crafted theory of change to serve as the foundation for a charity's program design and measurement plan. So naturally, it is the starting point in any good M&E process. Looking at the theory of change, brainstorm a long list of indicator metrics that could be used to test its assumptions and validate each causal step. This long list of indicators can then be narrowed down to the best ones based on factors such as feasibility and cost of measurement, susceptibility to bias, and so on.

**Phase 2:** Set up monitoring first to get the program operating smoothly

---

[75] Here's why: The median is the middle value in a data set, which means that ~50% of data points in the set lie above it and ~50% lie below. So if you pick 5 random data points from the set, the chance that they are all above the median is 50%^5 = ~3%, and the chance that they are all below the median is also 50%^5 = ~3%. This means that there is a 100% - 3% - 3% = 94% chance that the median is between the lowest and highest of those 5 data points.

[76] Douglas Hubbard, *How to Measure Anything: Finding the Value of Intangibles in Business*. Wiley, 2014

Conducting an impact evaluation tends to be a highly resource-intensive endeavor. As such, it's not worth investing in until you've nailed the basics of your intervention. Instead, focus first on monitoring: Are the activities occurring as expected? Are there signs of outputs and early outcomes? There are a million ways things can and will go wrong until you check and fix them.

For instance, in the case of distributing bed nets to combat malaria, you would monitor whether the nets are being purchased, whether they are the correct type, and whether they are being successfully delivered to people who do not already have nets in areas where malaria is prevalent. You would also ensure that the nets are in good condition upon arrival and that the beneficiaries are using them.

Monitoring allows you to establish smooth processes. Once this is achieved, it's time to evaluate. Although evaluation generally comes second, you need to think about it at the outset, as the evaluation approach may subtly affect your program design.

*One caveat is that sometimes it's possible to build evaluation in, for cheap, from the start (e.g. through randomisation or a natural experiment). If this opportunity presents itself, take it.*

**Phase 3:** Impact evaluation (Causal attribution is king!)

The final step in M&E is to conduct an impact evaluation. The classic mistake made during this step is to solely measure whether the desired outcome is occurring, such as a decrease in malaria incidence or an improvement in animal welfare standards in factory farms. While it's valuable to know that the world is improving, the purpose of M&E is to determine whether you are contributing to those improvements- in other words, whether you are causing them. To do this, you need to understand the counterfactual case, i.e. what would have happened without your intervention.

Sometimes the counterfactual case can be measured experimentally with a randomized controlled trial, in which the control group represents the counterfactual case. The design is straightforward: you randomly[77] assign one portion of the population to receive the intervention and another portion not to. If performed correctly, any observed differences can be attributable to the

---

[77] "Randomly" here means, specifically, through random sampling; it's important to eliminate all sources of possible non-random grouping.

intervention.[78] For example, suppose a bad rainy season caused an increase in the mosquito population such that the beneficiaries were worse off after the intervention than beforehand, but the control group who didn't get the intervention were even more, worse off. In that case, the relative benefit to the beneficiaries can be attributed to the intervention. By comparing the results of the intervention group with those of the control group, it becomes possible to isolate the impact of the intervention and determine whether it has made a significant difference. Conversely, if some other factor caused beneficiaries to be better off after the intervention, but the control group was also better off, an RCT would capture this and allow you to identify that the intervention had no benefit.

This is the top tier of evidence when it comes to causal attribution. However, RCTs are often too expensive or practically impossible. The next tier is various quasi-experimental methods, in which the counterfactual case is not measured directly. Instead, another case is measured that is assumed to be representative of the counterfactual case. Some specific techniques include:

- Difference-in-differences is a statistical method that can be applied to compare two groups that differ slightly from each other but experience similar changes over time, allowing one group to serve as a "natural" control group instead of a constructed control group in an RCT.

  Suppose you have child mortality data from two villages and are funding an intervention in just one of them. Although the two villages may differ in various ways, such as having different child mortality rates, they may experience similar changes over time, such as variations in the national economy, changes in the weather, and natural disasters. If the two groups change over time but in similar ways, the method returns a null result, suggesting that your intervention was ineffective.

- Discontinuity regressions take interventions applied to participants on one side of an arbitrary threshold and compare outcomes for participants just on either side of that threshold to determine the effect of the intervention. For example, if you were to tutor every student in a maths class who scored less than 70% on their first test, you could later look at the differences in

---

[78] This is subject to some caveats, like that the observed differences are statistically significant.

outcomes for those who scored 69-70% vs. those who scored 70-71% to get a sense of the effect of the tutoring.[79]

- Multivariate regressions compare individuals who received an intervention with those who did not whilst attempting to control for differences between the groups that might explain differences in the outcomes. For example, if it is known that older people are more susceptible to a certain disease, then you could adjust the observed difference in disease rate between those who did and didn't receive the intervention based on the relative ages of the two groups.

There are no hard rules about which types of quasi-experimental methods are better or worse. Instead, one needs to think critically about which method best mimics the counterfactual case in a given scenario.

One method that is rampant (both in the nonprofit and for-profit world) and which we want to urge a high degree of scepticism towards is the pre-post (aka before vs. afterwards) comparison. In this method, the outcomes for the same group are compared before and after the intervention, and any observed change is attributed to the intervention. For this causal attribution to make sense, we have to assume that outcomes would not have changed for that group otherwise. In reality, there are endless reasons that things might have changed, and it is easy to manipulate the start and end points to support a specific narrative. This method is most valid when the observed change is unprecedentedly large, and there is no other reason to expect the change to have occurred. On the other hand, when you come across something like a charity that gives primary school students iPads and compares the students' math skills to a year beforehand, and then attributes a 5% improvement in ability to the intervention (as if there's no other reason why a student might get smarter with age!), take it with a grain of salt.

---

[79] On average, we would expect the cohort students who scored between 70-100% on their first to outperform students who scored between 0-70%, as they likely have higher baseline maths skills. As such, comparing later performance of these groups wouldn't allow you to isolate the effect of the tutoring. However students who scored 70-71% would only have trivially better math skills than those who scored 69-70%, and such that the tutoring is the only significant difference between these cohorts. Therefore, comparing the performance of these groups should allow you to measure the impact of the tutoring.

## Principles for charities when designing their M&E plan

There are some best practice principles that charities should keep in mind when planning their M&E.[80] Beyond the "Goldilocks" principle of neither measuring too little nor too much, we recommend:

### 1) Prioritize validating the most uncertain step in your theory of change

If you could only measure one thing, it should be this. This is the crux of whether it makes sense to continue the program or not. You should measure it sooner and put more effort into it compared with other steps. Consider the bednet distribution example again:

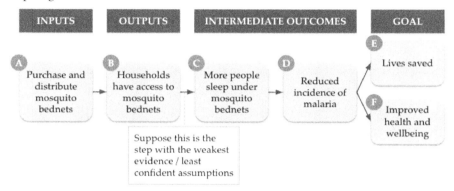

One can validate the most uncertain step by measuring on either side of it (i.e. between B and C), or by measuring as far to the right as possible whilst also including the tenuous step (i.e. between A and D/E, or both.[81]

There are pros and cons to measuring between A and D/E:

- Pros: Provides higher confidence that the end goal will be achieved because they don't have to rely on other people's evidence generalizing to their context (e.g. perhaps the effect size between C and D will be different in the population they're serving compared to the population in a study that was conducted thousands of miles away where there were different local levels of resistance to malaria).

---

[80] For further reading on this topic, we recommend the online courses offered by J-PAL (https://www.povertyactionlab.org/j-pal-courses)

[81] F can't be measured directly – rather you'll need to measure the reduced rate of malaria and use the research of others to convert that to improved health and well-being in your abstract impact metric (e.g. DALYs or WELLBYs).

- Cons: If the evaluation shows no or low impact, the evaluation won't provide any evidence of where the point of failure was or how weak/strong the effect size of each step in the theory of change is.

## 2) Only collect actionable data[82]

Collecting as much data as possible on an intervention is tempting. So long as the cost of measurement is trivial, this is a sensible heuristic. However, if you will never take action based on a measurement, then there is no point in allocating resources to collect it.

Two hurdles determine whether a given data point is actionable: The first is whether it provides meaningful insight about what action to take. The second is whether the organization is actually willing to change course based on the data. To ensure that the collected data is actionable, organizations should pre-commit to changing their course of action based on the results of the measurements. It's not sufficient to say, "If the data shows that X doesn't work, we will stop doing it," because this leaves it up to subjective judgment whether the data really shows that X doesn't work. Instead, the disciplined approach is to specify, in objective terms, the exact threshold for taking action, e.g. "If more than 5% of medicines don't make it to their destination, we will switch distributors."

## 3) Prioritize generalizable data[83]

There's a sense in which every program is unique, and so is every context that it operates in. But there are also important similarities between different programs and contexts that allow some insights to be generalizable from one to another. Whenever insights can be generalized in this way, a huge amount of effort can be saved in figuring out what will work. Significant resources can be saved that would otherwise need to be spent on more M&E. As a result, data that tells you more about whether a program will work in a different context (e.g. a different location or beneficiary population) or about whether similar programs will work (e.g. SMS nudges can increase vaccination rates, so perhaps they can prompt people to seek treatment for tuberculosis?) is more valuable, assuming all else is equal.

---

[82] Innovations For Poverty Action, "Goldilocks Toolkit: Impact Measurement with the CART principles", accessed 4 April, 2023.
[83] Ibid 71

### 4) Be as concrete as possible

It's not enough to just list a bunch of indicators you hope to measure in your M&E plan. That's the easy bit. It should also include specific and concrete details on how to collect data- such as who will collect it, how it will be collected, how often it will be collected, and how it will be processed. The devil is in the details, so don't neglect them.

### 5) Design to minimize potential sources of bias

There are all sorts of ways that M&E plans can introduce bias. Let's look at two of them:

- <u>Perverse incentives:</u> When choosing an indicator, think about whether it creates perverse incentives for those aiming to perform well. For example, imagine a charity trying to use a website to convince people to go vegan. They might use high website traffic as an indicator of good performance. This creates an incentive to solve for quantity over quality, which could involve advertising the website very broadly instead of focusing the advertising budget on the target audience most receptive to veganism.

- <u>Social desirability bias:</u> Any measurement tool that relies on human reporting is subject to social desirability bias. This is when people lean toward responses that put them and their organization in a positive light to avoid insulting or hurting other people's feelings. Sometimes, this bias runs the other way, with communities downplaying progress or exaggerating challenges in the hopes that services are continued or expanded.

  There are ways to reduce social desirability bias to some extent. One way is through anonymization, which can make people feel more comfortable providing honest answers. Another way is to frame questions in a neutral way so that respondents do not feel like there is a "right" or "wrong" answer.[84] Sometimes, you can sidestep this issue by using an objective metric as a proxy for a subjective one. For example, GiveDirectly has no easy way to figure out people's income without asking them. So instead, they use an objective

---

[84] Seven approaches for reducing social desirability bias in surveys are discussed in Anton Nederhof's *Methods of coping with social desirability bias: A review* which can be found at https://onlinelibrary.wiley.com/action/showCitFormats?doi=10.1002%2Fejsp.2420150303 , accessed Apr. 4, 2023

metric (one of many): whether the person's house has a metal roof.[85] In general, surveying housing characteristics is a common method of estimating poverty in developing-world contexts. This includes the materials of the roof, walls, and floor, the cooking method, and the availability of electricity and plumbing, amongst other criteria. It's important to remember how relying on these metrics alone can be misleading. For example, a particularly bad rainy season could motivate someone to buy a metal roof even though doing so is still financially uncomfortable. The most accurate (but also most expensive) approach involves triangulating both objective and subjective metrics.

## Quality hurdles for foundations when reviewing M&E plans

With the M&E planning process and design principles in mind, foundations can assess the quality of a charity's M&E plan by testing it against various quality hurdles.

1. Does an M&E plan exist at all? (Sadly, this is the most common point of failure)
2. Is the plan clearly built on their theory of change?
3. Is the plan concrete enough to demonstrate a way to actually pull it off?
4. Does the plan involve both process monitoring and impact evaluation?
5. Does the evaluation measure whether impact has been achieved, or only tell you about inputs and outputs?
6. Does it attempt to causally attribute impact to the charity?
7. How high is the quality of that causal attribution?

The fifth hurdle in this list is a particularly common stumbling block for charities, so we will explore it in a little more depth.

### *Why do so many charities' so-called impact evaluations consist of a bunch of input and output metrics?*

- **Ease**: It's far easier to measure the web traffic to your advocacy website than to do an RCT on whether it convinces people to go vegan. Thus, an increase in web traffic is often cited as a criterion for success, even when it may not be connected to the charity's real goals.

---

[85] Michael Faye, "Metal Roofs - A Lesson from the True Poverty Experts," GiveDirectly Blog, Aug. 6, 2013, accessed Feb. 20, 2023

- **Salience**: Identifying the most important metrics can be hard, particularly when a charity or grantee's goals are a bit vague. This is particularly true with younger charities, as well as charities with less of a clear focus. When a charity is unsure what the most important metrics are, it might instead report on a number of less helpful metrics.
- **Naive impressiveness**: Reporting on several metrics looks more impressive because they show more data – even if the data does not reflect the good being done. Additionally, the more metrics they have, the easier it is to cherry-pick the ones that are going well and downplay the ones that are not going as well. This kind of practice makes an organization more appealing to donors and members, even if it is ultimately an illusion.

### A concrete example

Imagine that you believe improving immigration in the US is important for economic growth and the welfare of immigrants. So your foundation gives a grant to an advocacy website that encourages people to write to their congressperson and urge immigration reform. How do you know if this project/website is effective?

The first way many foundations use is to ask the person running the project how they think it's going. Although this can be a useful first step, there are about 100 reasons for a person to be biased in a positive direction and very few for them to be negative. A slightly better approach is to analyze web traffic. While an increase in traffic could indicate positive outcomes, it does not necessarily translate to meaningful engagement, such as users following through to write to their congressperson.

Perhaps you could measure the number of letters that are delivered to congresspeople. While this does gauge your capacity to influence the public, what if the petitions are disregarded? How can you determine if the petitions lead to changes in legislation? What if the legislation was going to be changed regardless? Indicators such as web traffic and letters sent can aid in comprehending whether specific steps in your theory of change are functioning effectively. But they don't give you the full picture.

What you *really* want to measure is the counterfactual impact on legislation change. To do this, one method would be to construct an experiment where you randomly select some legislators to be targeted and some not to be. Then you see whether the targeted legislators are more likely to sponsor immigration reform than the non-targeted legislators. This approach is attractive because it uses a control group; however, it falls when you consider that legislators talk to one another, so there may be spillover between the treatment and control group. Not to mention the fact that you probably care a lot more about your ability to influence key individual legislators that are on the fence on the issue. Another approach, which is more targeted but also more susceptible to bias, would be to interview those decision-makers and (without asking leading questions) get their perspective on the influence of these letters on their stance on immigration.

Of course, this still assumes a final step in the theory of change, that immigration reform leads to economic growth and improved immigrant welfare, so this must already be substantiated by strong evidence for you to have confidence that the intervention is effective.

## 5.2.3. How much M&E should foundations ask for from grantees?

We've discussed how charities need to navigate the 'Goldilocks Challenge' of either measuring too little or measuring too much. But we haven't spoken about how foundations fit into the picture. Grantmaking foundations have an important role in establishing the norms for the level of M&E required for charities to receive funding. Meanwhile, the more high-quality M&E a foundation's grantees perform, the better the foundation can understand the impact of its grants. So how much, what type, and when should you ask for M&E from grantees? There are no strict rules, but in our experience, **most foundations demand too little from their grantees**. Here are some rules of thumb:

### 1) Expect an M&E plan as a condition before providing a grant

It may be the case that a project is deserving of a grant even though it is too young or small to do much in the way of M&E. However, as a grantmaker, you should know what you're getting in terms of M&E *before* you make the funding decision, not afterwards.

### 2) Expect more rigorous M&E for larger grants

As discussed earlier, charitable organizations should spend a fairly consistent percentage of the resources they consume (time and money), validating that they're using resources effectively. As a result, the larger the grant size and the larger the organization's total budget and team size, the more you should expect from them regarding M&E.

### 3) Expect more M&E when giving recurring grants

M&E is more decision-relevant for grantmakers if the grant is likely to be recurring, as you can use the results to inform whether to provide the recurring payment as planned, to double down (if the results are particularly strong) or to pull back (if the results underperform expectations).

### 4) Expect more M&E when there's a higher chance of causing harm

Whilst we generally caution against supporting interventions with a significant risk of causing harm, it's very common for even the best interventions to involve small risks. For example, perhaps an intervention that aims to increase veganism to reduce animal suffering risks creating a backlash that hurts animals more than it helps them. The higher the risk of these kinds of downsides, the more stringent the M&E standards need to be. Downsides, if they eventuate, can then be caught and stopped as soon as possible.

### 5) Encourage and be willing to fund more M&E when it can generate generalizable lessons

The M&E results on a particular project often have the potential to generate valuable lessons for the nonprofit sector. For example, if a project is implementing an intervention with a particularly limited empirical evidence base, then the results of a powerful M&E process could lead a foundation and the sector as a whole to significantly update how bullish they are about that intervention. It could generate lessons that are generalizable to similar interventions as well. The greater the potential information value, the more you should encourage and be willing to fund more rigorous M&E.

### 6) Don't ask for too much!

There is absolutely such a thing as asking for too much M&E, and the downsides can be significant. M&E is expensive, both in time and money, as is reporting on it to funders. So you should:

Only ask for decision-relevant metrics. Measuring everything you can or collecting data is often tempting because it seems interesting. However, there's no need to take a measurement if it won't help you increase impact. Unnecessary measurements cost charities in terms of design and administration. Collecting too much data from human beings also causes fatigue in respondents, hurting your ability to get the data you actually need in the long run. For each measurement, you should make explicit which decision it is helping you with.

Don't ask everyone for gold standard M&E. It might be tempting to ask all grantees to conduct an RCT, but this is not appropriate in many cases. For instance, no project should attempt an RCT in its first year of existence (unless it can be easily built into its pilot).

Avoid asking for bespoke reporting formats for no good reason. It's more efficient if the grantee can give one M&E report to all funders. As the Mulago Foundation puts it on its website, "The last thing we want is to waste time and energy of those who are trying to save the world. We ask for annual milestones and their impact methodology; beyond that, we rely on documents they should already have on hand."[86]

## 5.2.4. M&E for foundations

When foundations conduct M&E on themselves, it will look quite different to M&E for implementing charities. But one thing they both have in common is that they should be built on a solid theory of change. As discussed in 5.1.3, a foundation's theory of change will often involve the direct impact of providing grants to impactful organizations and some significant indirect impact through avenues like active grantmaking or thought leadership. It's possible to measure both of these types of impact.

### Measuring the direct impact of grants

While every foundation would love to know exactly how many DALYs it has saved through its grants, running a rigorous impact evaluation of each of its grantees to find this out would be unrealistic and inadvisable – after all, evaluations are often highly resource intensive. But this isn't a problem. The point of M&E for a foundation is to continuously improve the quality of your grantmaking decisions, and this doesn't require dozens of expensive evaluations. Instead, foundations should focus on measuring the quality of those decisions: which past grant decisions were

---

[86]The Mulago Foundation, "How We Fund," accessed Feb. 20, 2023, https://www.mulagofoundation.org/how-we-fund

successful? What aspects of the process work well, and which result in sub-optimal or wrong decisions?

If you have a systematic process for making grantmaking decisions (as we will discuss in Part C of this handbook), then this should be fairly easy. You should have some up-front assessment of each of the grants you considered making (ideally in reference to some quality benchmark, as we will discuss in Chapter 5.3). This will give you an initial "promisingness" score of how you thought different applications did. Going back at a regular time and reviewing your historical grants (once a year is a good habit) and seeing if you updated positively or negatively can be a solid start. You can also get a lot of value from just ranking past grants from best to worst, with a cut-off point below which you would not repeat your grant decision if you were to go back in time. (If you do not think you have made a bad grant in the past, you are being too easy on yourself! Even the best grantmakers make regrettable grants).

When you review a historical grant, you consider all the new information you have received since making it, including the recipient's own M&E reports, to see if you made the right decision in the first place, and update your own M&E based on these findings. The better the grantee's M&E, the better yours can become. This is yet another reason to hold grantees to high M&E standards.

## External grant evaluations

Another way to assess the quality of your grantmaking decisions is to have them externally evaluated. You can do this by asking an individual or foundation whose judgment you trust to evaluate your grants (e.g. order them from best to worst, alongside some benchmarks like AMF and cash transfers) and perhaps do this for them in return. We know a foundation that recently set up a blinded system where multiple trusted actors give their views on a number of grants made and almost made, so they can then identify correlations.

Semi-external grant evaluations can also be conducted by having a different staff or board member look at historical grants and give an evaluation from a slightly different perspective.

Judging old grants might seem less exciting than new ones. But given that you might want to re-grant to the organization or learn if your predictions came true, it is highly valuable to look at them. You will often be able to see trends (like it's often clear which application is the strongest after the first interview or that CEAs tend to be more predictive than the other models used).

## Measuring a foundation's indirect impact

A foundation might also have an indirect impact, as discussed in Chapter 5.1.3. It's hard to get high-quality data on this kind of impact, as it's hard to run clean experiments or construct control groups. But there are some methods for gathering evidence.

One means of gathering evidence is to run an external survey. Did other actors use your research? Did your request for proposals direct peoples' efforts towards an area they wouldn't have focused on otherwise? Did your announcement that you would fund animal welfare interventions in Asia give charities enough confidence in their funding security to start planning projects in that region? Asking some non-leading questions can start to give you a read of whether you had this kind of impact to a significant degree. One needs to design a survey like this carefully, as people often tell funders what they want to hear. Ideally, the survey can come from someone else, so people don't fill it out with the knowledge that you're using it for your impact evaluation. Instead of a survey, stakeholder interviews can be used to understand your influence in greater depth.

Another way of determining whether your foundation has had a significant indirect impact, which particularly applies to thought leadership, is to look at whether key phrases associated with your work are being used in the discourse (e.g. The Happier Lives Institute might look for an increase in the use of WELLBYs as an impact metric by other organizations since their publications on subjective well-being). A limitation of this type of evidence is that people adopting your language does not necessarily mean you are influencing their decisions.

One way to bring a bit of rigor to how you quantify this indirect impact is through the use of scenario analyses. For example, if you're trying to measure the extent to which your active grantmaking caused a given impactful project to come into existence, you could consider a few scenarios of what might have happened with or without your influence (e.g. the founders don't start the project, the founders start the project with funding from someone else in two years, the founders start a slightly different and ~50% less impactful project). You can assign different probabilities to these scenarios by triangulating the evidence available to quantify your impact.

Whilst it's sometimes possible to measure indirect impact in fairly precise terms (e.g. by determining how many dollars you're responsible for redirecting to more impactful charities and then converting that to an equivalent in dollars donated to a well-understood benchmark, like GiveDirectly), most likely you'll only be able to measure intermediate outcomes. This means you'll be reliant on some assumptions about the connections between those intermediate outcomes and impact. If those assumptions hold, then by tracking whether you are making more or less progress on those intermediate outcomes, you can steer your foundation toward greater expected impact.

## 5.2.5. Summary

- Monitoring and evaluation are both methods for using empirical evidence to improve your estimates of the impact a nonprofit is having. They both help you validate whether a hypothesized theory of change plays out as hoped when put into practice.
- Evaluation is the process of using empirical evidence to determine whether a program has achieved its predefined goals and to continue (and perhaps scale up), overhaul or discontinue it. It is a time-bound exercise conducted periodically.
- Monitoring refers to the ongoing, systematic process of taking measurements at various steps across a theory of change to (a) track and improve the efficiency of the implementation and (b) estimate its impact on an ongoing basis.
- Because M&E is crucially important but uses resources that otherwise could be spent on the programs themselves, nonprofits face the 'Goldilocks Challenge' to neither measure too little nor too much.
- The process of setting up M&E for a charity involves:
    1. Starting with a theory of change and building towards indicators
    2. Setting up monitoring first to get the program operating smoothly
    3. Performing an impact evaluation, in which causal attribution is king
- Recommended design principles for charity M&E plans include:
    1. Prioritize validating the most uncertain step in your theory of change
    2. Only collect actionable data, and pre-commit to how you will act based on the results
    3. Prioritize collecting data that can generalize to other contexts or programs
    4. Be as concrete as possible: How will the data be collected? By whom? How often?
    5. Design to minimize potential sources of bias (e.g. check for perverse incentives, minimize social desirability bias)

- In terms of your expectations from grantees:
    - Expect an M&E plan as a condition before providing a grant
    - Expect more rigorous M&E for larger grants
    - Expect more M&E when giving recurring grants
    - Expect more M&E when there's a higher chance of causing harm
    - Encourage and be willing to fund more M&E when it can generate generalizable lessons
    - Don't ask for too much! – M&E is costly
- Foundations should conduct M&E on themselves by (a) systematically reviewing their grantmaking decisions and (b) measuring indicators of indirect forms of impact (e.g. thought leadership)

# 5.3. Benchmarking

Deciding how good is 'good enough' can be tricky. When amateurs build something, they tend to decide what's 'good enough' by gut feel – after all, the stakes aren't that high. But professionals need to consistently meet high standards, so they will compare what they're building to some kind of benchmark.

Suppose a professional carpenter is designing a chair; they have to consider what chairs are on the market to compete with. What is the price point of the chairs at IKEA? What is the quality of their design and construction? How can a new design outperform this standard? A master craftsman who has outperformed IKEA many times might keep one of the best chairs they've designed in the workshop to compare their latest work side by side. That way, they can tell if their new work is actually an improvement or if they should spend their resources reproducing previous designs.

Similarly, grantmakers should use benchmarks to make more informed and consistent decisions about which grant opportunities are up to scratch. Like the carpenter, a grantmaker may have different benchmarks for different purposes (we'll discuss these below). The best benchmarks make it possible to compare a wide range of projects against a common standard.

In addition to improving the quality and consistency of your grantmaking decisions, benchmarks help save time when vetting grant applications. Instead of ranking every application you receive from best to worst, you can dismiss those that clearly won't meet your benchmark (e.g. the applicant's cost-effectiveness estimate is too low or their evidence base is just too poor) and just rank those that might meet the bar.

Being public about the benchmark you use also makes it easier for applicants to decide whether they're a good fit to apply for funding. If your benchmark is high, it sends a strong signal to implementing organizations about the standards they ought to strive for.

There are two types of benchmarks that you might use in your grantmaking decisions: guardrail benchmarks and target benchmarks.

# 5.3.1. Guardrail or 'opportunity cost' benchmarks

The guardrail benchmark represents who you'll give to if you can't find anything better within a certain period. They're helpful when you've committed (for legal or strategic reasons) to give a certain amount at minimum per year. Your guardrail benchmark should be the best option available within your foundation's scope, with enough room for funding to absorb your minimum spend. For example, within the cause area of global health, you might pick the Against Malaria Foundation, which saves lives at a cost of ~$5,500[87] and has significant room for funding.

To illustrate, suppose it's your foundation's first year of operations, and you've decided to deploy at least $5M of funding this year. Suppose that before you begin assessing grant applications, you're already aware of three projects that you could give to, all of which have a solid level of cost-effectiveness (although you expect you can find better):

| Option | Cost per DALY | Room for funding | Can absorb min. spend? |
|--------|---------------|------------------|------------------------|
| A | $90 | $0.1M | No |
| B | $100 | $50M | Yes |
| C | $110 | $1M | No |
| D | $120 | $100M | Yes |

A and C aren't viable guardrail benchmarks because if you only find $1M in opportunities that beat it, they can't absorb the rest of your minimum spend. Although D can absorb the full $5M if need be, it's not the most cost-effective option that can do this. Therefore, B is the best choice.

---

[87]GiveWell, "How We Produce Impact Estimates," last modified Sept. 2022, accessed Feb. 20, 2023

One might object to the need for a guardrail benchmark by pointing out that if you have to spend a minimum of $5M in a year, you could just rank your opportunities and give the most cost-effective options with $5M total room for funding. This is true, but we think it's very important to explicitly set a benchmark and include it in your decision-making process anyway. This is because it's easy to get excited by all the new projects and organizations you come across each year. You can end up making grants to some of these opportunities that aren't as strong as some of the older ones, which may seem a bit vanilla but are still highly cost-effective and can absorb more funding. Using a benchmark forces disciplined grantmaking decisions: Is this new project on the block a better funding use than your "old faithful"?

A foundation's guardrail benchmark will hopefully change over time as they discover new opportunities that are more cost-effective than their previous benchmark and also have significant room for funding. Another reason it may change is that your previous benchmark's room for funding decreases, or their cost-effectiveness goes down (hopefully because they've solved most of the problem!) For this reason, it's important to revisit your benchmark roughly every year.

## 5.3.2. Target benchmarks

Many foundations are itching to solve the world's problems, so they want to spend significantly more than the minimum annual amount they've committed. We commend them! These foundations will also have a maximum annual spend based on their stance on the 'spend now vs. later' spectrum (discussed in Chapter 7.1.1) and because of liquidity constraints. How should you decide how much to spend between your minimum and maximum each year? This is where target benchmarks come in.

In some cases, the guardrail benchmark may be sufficiently ambitious such that a foundation can simply fund all opportunities that beat it each year ($15M in the below example). In other cases, these opportunities may exceed your maximum annual spend (e.g. $10M), in which case you need to set the bar higher (e.g. setting the bar at 1.1x the guardrail benchmark would mean the top three applicants are funded to a total of $7.5M).

| Option | Cost per DALY | Room for funding | Cumulative $ |
|---|---|---|---|
| Best grant applicant | $70 | $2M | $2M |
| 2nd best applicant | $87 | $1.5M | $3.5M |
| 3rd best applicant | $89 | $4M | $7.5M |
| 4th best applicant | $94 | $3M | $10.5M |
| 5th best applicant | $97 | $4.5M | $15M |
| Guardrail benchmark | $100 | $50M | $65M |
| .... | ... | ... | ... |
| 50th best applicant | $20,000 | $10M | $200M |

The right number to pick as a target benchmark is much less obvious, particularly because it requires a view of how the quality and quantity of opportunities available will likely change in the short-to-medium term. As a foundation matures and the philanthropic landscape changes, the target benchmark will also change.

## 5.3.3. Real-world examples

### GiveWell

GiveWell has set a benchmark based on GiveDirectly, a charity that distributes cash directly to some of the world's poorest people. GiveDirectly is highly impactful and can absorb all the funding that GiveWell has. In this sense, GiveDirectly represents how GiveWell could happily deploy all of its funding if it had to spend it all today. GiveWell scores other charities by comparing their impact with GiveDirectly (e.g. CharityZ is 8x GiveDirectly), which also serves as a tangible way to describe impact: "8x as impactful as giving cash to some of the world's poorest people".

Cash benchmarks have also been picked up by some international aid organizations and governments as a clear "bar to beat." This is a pretty reasonable lower bound to set as a benchmark for most foundations. Many have argued that setting cash transfers as a benchmark for all of global health and poverty would make a lot of sense[88] (although others have argued this bar is too low).[89]

It would be nice for GiveWell to be able to set their bar at 100x GiveDirectly. But they would find almost no evidence-based opportunities at high levels of scale with that level of expected cost-effectiveness, given the amount of research and scrutiny they put into their evaluations.

Typically, foundations making smaller grants can set a higher benchmark: Finding an opportunity that can absorb 1 million dollars at 100x GiveDirectly is much easier than finding an opportunity that can absorb $500 million at that level.

## Open Philanthropy

Open Philanthropy has a target benchmark of "1,000x returns".[90] This means "it must be 1000 times as cost-effective as giving a dollar to someone with $50k of annual income (the average U.S. citizen)." This roughly translates to about 10x GiveDirectly. This bar is based on OpenPhil's opportunity cost (e.g. giving more to GiveWell) and on what they think is a high but realistic level of ambition.

Sometimes Open Philanthropy will also use other benchmarks, depending on the cause area, as some areas will be difficult to compare to "1,000x returns." For example, in the context of animal welfare interventions, they may use cage-free campaigns as a benchmark, given their high estimated level of cost-effectiveness.

## Charity Entrepreneurship (in its infancy)

Benchmarks can still be used when hard data on cost-effectiveness is scarce, for example, by qualitative comparison. When Charity Entrepreneurship was first starting out, our benchmark was to start charities that were roughly the quality of Fortify Health (our first incubated charity). This gave us a sense of the quality bar we were aiming for and had the advantage of allowing us to compare charities in very different areas (with very different impact metrics).

---

[88]Center for Effective Global Action, "Cash Benchmarking," CEGA, accessed Feb. 20, 2023, https://cega.berkeley.edu/initiative/cash-benchmarking/.

[89]The Mulago Foundation, "Cash Benchmarking: A Solution in Search of a Problem," accessed Feb. 20, 2023, https://www.mulagofoundation.org/blogs/cash-benchmarking-a-solution-in-search-of-a-problem.

[90]Peter Favaloro, Alexander Berger, "Technical Updates to Our Global Health and Wellbeing Cause Prioritization Framework," Open Philanthropy, Nov. 18, 2021, accessed Feb. 20,2023

## 5.3.4. Summary

- Using benchmarks has benefits in terms of the quality and efficiency of your grantmaking decisions and in terms of communications:
  - o Quality decisions: Ensures you're assessing grants against a consistent standard and giving to organizations whose value is less than the opportunity cost.
  - o Efficient decisions: You can save time by only thoroughly vetting opportunities that can't quickly be eliminated by comparison to the benchmark.
  - o Communications: (a) Helps would-be grantees understand whether they're a good match and should get in touch, and (b) sets high standards for charities to strive for.
- There are different types of benchmarks for different purposes:
  - o Guardrail benchmarks are for when you have a minimum annual spend. It should be based on the opportunity cost of each grant, i.e. the most cost-effective organization that could absorb all of your minimum spend.
  - o Target benchmarks are for when you have a floating annual spend (within a range) and need a means of determining how much funding to deploy each year. It should be chosen based on how you expect the quality and quantity of opportunities to change in the short-to-medium term.

# PART B
# Key decisions for new foundations

If a foundation is to reach its full potential and have a massive positive impact on the world, then some key decisions must be made first. These decisions can be grouped into three themes:

1.  **Scope**: Identifying what counts as impact, given your values. Deciding where to direct your funding (cause areas, locations and types of recipients) so that you can have as much impact as possible.
2.  **Structure**: How to organize your organization to effectively make change within its given scope. Decisions such as how quickly to deploy funding, how much to spend on staff vs. the grants themselves, and how involved to personally be in your grantmaking.
3.  **Strategy**: How your foundation will achieve impact. You will need to decide things such as how much risk you will take in your grants, whether to use open or closed applications for grants, and how to incorporate considerations like "counterfactuals" and "leverage".

In this chapter, we will go through each of these high-level decisions and discuss the trade-offs you will encounter.

When making these decisions for your foundation, it can be helpful to consider examples of existing foundations, like those summarized on pages 177 and 178.[91] How explicitly have they made these decisions? What about their circumstances led

---

[91] Notes: (1) This table is based on publicly available sources (e.g. foundation websites) and conversations with foundation members. Our general level of confidence in the details is low and we have included error bars to at least partly account for this. (2) This is not exhaustive of every key decision we discuss in this section – some of these don't lend themselves to summary in this table. (3) Geographic focus here refers to where the interventions occur in practice, as opposed to the foundations' explicit geographic scope (most of these foundations don't explicitly limit scope by geography).

them to make the choices they did? How do your circumstances differ, and what implications does that have for how you should make these decisions (perhaps differently)?

It's interesting to note that whilst you might expect decisions on these dimensions to be largely independent, in practice, some are correlated. For example, foundations that aim to deploy a lot of funding each year tend to give larger grants to more mature organizations rather than hiring an army of grantmakers to make many small grants to early-stage organizations. This bias is somewhat defensible; foundations with the means to fund large grants have a comparative advantage in addressing those kinds of funding gaps relative to foundations with more limited spending power. However, it's possible to fund both large and small grants. And it would be a shame to miss out on opportunities to do more good by needlessly ruling out funding small grants, no matter how potentially transformative they might be.

Every foundation will have its own comparative advantages based on the worldview, motivation, skills and life experience of its team. When you understand these comparative advantages, you can choose the scope, structure and strategy that will allow you to have the most impact.

Examples of some real world foundations' key decisions (1 of 2)

| | | Givewell | Open Philanthropy | EA Animals Funds |
|---|---|---|---|---|
| | **Comparative advantage** | Highest standards of scientific evidence and cost-effectiveness analyses in the area of health and development direct delivery | Biggest cause-agnostic EA-minded foundation; Focus on worldview diversification, with program officers siloed by cause area | Brings together five fund managers from different organizations with distinct perspectives; Open process for animal orgs to seek funding |
| **Scope** | **Cause areas and interventions** | Humans, near-term. <br><br> Cause areas: Global health & development. <br> Interventions: Direct delivery | Humans and animals, near and long-term. <br><br> Cause areas: Biorisks; EA community growth; Farm animal welfare; Global health & development; AI safety; Scientific research; South Asian air quality; Global aid policy | Animals, near-term. <br><br> Cause areas: Farm animal welfare; Wild animal welfare; Sentience research; Alternative proteins |
| | **Geographic focus** | Africa and South Asia | Global (incl. developed nations for causes such as policy, research, farm animal welfare etc.) | Global (incl. developed nations for interventions like research, corporate advocacy etc.) |
| | **Typical recipient size** | Large (~$20-120 M/yr) | Small - Large (~$0.5-100 M/yr) | Seed - Mid (~$0-1 M/yr) |
| **Structure** | **Run-down rate** | n/a - donation based | Within founders' lifetimes | n/a - donation based |
| | **Grantmaking $/hr ratio** | | | |
| | **Founder involvement** | | | n/a |
| | **Team size** | | | |
| **Strategy** | **Evidence vs. hits** | | | |
| | **Active vs. Passive** | | | |
| | **Open vs. Closed** | | | |
| | **Use of leverage** | | | |

| | | Mulago | Bill & Melinda Gates | Woodleigh Impact |
|---|---|---|---|---|
| | **Comparative advantage** | Providing unrestricted funding to early stage organizations led by high-potential leaders with the capacity to scale | Brand recognition and size means they can coordinate large actors & governments (e.g. setting up GAVI); Expertise in tech solutions | Helping early stage orgs to collect evidence on their program, then helping them scale and find larger / end-stage funders |
| **Scope** | **Cause areas and interventions** | Humans, near-term.<br><br>Cause areas: Global health & development, more specifically: Early education; Smallholder farming,; Primary healthcare; Water and sanitation; Energy | Humans, near-term.<br><br>Cause areas: Gender equality; Global health, development, policy & advocacy; U.S. Program | Humans and animals, near-term.<br><br>Cause areas: Global poverty (80%); Climate change (20%); Tentative plans to add farmed animal welfare in 2023. |
| | **Geographic focus*** | Global South | 130+ countries, incl. developed nations like U.S & United Kingdom | India and Sub-Saharan Africa but planning to narrow down over the next three years |
| | **Typical recipient size** | Small - Mid (~$0.5-5 M/yr) | Mid - Large (~$0.5-5 M/yr) | Seed - Small (~$0.5-1 M/yr) |
| **Structure** | **Run-down rate** | Not public. Possibly perpetuity | Within 20 yrs of founders' deaths | 5-10 years |
| | **Grantmaking $/hr ratio** | | | |
| | **Founder involvement** | | | |
| | **Team size** | | | |
| **Strategy** | **Evidence vs. hits** | | | |
| | **Active vs. Passive** | | | |
| | **Open vs. Closed** | | | |
| | **Use of leverage** | | | |

# 6. Scope

Every foundation has a key decision to make on how it will set its scope. There are hundreds of possible cause areas and locations and just as many types of interventions, projects and organizations to consider funding. You can't solve every problem, so which ones to focus on is a big question. Even the biggest and most high-performing foundations can't build the depth of knowledge necessary to make expert decisions across such a wide domain. In fact, the difficulty of making excellent grantmaking decisions in any one niche is underrated. Choosing your scope very intentionally will allow you to consistently fund the best opportunities within your niche.

It's important to narrow your scope, but figuring out how narrow to be can be a hard task. On the one hand, too narrow a scope will limit your options to a very small number of charities to support. This means you might rule out otherwise great opportunities. For example, a foundation set its geographic scope to be organizations with an HQ based in Atlanta (a city in the US) that work in the DRC (a country in Africa). As you can imagine, a scope this narrow meant only a couple of charities fit the criteria. They ruled out many more effective organisations in their work but did not have their HQ in Atlanta.

On the other hand, too broad a scope can result in low expertise and unclear priorities. If your foundation's scope is "we want to do the most good in any way we can," it won't inadvertently rule out high-impact projects. But it *will* make it difficult for charities to know whether their values or goals align with yours. With less confidence in their prospects of being a good fit and no reason to send their application to your foundation in particular, fewer organizations will get in touch. Those that do will likely have a wide range of views on what the 'most good' means and be less focused, reducing the percentage that are a good fit for you. In practice, even if an existing foundation's scope is very broad, typically, there will be specific types of organizations or interventions that they feel more optimistic about, and it would be very beneficial for them to share that preference publicly.

Foundation founders tend to be passionate people who can easily get excited about many ideas simultaneously. As a result, the natural bias will be towards going too broad in scope rather than too narrow. Keep this in mind when trying to find the right balance for your foundation.

We urge you to be as transparent and specific as possible about the types of organizations and projects you are interested in funding. In addition to giving organizations the confidence and a reason to send their application to you, it will also signal the types of ideas worth fleshing out into project applications, influencing what types of project ideas come into existence.

Larger foundations tend to have broader scopes, but no hard and fast rules exist. A decent heuristic is to dedicate at least one FTE (full-time-equivalent staff member) per focus area.[92] For example, suppose you are a foundation giving away $5 million a year and plan to have two program officers plus the founder's time. In that case, setting two to three scope focuses for your foundation to narrow in on might make sense. Having each program officer focus on one area, instead of having each of them be generalists across the set of areas, allows them to build stronger networks and deeper expertise. This helps to source better opportunities and vet them more effectively.

There are a lot of ways of breaking up scope, with the most common being cause area (e.g. farmed animals vs. global health) or geographic focus (e.g. focusing on North India). This chapter will introduce and consider the following ways to break up scope:

- Values
- Cause area
- Geographic focus
- Recipient organization size

---

[92] Of course, one can divide the world up into focus areas of very different sizes. Here, we have in mind areas of the size of "global poverty", "farmed animal welfare" and "biorisks".

The narrower you focus your scope in one of these dimensions, the broader you need to set your scope on other dimensions. This ensures that there is a large enough pool of charities within your scope for there to be sufficient quality projects to fund.

Let's start with one of the most fundamental ways to consider narrowing scope: your values.

# 6.1. Values

Knowing your goals is key to accomplishing them efficiently. So what is the goal of being a grantmaker? It might seem simple: give funding to effective projects that help others improve their lives, thus helping the world and doing good. But what is good, and who counts as others? What does it mean to help them? Different people's values point them in different directions on these questions. The answers you choose, based on your values, will have important ramifications for how you operate your foundation.

You don't need to know your exact values or have a deep understanding of ethics to see that certain charity work is doing good, e.g. curing diseases and reducing child mortality are fairly morally safe. Because ethics is such a tricky subject to master, there is a case to be made that it may be safest to support the types of charities that look good across a wide range of values. But if you're ambitious in your altruism, it's worth giving your values some serious thought; progress in this area could allow you to identify specific opportunities far more impactful than a 'safe choice.' So let's dig a little deeper.

## 6.1.1. What does it mean to improve lives?

When folks talk about 'helping people,' they're generally talking about improving lives. But what does it mean to improve lives? What do we fundamentally mean when we say someone has a high quality of life, or that a state of affairs is good for them? Do we mean that they are happy, that they approve of how their life is going, or something else entirely? What does well-being consist of?

184 VALUES

There is a lot of disagreement about what specifically makes up well-being or 'quality of life.' But people are unanimous that some aspects are only important in so far as they affect others. For example, money can be useful for making life go well, but possessing money does not in *itself* make life good — money helps you access the things that ultimately make life good (for example, you might include good health, pleasant mental states, or satisfied preferences in that category).

Disagreements about what counts as improving lives are not only relevant for philosophers; they can affect philanthropists' decisions often enough to justify building a basic understanding of the most common[93] philosophical views.

## Hedonic views

These views hold that well-being is all about the quality of an individual's subjective experiences, i.e. how positive or negative their mental state is. Most everyone agrees that the quality of an individual's subjective experience is an important part of well-being. However, hedonic views are defined by thinking that this is *all* there is to well-being.

There are a number of perspectives on what constitutes a high-quality mental state. For example, the classical hedonic view is that quality mental states are characterized by the presence of emotions like happiness and pleasure and the absence of emotions like sadness, pain, and fear. On the other hand, the tranquilist view is that the highest quality mental states are those characterized by contentment (i.e. absence of cravings or desires for change).[94] Tranquilism, similarly to Stoicism and Zen Buddhism, sees the quality of your mental states as being determined not by their *content* (e.g. happiness or sadness) but by your *judgment* of that content as 'good' or 'bad.'[95] An implication of tranquilism is that non-existence (which is a state that is absent of desire) is no worse than any mental state. Therefore, a grantmaker

---

[93] Note: We will not discuss Objective List Theories of well-being, because in our experience they're too uncommon among philanthropists to justify discussion here. For reference, these views on well-being think that there is a finite list of things that make up quality of life, regardless of whether they make people's subjective experience better, or whether people prefer to have those things. Classic examples of items on this list are happiness, freedom, health, knowledge and friendship.

[94] Lukas Gloor, "Tranquilism," Center on Long-Term Risk, June 15, 2020, accessed Feb. 20, 2023, https://longtermrisk.org/tranquilism/.

[95] Tranquilism says that pleasure can be instrumentally valuable, because it can temporarily satisfy a desire for change; however, if one is already content in a given moment, then making their subjective experience more pleasurable would not improve their well-being.

whose values align with tranquilism might not want to fund interventions that lead to more people existing, as they would see this as neutral at best and harmful at worst.

## Preference views

These views hold that well-being is about more than just one's mental state. Specifically, they hold that an individual's well-being is about satisfying *their* preferences. For example, in addition to preferring mental states that are free from pain, people often have preferences about privacy or what happens to their bodies after their death. So if one foundation holds hedonic views, and another has preference views, how might their grantmaking decisions differ? When deciding whether to fund family planning (e.g. Maternal Health Initiative) or chemo-prevention of malaria (e.g. Malaria Consortium), if the options tied on their cost-effectiveness in improving mental states by preventing health issues, the foundation with the preference view might place some weight on the satisfaction of women's preference for reproductive autonomy, tipping the scales in family planning's favor.

## Negative views

Sometimes called 'suffering-focused' views, these views hold that reducing negative well-being is more important for improving lives than increasing positive well-being. Negative views are consistent with both hedonic and preference views about what well-being actually is.[96] In practice, focusing on reducing suffering tends to lead to supporting similar interventions to focusing on both positive and negative well-being because it is generally more cost-effective to meet basic needs than higher needs, and this usually involves reducing suffering more than increasing pleasure. So where might the grantmaking decisions of a foundation with suffering-focused values differ from other foundations? One area is on interventions that change how many people will exist: Grantmakers with the most intensely suffering-focused conception of well-being would strongly prefer interventions that lead to fewer lives

---

[96] Negative views come in all sorts of flavors, from the most intense position that reducing any amount of negative well-being (e.g. suffering, or thwarted preferences) is more important than adding any amount of positive well-being (e.g. happiness, or satisfied preferences), to the more moderate position that there is some kind of exchange rate between reducing suffering and increasing pleasure, and suffering is 'worth more'. In fact, the tranquilist view discussed earlier, which defines well-being in terms of the absence of something negative (desire for change), is a negative view of well-being. There is also prioritarianism – the view that we should give more weight to helping those who are the worst off – which isn't necessarily a negative view, but has many aligned practical implications.

being lived (even if people would generally consider them 'lives worth living'), such as family planning. More moderate suffering-focused grantmakers might simply place less emphasis on interventions that aim to increase the number of happy lives that exist, such as those focused on space colonization.

Hopefully, this discussion, whilst very simplistic and incomplete, has given you a sense of how subtle distinctions in what counts as 'improving lives' according to your values can have large ramifications for what you ought to fund.

# 6.1.2. Whose lives matter?

## Moral circle expansion

A famous thought experiment by the moral philosopher and Professor of Bioethics at Princeton University, Peter Singer, puts the choices we make every day into perspective: He asks us to imagine walking past a shallow pond only to see a child drowning. The child would be easy to save, but at the cost of your clothing, your watch, and your phone in your pocket all being destroyed.

Almost everyone agrees that the tradeoff of saving the drowning child is not simply the right thing to do – it's the only ethical choice. It doesn't matter if someone else could have saved the child or even if five children were drowning; you would do everything in your power to save as many children as you could.

Although coming across drowning children might be rare, a slight shift in the question makes it relevant to our everyday lives: What if you could donate the cost of your clothing and gadgets and be certain that the money would save someone on the other side of the world? GiveWell currently suggests that a life can be saved for around \$3,000-5,000.[97] They use a highly rigorous process to ensure that each dollar donated does, in fact, make that difference. The power to save lives for such a small trade-off gives us both an opportunity and, arguably, an obligation to help others where we can.

---

[97] GiveWell, 'Our Top Charities', accessed Feb. 20, 2023, https://www.givewell.org/charities/top-charities

Singer connects this point to W.E.H. Lecky's concept of the expanding moral circle – the idea that the number of individuals we, as humans, consider it reasonable or even morally obligatory to help is growing over time:[98]

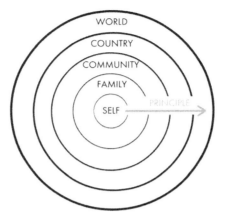

Long ago, the expectation was that you would support yourself and your family. Animals, neighbors, and faraway humans would be considered a tool at best or a threat to be eliminated at worst. But as time passes, we recognize more and more beings as deserving of our help. The importance of caring about our community grew into caring about our nation and, over time, caring about humans all around the globe just in virtue of them being fellow human beings.

It's tempting to think that we're at the end of history and our circle now includes everyone we should care about. But there are many beings who, for all intents and purposes, remain outside most people's moral circles. One example is people many generations in the future. Whilst many people have started giving more moral consideration to humans far away in space (i.e. on the other side of the world), few give the same degree of consideration to humans that are far away in time (i.e. ten generations into the future). Whilst there are practical constraints on our ability to help far future people, we don't see any good justification for excluding them from our moral circle.

Another example is (nonhuman) animals, who fall into an even more distant ring in people's moral circles, despite compelling evidence that many, if not all, animals suffer in very similar ways to humans. We treat the animals closest to us, such as dogs and cats, with an extremely high level of concern, often seeing them as beloved family

---

[98] Peter Singer, *The Life You Can Save: Acting Now to End World Poverty* (Melbourne: Text Publishing, 2023).

members. But we give other animals far less ethical consideration. One of the most abused populations in the world right now is the billions of animals in factory farms who suffer intensely for much of their lives. Suppose moral circle expansion continues on its trajectory. In that case, future generations will likely look back on our cruelty to farmed animals with shame.

Perhaps there are evolutionary reasons why we care about those closest to us - but does that make them right, ethically? After all, many claim that there are evolutionary reasons why humans are predisposed to violence, yet we actively try to reduce this in society.

Let's consider another thought experiment: As suggested by the famous philosopher, John Rawls, imagine you are behind a "veil of ignorance," from which vantage point you know nothing about yourself, your natural abilities, or the position you will hold in society when you are born. You might be a human from any country or even (to take Rawls' ideas even further) an animal. What system would you want to design? How would you want others to act? If we knew nothing of our position in the world, we would probably not want to roll the dice and end up on the edge of the moral circles of those with power and resources.[99]

For the average person in the Western world, people living in the most extreme poverty fall at the outer limits of their moral circle – out of sight and out of mind. More and more actors are realizing the unacceptability of this fact. The Gates Foundation believes "all lives have equal value," and the organization's resulting actions focus on locations and people with the highest need, often far from its Seattle base.[100] This is quite different from the adage "charity begins at home" and closer to a policy of "charity begins with those in the most need."

Ultimately, being geographically or temporally close to, similar to, liking, or agreeing with a group doesn't affect how much moral concern we should give to it. Someone who thinks differently from us in all ways or looks different still feels the same pain from injury. If it's in our power to prevent suffering and make the world a better place, we ought to do so. It does not matter how different they are or who caused the injury. Our moral circle should include all those who *feel*.

---

[99] McCombs School of Business at the University of Texas at Austin, "Veil of Ignorance," Ethics Unwrapped, February 21, 2022, accessed Feb. 20, 2023, https://ethicsunwrapped.utexas.edu/glossary/veil-of-ignorance.

[100] Bill & Melinda Gates Foundation. "Our Story," accessed Feb. 20, 2023, https://www.gatesfoundation.org/about/our-story

## Population ethics

Another consideration we may want to give some thought to is that our actions can increase or decrease the number of people that will exist (e.g. by saving lives, increasing access to contraception, or mitigating existential risks). If these additional people would have good lives, have our actions made the world better? If they would have bad lives, have our actions made the world worse? Do the lives of these 'potential people' matter? Population ethics is the attempt to make sense of questions like these that arise when our actions affect who and how many people are born and at what quality of life.

Population ethics is a notoriously difficult area to make sense of. Delving into it in depth here would be a distraction – and a very dry read! To keep things as simple as possible, the key question to consider is which statement is a better match for your moral intuitions: (1) A higher number of happy lives existing is a good thing, all else being equal; (2) It is good to make people happy, but at best neutral to make happy people.

If the first statement better matches your values, then you may be more sympathetic to funding interventions that grow the global population or prevent existential risks. This, of course, assumes that you think the additional lives will be good ones and that there are interventions with good enough evidence for their efficacy to justify funding them. If the second statement better matches your values, then you may be less interested in preventing existential risk and you may have fewer qualms about interventions that may reduce how many lives come into existence (e.g., family planning). In practice, though, regardless of which view you hold, you probably think that preventing nuclear war, climate change, or pandemics is a good thing because both involve making life worse for many people – at most, population ethics adds another (albeit very important) reason to think these causes are important. In practice, population ethics will only tend to make a big difference in fringe cases, like the question of whether it's important for humans to colonize the stars.

# 6.1.3. Navigating conflicting values

When attempting to improve the world, you'll likely encounter situations where different things you value pull you in different directions. Navigating these situations can be very difficult.

There is a well-known example of 'trolley problems,' where a runaway train ('trolley') is hurtling towards two people tied to the track. You can either let these people be killed or pull a lever to divert the train to a different track where just one person will be killed. In this thought experiment, many people experience a tension between a value that says 'take actions that lead to the best consequences for the most people' and a value that says 'don't kill others.'

There are also more practically relevant examples, like family planning: Providing family planning support has direct benefits that most people see as valuable, such as women's education, income, autonomy, and maternal and neonatal health. However, if this is all you value, other interventions may be more cost-effective. But, of course, family planning has many more flow-through effects, which you may deem positive or negative depending on your values. For example: How does one fewer unplanned child being born affect a low-income family that may already be struggling even without another mouth to feed? Would that child's life have been happy - if so, maybe it's bad they did not come into existence? Or would their life have been filled with more suffering than joy, so that it's perhaps a good thing they were not born? Taking a step even further out, how would that child affect their country and the broader world? Would they help or hurt the economy of the country? What would their environmental impact be? What about their effect on animals? The ripple effects of such an intervention can be highly complex. Depending which way your values pull you on these questions, family planning could look like the clear winner among ways to help the world, or you could be left deeply conflicted about whether it is positively impactful at all.

We will discuss two tactics for navigating these kinds of value conflicts.

**Introspection:** Sometimes, apparent conflicts in values can be resolved through a process of introspection. For each apparently conflicting value, we can ask ourselves: why do I value this? This will often lead us to realize that this thing is merely a means (instrumental) to something more fundamental that we value intrinsically. We can then ask ourselves why we value that thing, and so on, until we land on one or more things we value intrinsically, such as 'truth' or 'preventing suffering.' Often, this process allows us to look back at the apparent conflict in values (some of which may be instrumentally valuable) and resolve it in terms of our intrinsic values. For example, in the classic trolley problem scenario, introspection may lead us to realize that the value 'don't kill others' is not actually an intrinsic value but rather is a heuristic that serves as a useful rule of thumb for acting in accordance with a more fundamental value, such as 'maximise the well-being of all sentient creatures.'

But sometimes, having made all the progress you can through introspection, you may find that your intrinsic values are still in conflict. Or you may be uncertain which of your values are the most fundamental. At this point, you need another solution.

**Moral parliament:** One way to think through intractable value conflicts is imagining a busy parliament house filled with 100 members. But instead of political parties, these members represent moral theories. You might put quite a bit of weight on some theories, and so many of your ministers are in that party. For example, for many of the team at CE, one of the largest parties in our moral parliaments is some form of consequentialism[101], while the rest of the seats are taken by other ethical theories. When they come together, just like politicians, they make trades and alliances.

Your major parties might not care about some issues that more minor parties find very important. For example, most of us at CE do not eat animal products, and many of our moral parties think this is the right thing to do. However, if an animal was raised in good conditions and treated well, eating meat would no longer be a significant ethical issue for some of our parties (including the largest ones) – it might even be slightly net positive if it brings a happy life into existence. But smaller parties in the moral parliament, such as deontological parties, may have a rule that allows no exceptions to the maxim: "Do not kill." They would thus still strongly maintain that we should not eat meat. Still, other parties might be indifferent: The parliamentarians from virtue ethics parties might know that we have good intentions in both cases and thus abstain from any votes.

Having a sense of your fundamental ethics in this way is a helpful exercise. And reading up on ethics can be a way to understand how you want to do good in the

---

[101] Stanford Encyclopedia of Philosophy, "Consequentialism," accessed Mar. 16, 2023, https://plato.stanford.edu/entries/consequentialism/

## 6.1.4. Living your values

### Being ambitious in your values

Almost everyone wants to do good, and most NGOs do *some* good. However, chances are that if you are reading this book, you want to aim higher. CE wants to create and support foundations that do the most good – foundations with the ambition to not just be decent but be standouts in their field.

If saving one life is good, saving two lives is no less than twice as good. Most people will agree with this simple statement, but our emotions often don't align with this sentiment. A well-known quote says, "A single death is a tragedy; a million deaths is a statistic."[102] The point is that our brains have trouble comprehending large numbers of suffering, and we certainly do not feel a million times sadder hearing about a million deaths than when hearing about one. Humans evolved in small groups, caring deeply about those closest to us. We did not evolve to handle large numbers or to emotionally understand the global community we are now a part of.

Let's go back to Singer's thought experiment on the drowning child. What if two children were drowning? Does that change your actions? Even if so many children were drowning that you could not possibly hope to save them all, you would swim until your arms gave out. Nearly all of us feel this moral imperative to do the most good we can. There is so much pain and suffering in the world that a fantastic organization could work as hard as it can, and there will still be problems. But that hundredth child saved, the last one you manage to rescue before your strength gives out, matters just as much as the first.

Doing the *most* good you can versus doing *some* good makes all the difference when we look at individual lives. Your granting work may feel more abstract than saving the drowning child, but the stakes are no less high.

---

[102] Attributed to a French diplomat in the essay "Französischer Witz [French Wit]" in Vossische Zeitung 23 Aug. 1925, according to Susan Ratcliffe, *Oxford Essential Quotations*, 4 ed. (Oxford University Press, 2016).

## The challenge of living your values

*"There is a fight going on inside me." Whilst she was used to her grandfather being a little melodramatic, this unusual statement piqued her interest. Clearly, he was about to give one of his infamous cryptic lessons. "It is a struggle between two wolves. One wolf is selfishness – he is my greed, my callousness, my self-importance, my closed-mindedness, and my excuses. The other is altruism – he is my kindness, generosity, compassion, humility, commitment, and sense of justice." She looked at him, confused. He continued, "And the same fight rages on inside of everyone – even inside of you." She chewed her lip thoughtfully as she tried to digest the meaning of his words. "Which wolf will win?" she asked. The grandfather looked at her intensely and replied, "The one you feed."*

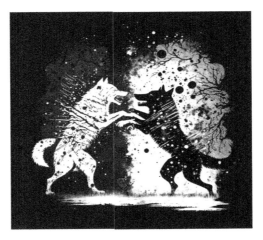

Living your values can be hard. As a foundation leader, sometimes the part of you that wants to pursue your moral values will be in tension with the part of you that wants other things. For example, pursuing impact may be in tension with pursuing personal passions, making correct calls may be in tension with making popular ones, and maximizing impact may be in tension with work-life balance.

Personal passion or interest in a project may be important as motivation, but given that humans in far-flung countries and nonhuman animals at the fringes of the moral circle need our help most, how important is that personal passion relative to starting a project that could help others even more? Can you inspire yourself to pursue and become passionate about a more impactful area if your passion does not align with where there is most need?

194 VALUES

The right choice for the world and all those suffering may not be the one that makes you look the best or that makes your family and friends the happiest. As a foundation leader, sometimes you will need to make hard calls. Firing an underperforming employee whom you really like is the right thing to do for the world. But for you personally, it's far less pleasant than keeping them around. Your team will also have to do unpleasant tasks that are important to your organization's progress.

In addition to such broad considerations, moral considerations will factor into many of the day-to-day decisions you'll make as a foundation. If you are the founder, you will have no boss and thus have considerable flexibility about how you work. What is the best way to think through choices where your personal well-being or interest might not always line up with the path to making the greatest difference? There is, of course, a limit to how hard we can, or should, push ourselves. But not all people find that limit – and it's worth exploring for the sake of those many individuals we are in a position to help.

Sometimes the choice that helps others the most is at a cost to yourself or those closest to you. These can be the choices that separate good from great grantmakers. Choosing the right balance and motivating yourself to live by that choice will be one of the key challenges you face as a foundation entrepreneur.

## Avoiding value drift

Priya is in her first year of university when she starts getting interested in effective philanthropy. She gets excited about the idea through her university's Effective Giving society, and her family has the financial means to make philanthropy a real option for her one day. She takes a pledge to donate some of her income and accepts an internship at a young but promising foundation over winter break to improve her skills. So far, Priya is on a great track to work in the philanthropic sector and holds it as one of her major life goals.

When Priya returns from break, she hits a particularly rough year of school and has to focus on keeping her grades up. Her involvement with the university society drops off – she's too busy. The silver lining at the end of this rough year is that she starts a relationship. The person is smart and well-suited to her but does not share her charitable interest. Over time, Priya stops reading the NGO content she used to and never gets back into attending chapter meetings. After she gets her degree, she takes a job in consulting to build up some skills, planning to work on helping others later in her career. But she has a sense in her heart that it's unlikely to happen.

Priya's story is not uncommon. Knowing your values is only half the battle. The other half is actively making choices that support and reinforce them.

We tend to think that the person we are today is who we will be in the long term. However, if you look back at who you were five years ago, you'll probably realize that your lifestyle and views have changed significantly. This applies to your values, too.

Sometimes change is neutral or positive, as you may deepen and confirm your understanding of your values. Other times, you might drift in your views or behavior away from your values, much like a healthy eater might drift toward junk food.

Value drift may be a problem that concerns the future you, but just as you want your future self to be healthy, you want your future self to live a morally good life. Thankfully, there are many ways to support your values and make it easier to remain the person you wish to be ethically.

**Setting specific guardrails**: Often, bad habits sneak up on us one inch at a time. Drawing a clear line in the sand, such as "I will always donate XX% of income," might seem overly restrictive. But there is a lot of evidence in psychology that setting specific guardrails or goals greatly increases the chances of sticking to positive habits.[103] Many of the most successful grantmakers we know set specific goals for themselves for hours worked or other aspects that are otherwise easy to let slide when founding a new project.

**Adapting your environment**: Studies show that you can change your environment to support the actions you wish to do: Something as simple as putting healthy foods in a glass bowl or putting cookies on a hard-to-reach shelf can significantly improve your odds of choosing healthier foods (a great book on this is Sunstein & Thaler's Nudge).[104] Adopting automatic systems can make doing good the easy default action, such as setting up automatic donations instead of having to remember each month. When it comes to starting any project, put yourself in an environment that will make it easy to keep doing the actions you wish to do; for

---

[103] James Clear, *Atomic Habits: An Easy & Proven Way to Build Good Habits & Break Bad Ones*. Avery, 2018

[104] C.R. Sunstein and R.H. Thaler, *Nudge: Improving Decisions About Health, Wealth, and Happiness*. Penguin Books, 2009

instance, working at a coworking office or in a city with a strong drive toward charity and doing good, or building skills that are more useful in altruistic careers than others.

**Public commitment**: Publicly committing to your plans creates social pressure for you to stick to your ethical goals even when it's hard.

**Surround yourself with motivating, inspiring people**: There's a saying that you become the average of the five people closest to you. Lots of people vastly underestimate the impact of the social connections around them. But your relationships can shape huge aspects of your personality. Surrounding yourself with people who motivate and inspire you in your altruistic pursuits can be one of the best ways to have an impact long term. Meeting up regularly with others focused on charitable giving and doing good can have a huge positive effect. Besides your friendships and close colleagues, you could make an effort to have regular social interactions with value-aligned people (e.g. meet for lunch/dinner/coffee), engage with or start an altruism meetup or volunteering activity, attend conferences or social events, take part in a funders circle, or get in touch with value-aligned people and communities online.

For the more adventurous, even something as radical as moving cities can be a fair idea to increase the community connection you want to build. Currently, a large hub for charity entrepreneurship and philanthropy is in London, UK., but there are altruism-focused, philanthropic, and charity hubs all over the world.

# 6.2. Cause areas

Many people work in areas based on causes that have personally affected them. But given the size of the world and its range of problems, it's highly unlikely that the *best* way to save lives will be something that affects you personally.

Most of the strongest charities and most impactful foundations choose cause areas using a systematic process. You can use decision-making tools to create a systematic comparison and make an informed decision of which cause area(s) the world needs you to support the most.

In this chapter, we will investigate a number of common and rising cause areas you might consider focusing your grantmaking on. We will compare them in terms of their profiles, a weighted-factor model quantifying their performance on central criteria, their cause area-specific key strengths and weaknesses, and underlying ethical and epistemic assumptions.

## 6.2.1. Comparing cause areas

"Cause area" is the umbrella term for a broad problem. To clarify, mental health would be a cause area, cognitive behavioral therapy would be an intervention, and creating a cognitive behavioral therapy app to reduce postpartum depression in low-income countries would be a charity idea. Beyond doubt, the area that has received the most cost-effectiveness estimates, evidence evaluation and external review to date is global health. But many other cause areas might turn out to be similarly or more effective than the top global health charities and are starting to become more mainstream in the charity world.

Each cause area has its strengths and weaknesses, and it's hard to compare them reliably due to the many assumptions (both ethical and epistemic) that must be made. This chapter offers a starting point for such comparisons.

## Mental health

Mental health interventions directly influence experienced happiness and can fill large happiness gaps in high- and low-income countries. Despite limited historical work on determining the most cost-effective interventions, the evidence-base looks promising. Interventions within this cause area could include delivering guided self-help for mental illnesses, distributing antidepressants such as SSRIs, or training local stakeholders to help prevent suicide.

## Animal welfare

Farmed and wild animals are victims of huge suffering and extreme neglect. The animal movement is smaller and newer than the global health and development space, but large strides have been made for animal welfare in recent years, with many governments starting to ban some of the most egregiously inhumane conditions for farmed animals. However, the best ways to help animals remain unclear despite the enormous amounts of suffering humans cause animals every day – we simply don't have enough evidence on what works and what doesn't work in the space. Now seems like a uniquely good time to support new animal organizations to tackle this gap between supply and the need for research. Example interventions include addressing footpad burn and feather pecking among factory-farmed birds, improving water quality for farmed crustaceans, and campaigning for more humane rodent control.

## Family planning

Family planning has a range of positive effects on health, wealth, empowerment, and more. The area looks highly promising and is growing dramatically, but has not yet received as much analytical attention as other areas of global health. Ideas could include offering family planning services to women postpartum and post-abortion, providing vouchers for contraceptives to increase access, and implementing a social and behavior change media campaign.

## Global health

Global health (both direct delivery and policy) can be highly effective and has amongst the strongest evidence bases in the charitable world. Leveraging government resources can make a significant, large-scale impact. This could include ideas like campaigning for lead paint regulation, distributing mosquito bednets, lobbying for higher taxes on alcohol, or vaccination-related interventions.

## Biorisk mitigation

Effectiveness-focused philanthropists had been sounding the alarm about biorisks for years before the COVID-19 pandemic exposed the costs of under-preparedness. Even with the pandemic fresh in our collective memory, the resources invested in mitigating future risks are woefully low. Mitigating the risk of man-made pathogens, which have the potential to be far more infectious and lethal than the worst evolved pathogens, is even more under-resourced. Promising interventions in this area include early detection systems, technological solutions to prevent and treat infections (e.g. vaccines, PPE), improved governance of gain-of-function research, and strengthening of international commitments to abstain from developing or using biological weapons.

## Artificial intelligence safety

Some AI experts believe we will develop general artificial intelligence technology within our current lifetimes. If we can ensure that AI technology is safe and aligned with humanity's interests, it could result in unprecedented benefits. Conversely, executing this technological shift poorly could result in unprecedented suffering and pose an existential risk. Commonly pursued interventions in this space include technical AI safety research and improving governance and regulation of organizations developing AI.

## Climate change and environmental sustainability

Environmental damage risks massive costs to the health and well-being of humans and non-humans alike. This cause area has the benefit of a large existing body of research and a high amount of public support and resources committed. This means that additional support may be more replaceable than other relatively neglected causes. It's also a highly politicized area, which can be challenging.

## Nuclear war and great power conflict

Armed conflict between the world's most powerful nations and those with nuclear weapons risks causing huge amounts of suffering, reversing economic development (at best) and risking human extinction (at worst). Near misses in the context of nuclear war, like the 1983 Soviet nuclear false alarm incident where the caution of one man, Stanislav Petrov, prevented the likely full-blown nuclear war between the USA and USSR, show that this cause area ought to be taken seriously.

## A multi-factor comparison of cause areas

Let's start to compare these very different areas. The table below shows our multi-factor model framing for each of these cause areas. Each area is color-coded from strongest (dark) to weakest (light). The criteria considered are the following:

- Marginal cost-effectiveness: The estimated cost-effectiveness of giving an additional dollar to an organization that successfully implements the best interventions in this area
- Relevant evidence: The quantity and quality of evidence available to inform decisions about what interventions or organizations to funnel resources into to maximize impact
- Limiting factor: What generally keeps this cause area from scaling its impact?
- Execution difficulty: How likely is a venture focused on this cause area to be successful?
- Indirect flow-through effects: How significant and positive are the ancillary effects of this initiative? e.g. animal welfare interventions are typically appraised based on their cost-effectiveness in reducing animal suffering. But there may be significant other impacts, e.g. human health, climate change, or pandemic prevention.

| | Marginal cost-effectiveness | Relevant evidence | Limiting factor* | Execution difficulty | Indirect flow-through effects** |
|---|---|---|---|---|---|
| **Mental health** | Moderate | Some | Funding (1) | Easier | EA movement (3) |
| **Family planning** | Low | Moderate | Contraceptive supply chain (4) | Complex | Child, animals (4) |
| **Animal welfare** | High | Low | Talent, Proven interventions (2) | Easier | Bar setting (2) |
| **Health policy** | High | High | Funding (3) | Moderate | Precedent (1) |
| **Biorisk mitigation** | Moderate | Moderate | Supply chain of PPE (4) | Complex | Other health effects (3) |
| **AI safety** | High | Low | Talent (1) | Complex | Technology governance (1) |
| **Climate change & environment** | Low | High | Technology (3) | Moderate | Broad positive (5) |
| **Nuclear war & great power conflict** | Moderate | Low | Funding (1) Proven interventions (2) | Very complex | Economic development (5) |

*If the number accompanying the limiting factor cell is low, this means that the limiting factor will be met very quickly. Higher numbers mean that the factor will not soon become relevant. Shading is dictated by (a) how quickly the limiting factor will be hit (b) whether foundations could easily address the limiting factor, e.g. funding bottlenecks are relatively easy to address and so tend to score higher (shaded darker).

** If the number accompanying the indirect flow-through effect is high, this means that the flow-through effects are large and positive. If the number is low, this means that the externality is small.

We can also frame cause area comparisons in terms of more specific key strengths and weaknesses:

# List of key strengths and weaknesses by cause area

## Mental health

| Strengths | Weaknesses |
| --- | --- |
| • The directness of the subjective well-being metric and possible underrating of the area by other metrics<br>• Possible promising cost-effectiveness for both low and high-income countries<br>• Strong to moderate evidence- base and background research but limited prioritization work of interventions<br>• Could encourage EA movement to consider more cause areas long term | • Uncertain cost-effectiveness compared to top global health interventions<br>• More theoretical and philosophical work is required for assessment<br>• More limited funding base, particularly in the EA movement<br>• Evidence base has a wider range of metrics used, making it more difficult to compare |

## Family planning

| Strengths | Weaknesses |
| --- | --- |
| • Strong funding outside of EA for scaling up new organizations with counterfactually clean funding<br>• Moderate evidence base<br>• Diverse range of positive effects (e.g. women's empowerment, unborn child benefits, family benefits, income benefits, animal effects, etc.)<br>• Could be extremely impactful under certain ethical views<br>• Relatively neglected because comparative CEAs generally don't capture the diverse benefit | • Maximizing multiple positive effects makes the charity harder to run<br>• Evidence is spread out between a wide range of metrics; thus, speculative conversions and comparisons need to be used<br>• Can be controversial<br>• Size of impact depends in part on questions of population ethics where there is little consensus |

## Animal welfare

| Strengths | Weaknesses |
| --- | --- |
| • Naive cost-effectiveness estimates generally show extremely high cost-effectiveness<br>• High levels of historical neglect mean many promising charity ideas are not yet founded<br>• Strong support both within and outside of the EA community<br>• Very strong case that animals should be given moral weight | • Low evidence base for what actually works compared to other areas<br>• Some talent shortages in the movement that impair key charities<br>• More limited externalities and flow-through effects than other cause areas<br>• High rate of non-effectiveness-minded activists and actors in the area |

## Health & development policy

| Strengths | Weaknesses |
| --- | --- |
| • Naive cost-effectiveness estimates show higher cost-effectiveness than standard global health interventions and maybe all other human-focused areas<br>• Evidence base fairly strong if confidence is established in a causal relationship of lobbying | • Extremely complex space resulting in a much higher-than-average chance of a charity having limited or no impact<br>• More limited externalities and flow-through effects compared to other cause areas<br>• Very high bar of charities already working in the space |

## Biorisk mitigation

| Strengths | Weaknesses |
| --- | --- |
| • Interventions have broad positive health and tech/weapons governance benefits<br>• Now is a uniquely promising time to work on biorisk due to the recent covid scare.<br>• Interventions are uniquely strong in feedback loops relative to other more long-termist cause areas | • Unclear cost-effectiveness. Many biorisk interventions are based on relatively limited evidence and data and have unclear future utilization potential<br>• Difficult counterfactuals. Biorisk interventions often involve many different actors, including researchers and multiple governments, making counterfactuals difficult to estimate |

## AI safety

| Strengths | Weaknesses |
|---|---|
| • Naive expected value calculations can be extremely promising<br>• Is a highly socially appealing area to work in, with interesting challenges and growing levels of events and support for actors in the field<br>• Could affect high-resource people, making it easier to build buy-in from non-altruistic actors | • Extremely poor feedback loops. Risks from AI are unprecedented, and quite hard to get verifiable or falsifiable evidence on what works to mitigate them<br>• Getting the wider public to take something that sounds like sci-fi seriously is a challenge. Very far outside of the typical philanthropy mandates<br>• Limitations in the supply of talent that are hard to fix with funding |

## Climate change and environmental sustainability

| Strengths | Weaknesses |
|---|---|
| • Growing public support<br>• Some alignment between human and non-human interests<br>• Market solutions exist (need policy support to cost externalities) | • Already well-resourced (funding, research, executors)<br>• Often heavily politicized<br>• Some tension between human and non-human interests, e.g. climate considerations lead people to eat less cows but many more lower-welfare chickens |

## Nuclear war and great power conflict

| Strengths | Weaknesses |
|---|---|
| • Addressing it is in all peoples' self-interest (which helps with generating support)<br>• Preventing nuclear war is neglected, and funding has recently declined | • Long and weak feedback loops mean it's hard to know what interventions work<br>• Heavily politicized<br>• May require local actors to have influence (e.g. within China, within the USA, within India) |

## Effects of ethical and epistemic assumptions

Another way to compare these cause areas is to consider key ethical and epistemic assumptions. Here are four examples of controversial ethical dilemmas that might rule out or strengthen certain areas (some of them will be familiar from our discussion in the last chapter on values):

1. Animal vs. human lives
2. The lives of unborn people vs. existing lives
3. Happiness vs. health vs. income
4. Cluelessness and priors

We will go through the shallow considerations within each dilemma. But it's worth the time to dive deeper and form your own opinions regarding these questions before you make a final decision on which cause area(s) to focus your grantmaking on.

## Animal vs. human lives

- **Assumption: Ethical**
- **Issue: Moral circle**

An increasingly outdated view is that certain nonhuman animals do not feel pain or suffering. However, this is becoming rarer and rarer in regard to larger animals (especially mammals such as dogs, cats, pigs, and cows). The view is still common when considering animal species further from humans in the evolutionary tree. Should shrimp and insects be given moral consideration? Often, the same sum of money can save either many smaller animals or just one larger animal – but how can we weigh this trade-off ethically?

Another difficult question: even if you agree that the suffering of nonhuman animals matters, could you motivate yourself every day to put energy into saving nonhuman animals when humans are still suffering? If not, this could rule out animal welfare as an area. However, animal advocacy could be a good fit if you're keen to help neglected beings who would otherwise receive little attention. The movement has a lot of momentum, and among the billions of farmed animals suffering every day, there are outstanding opportunities to create change. And if you morally value animals such as fish, shrimp, or bugs, you can help truly staggering numbers of beings by working in the animal space. Those interested in the arguments for valuing animal lives might want to read *Animal Liberation Now* by Peter Singer.[105]

## Lives of potential people vs. existing lives

- **Assumption: Ethical**
- **Issue: Population ethics**

Some interventions save lives, while others affect potential people. Family planning has measurable benefits for the mother's health and harder-to-measure benefits for her autonomy. It also impacts how many people come into existence, and some believe that if they would go on to live good lives, this should be a consideration in determining the net impact of family planning. Family planning raises many questions: In the longer term, do we want more humans on earth (this may be good for the additional humans and economic progress) or fewer (this may be good for animals, the environment, and perhaps existing humans)? Does the well-being and/or preference of an existing being matter more than the hypothetical well-being or preference of a potential future being that may never come into existence? Most will agree that it's good to make people happy, but is it good (or merely neutral) to make happy people? Intuition on these sorts of questions can make family planning or cause areas focused on existential risks look either promising or not very promising.[106]

## Happiness vs. health vs. income

- **Assumption: Epistemology**
- **Issue: Measuring well-being**

Very few people would deny that happiness, health and income all have an influence over someone's well-being (even if the effects of income on well-being see sharply diminishing returns). However, people have different views on how we might be able to measure well-being, to what extent measures of happiness, health and income are important and how we might be able to cross-compare or make trade-offs between them. The DALY is used across many health interventions, but comparing it to income or subjective well-being (self-reported happiness) is difficult. Certain

---

[105] Peter Singer, *Animal Liberation Now*. Bodley Head, 2023.

[106] If you are interested in the case for moral obligations towards future people, we recommend: William McAskill, *What we owe the future*, (New York, New York, Hachette Book Group, 2022).

cause areas do much better on one metric than others: Mental health looks extremely important from a subjective well-being perspective but less so from a DALY perspective. We discuss the choice of impact metric in more depth in Chapter 4.1.4.

## Cluelessness and skepticism

- **Assumption: Epistemology**
- **Issue: Standards of evidence**

<u>Skepticism:</u> Everyone has a prior view on something, that requires evidence in order to update. These priors tend to dictate how quickly one changes and how much evidence they require to change. Calling someone close-minded or naive are often an informal way of gesturing at someone's priors being too heavy (and thus hard to move) or too light and quickly updated, respectively. People with heavier and more skeptical priors are less likely to buy into the importance of a cause area they find unintuitive (like preventing catastrophic risks from AI) based on a given amount of evidence.

<u>Cluelessness:</u> The more quickly you think people descend into perfect cluelessness (e.g. not knowing if some action or intervention will be predictably net positive or net negative in the long run), the more negative you will be towards far-future interventions. In many cases, there is agreement on some aspects of the issues, e.g. although a butterfly flapping its wings may create a tornado, we are clueless as to these effects. On the other hand, the confidence that our actions or interventions can predictably affect something like an important value being preserved over time, or an existential risk being prevented, are more debated topics. The more complex and unpredictable you think long-term effects are in the world, the more skeptical you will end up being towards longtermist[107] interventions.

---

[107] Longtermism is the view that because the majority of the people that might ever exist will do so millions of years in the future, the best way to do the most good is to focus on interventions that will improve things for those people in the far future. However, if cluelessness means we're particularly unable to predict the impact of our present actions on that long term future, then longtermism is a less compelling view.

## 6.2.2. Comparing interventions

Foundations don't have to just specialize by cause area – they can specialize by intervention as well, or instead. Specializing by intervention tends to involve fewer ethical considerations and more evidence-based considerations. The reasons a foundation might want to specialize by intervention are similar to why they might want to specialize by scope: It allows the foundation to build deep expertise in that area, it makes lessons from each grant more generalizable to the others, and all-in-all leads to more rigorous, better quality grantmaking decisions.

Below is a high-level summary of the general strengths and weaknesses of some types of interventions. Granted, you can divide up the types of interventions in many equally valid ways and at different levels of granularity, and the results of the comparison would differ. Your foundation's risk appetite and the importance you place on strong feedback loops may push you towards or away from certain types of intervention.

| | Marginal cost-effectiveness (if successful) | Risk profile | Feedback loops | Limiting factor | Indirect flow - through effects |
|---|---|---|---|---|---|
| **Direct delivery** | Relatively low* | Low | Strong | Funding (3) | Weak |
| **Policy advocacy** | Very high | High | Weak - Middling | Policy windows (1) | Middling |
| **Institutional advocacy** | Middling | High | Weak - Middling | Talent (1) | Middling |
| **Public outreach** | Middling- High | Middling | Middling | Evidence (1) | Strong |
| **Meta** | High | High | Poor | Talent (5) | Strong |
| **Research** | Relatively low | Middling | Poor | Funding (2) | Strong |

*Keep in mind that the marginal cost-effectiveness of the best direct delivery charities (e.g. those recommended by GiveWell) is excellent. It's only low relative to some other high-leverage interventions like policy interventions, which are necessarily more cost-effective when you factor in the high risk of failure.*

To clarify what these different types of intervention are:

- Direct delivery interventions involve providing a service directly to beneficiaries, like giving cash transfers to impoverished people.
- Policy advocacy involves attempting to influence government legislation or spending to improve the lives of beneficiaries.
- Public outreach involves attempting to influence individual consumers to make choices that help beneficiaries (e.g. by going vegan) or improve the world (e.g. by emitting less $CO_2$). Often public outreach is a tool used as part of policy or institutional advocacy interventions to put pressure on these stakeholders to make desired changes.
- Institutional advocacy involves attempting to influence any institutions other than the government or the public to improve the lives of beneficiaries. For example, animal advocates have lobbied a range of stakeholders, from corporations to schools, hospitals, and jails, to remove cage eggs from their supply chains.
- Meta-interventions are one step removed from doing good directly. For example, Charity Entrepreneurship's training program does not cause impact directly. Instead, it supports charities that then go on to cause impact. Meta-interventions include charity incubation, charity evaluation, and grantmaking.
- Research involves generating and disseminating evidence that others can use to make better decisions that serve the interests of beneficiaries.

Keep in mind that whilst many attributes of interventions generalize across cause areas, some don't. For example, it's our understanding that the marginal cost-effectiveness of public outreach in the family planning space is strong (e.g. Family Empowerment Media was recently estimated at 26x the cost-effectiveness of cash transfers).[108] But in the animal welfare space, the cost-effectiveness of public outreach like adverts promoting reducing animal consumption remains uncertain – there haven't been any clear winners, but the idea hasn't been explored thoroughly enough to reach a verdict.

---

[108] Rosie_Bettle, "Mass Media Interventions Probably Deserve More Attention (Founders Pledge)" EA Forum, Nov. 17, 2022, accessed Feb. 20, 2023.

Next, let's compare examples of policy and direct delivery interventions within global health and farmed animal welfare, respectively, to get a sense of how these types of interventions' strengths and weaknesses play out.

**Global health** (same intervention through direct delivery vs. policy)

| Intervention | Strengths | Weaknesses |
| --- | --- | --- |
| Direct delivery of flour fortification | • Focusing on helping mills transition to fortified flour has quick feedback loops<br>• Strong track record of similar interventions<br>• Highly scalable (i.e. could absorb $10m+ a year) | • Going mill to mill is expensive and requires a large team that takes time to scale<br>• Higher cost than a policy mandate |
| Policy advocacy for government to mandate flour fortification | • Governmental actors are sympathetic to this idea, and it's relatively uncontroversial<br>• The scale of current large-scale government food programs allows a large population to be reached almost immediately once policy is changed<br>• A relatively small team is all that is needed to test this idea | • The government is slow to change<br>• The government brings implementation restrictions (e.g. only working via school feeding programs)<br>• High risk of failure |

**Farmed animal welfare** (two different interventions)

| Intervention | Strengths | Weaknesses |
| --- | --- | --- |
| Partnering with individual farmers to improve fish welfare (direct delivery) | • Strong evidence base relative to other interventions in the space<br>• Ability to learn from the implementation of each farm and improve the process<br>• Necessary first step as a proof of concept before other interventions can be executed at a large scale | • High variability of farms means no one-size-fits-all solutions<br>• Requires a large staff team with solid industry connections<br>• Requires heavy ongoing monitoring & evaluation to ensure welfare improvements have intended effects |

| Banning the import of animal products below local welfare standards (policy advocacy) | • Very high cost-effectiveness if successful<br>• Uniquely tractable in that farmers in high welfare countries are in favor<br>• Could likely work in multiple countries simultaneously, given the narrow scope of the project<br>• Strong precedent-setting value | • A limited number of countries are applicable for this intervention (countries with high welfare standards but a lot of importing)<br>• Not a proven intervention |
|---|---|---|

# 6.2.3. Making the decision

Picking a cause area is a complex choice that merits deep research and conversations with people who have worked in the space or faced similar choices. Some cause areas might not look as effective as you first thought once you review the cause area profile and current state and compare their performance on central criteria. Always try to keep in mind the fundamental goal: saving or improving as many lives as possible.

Every foundation will need different guidance, but there are a few pieces of cross-applicable advice that could benefit virtually all organizations:

### *Compare at least ten options*

There are untold numbers of cause areas out there; the odds are vanishingly low that anyone is obviously the optimal one. Furthermore, your choice can only be as good as the best option you have on the table. If you consider only two cause areas, that puts hard limits on your potential upside. So, to come up with a truly impactful cause area, think of at least ten different options.

The "at least" is important. Ideally, you should try to think of dozens and then whittle them down with good decision-making tools. The more ideas you generate, the more likely you'll come across something truly outstanding.

Supporting a cause area long term is a really big commitment, and the interventions you choose to support are the largest driver of how impactful your grantmaking will be. You could execute flawlessly, but if you're supporting a charity distributing homeopathic medicine, you won't be helping anybody; you want to make sure you're committing to something worth the effort. Changing your direction later on is difficult, both logistically and psychologically.

### Use a range of decision-making tools.

In Part A of this handbook, we discussed tools for making good decisions in considerable depth. You will need to use many of these tools when choosing your scope. We recommend using a weighted-factor model to combine scientific evidence, philosophical arguments, the perspectives of experts, and the most helpful heuristics.

### Test out multiple areas.

People tend to start work in one area and quickly become attached to it. If at all possible, explore multiple areas for a while before settling on your choice (e.g. hiring a full-time staff to work in this area). This can even be worthwhile for areas you are pretty confident you will support.

### Research your cause area— then try to destroy it.

This may seem obvious, but most people we have spoken to have not really done this. They stumble into an idea, then ask a few people what they think. Those people often don't want to be critical and "crush your dreams" (people are particularly wary about critiquing the ideas of funders), so you might be tempted to dive straight in. Destroying an idea you are considering is emotionally difficult but essential if you want to do the most good you can.

The most important point here is that you want to rule out suboptimal cause areas before you become emotionally invested, or it will be far less likely that you'll ever be able to see that it's not a good idea. This is one of the greatest dangers lurking in the waters of grantmaking. If you run a for-profit and it isn't making money, you'll eventually find out, no matter how much it hurts to admit it. With a foundation, the results are very rarely obvious. You could run something that has no impact indefinitely and fool yourself into thinking it's working great.

# 6.3. Geography

Having a geographic focus is extremely common in the foundation world. It can allow foundations to develop a stronger understanding of the cultural factors and stakeholder landscape (e.g. governments, charities, funders, the private sector, and recipients) in specific regions, as well as a stronger network in those regions. This can enable better identification and vetting of grantmaking opportunities. However, foundations often over-weight the value of this relative to factors like the scale and tractability of the problem in that region. It is not necessary to narrow your foundation's scope to the location dimension, but should you decide that it makes sense for your foundation, make sure you choose a focus that is narrow enough for you to genuinely specialize (i.e. 'Asia' is probably too broad) but where the problem is large enough to enable impact at scale (i.e. 'Fiji,' or any location with <100 million people is probably too small for a large foundation). Also, remember that once you pick a location, it can be difficult to change it. Many location-specific networks and skills may not transfer from place to place.

Before deciding if your foundation should focus its scope on a location and where it's crucial to consider how many potential beneficiaries in that area stand to benefit from the type of interventions you plan to fund - including considerations about limiting factors (discussed previously). When working on global health interventions focused on humans, you can usually help the most people if you work in an area with a large population that suffers from severe poverty, especially where people suffer from easily preventable health issues. A proportionately smaller number of people in need live in more affluent locations such as New York, London, or Tokyo. And it is generally far more difficult to alleviate those types of suffering without spending a large amount of money.

When considering overall need, it is important to consider neglectedness, total need, and need density (incidence rate) all together. If you look at any one of these factors in isolation, you will often end up with the wrong geographic focus:

- If you focus only on neglectedness, you would typically end up in a country that is underfunded for valid reasons, e.g. the Democratic Republic of Congo might look promising on a number of dimensions, including neglectedness, but it is extremely hard to operate in.
- Look at total need only, and you will almost certainly arrive at China, India, or Nigeria as the place to focus due to their high populations. However, countries of this size are often diverse enough that they would need to be approached at a state level anyway, where their scale is less dominant compared to other countries
- If you look at incidence rates alone, you will often end up favoring very small locations with extremely high incidence rates but highly limited options for impact at scale (e.g. Lesotho or Samoa).

As seen in the table below, a country can score highly in at least one dimension but poorly in at least one other. It's worth considering whether the dimension a country scores poorly on is a strong enough limiting factor to negate the dimensions it scores well on.

|  | Neglectedness | Incidence Rate | Total need |
|---|---|---|---|
| **Samoa** | High | High | Low |
| **China** | High | Low | Very High |
| **USA** | Low | Mid | High |
| **Ghana** | High | High | Mid |

A geographic focus does not have to be a country - it can be any group of locations that are sufficiently homogeneous when it comes to the key factors that make one geography more attractive than another (like neglect, total need, incidence rate, tractability, etc.) For example, India is a large enough area to have it as a solo focus, but even Ghana (>30 million people) does not have the population to be the solo focus for a large foundation, so it should likely be considered as part of a grouping of countries in West Africa instead.

# 6.4. Grantee size and maturity

Another way to break down scope is based on the size of recipient organizations. This is intuitive to many organizations. A proposal you might receive from an organization in its first six months seeking $50,000 will look very different from one from an organization that has been running for six years and is seeking $5 million.[109] Likewise, how you process and what you look for can change substantially based on the size of organizations you think are most promising to support (see Part IV on vetting for more on this).

There are a few different categories of organization size that a foundation could specialize in. Foundations typically think of recipient organizations as being small, medium or large based on their annual budgets. These tiers roughly line up with those laid out by DIV (Development Innovation Ventures) and GIF (The Global Innovation Fund). Interestingly, most charities are relatively small (92% running with a less than $1 million yearly budget). But the total money donated is not distributed evenly, with a few large charities receiving a huge proportion of total donations.

Let's take a look at your options when choosing what size organizations to focus on, the pros and cons of each, and the implications of the choice.

---

[109] Note that whilst a charity's age, annual budget and grant size are correlated, this isn't a strict rule. A brand new charity can seek a $10M grant. A veteran charity with a $100M budget can seek a $50k grant restricted to a specific pilot project.

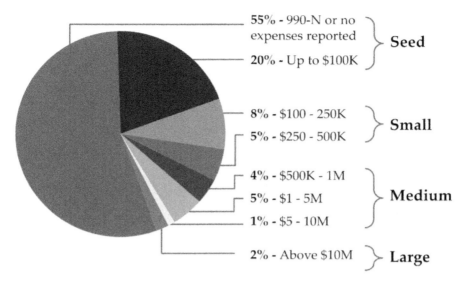

*Charitable nonprofits by size (501(c)(3)s, excluding private foundations)*[110]

## Seed

An organization in its seed stage is typically very young; in many cases, you might be the organization's first funder. Seed-stage organizations typically have a founder and an idea but little else outside of that. We also lump pre-seed charities (e.g. actively getting a new charity started) into this category, as the same funders often cover these two sizes. The benefit of supporting an organization at seed level is that your influence could mean the difference between a high-impact charity flourishing or never even getting off the ground. The downside is that your investment is much higher risk. The vetting process for these organizations would be more about the quality of the founders and the theoretical evidence base for the intervention rather than the intervention's track record.

## Small

'Small' generally describes organizations under (and sometimes well under) $500,000 a year. A grant to charities in this range could be $20k to $200k. These organizations will typically be pretty young (e.g. under three years) and have a bit of a track record. They may be looking to run a more formal pilot or test on their

---

[110] National Council of Nonprofits, "Think you know everything about charitable nonprofits? Think again!" accessed Feb. 20, 2023, https://www.nonprofitimpactmatters.org.

activities, but they will be characterized by more of a "we are still figuring this out" attitude relative to larger projects. These small organizations can also be exciting to fund, as any extra resources they receive can have highly tangible, measurable results. Supporting them can mean the difference between them having to shut down, being mediocre, or becoming high-impact. Focusing your scope on small charities would give you the widest range to choose from, as well as a higher possibility of finding neglected ones. Much as with seed-stage organizations, small charities carry more risk than larger ones but can be much more cost-effective.

## Medium

Medium-sized organizations are where you start to get established track records; commonly, they will be three to ten years old and are pretty stable. Much of the time, you would be one of many funders that support them. Their budgets might range from $500,000 to $10 million annually. Medium organizations can provide a good middle ground between reward and risk. As you start considering these bigger organizations, you need to consider whether you are having the most impact possible; would the organization easily secure funding if not for you, and if so, are you better off looking for a gap elsewhere?

## Large

There are fewer of them, but large organizations are typically the ones we hear most about (Save the Children, Oxfam, BRAC, etc.) They are organizations with operating budgets of over $10 million a year. Often they have been running for a long time and have slowly built up to cover a huge number of areas. Very rarely does a single funder cover the entire organization at this size; funding is usually spread out between a large number of individuals, foundations, and governments. Large organizations are the least likely to collapse and can absorb a lot of funding. However, you need to seriously consider if donating to such large organizations has the highest impact possible; they are rarely as cost-effective as smaller organizations. Large organizations also tend to perform a wide range of interventions with varying levels of cost-effectiveness, but it can be difficult to selectively fund just the effective ones (see Chapter 8.2.2. on restricted funding).

## No size constraints

A final approach is to not have any size constraints. This, of course, gives the most options but also reduces your organization's specialization. We think this makes particular sense for cause areas already really small (e.g. an area that only has 10 charities in total might not allow for size specialization anyway). Suppose your scope focuses on such a cause. In that case, you may want to heavily specialize in ways other than organization size, such as values or geographic area.

| Charity size | Example | Typical age | Typical budget | Benefits of funding | Downsides of funding |
|---|---|---|---|---|---|
| Seed | CE incubatee | <1 yr | <$0.1M /yr | • Your funding could be the difference between failure and the opportunity to become a world-leading charity long-term | • Highest risk of minimal impact<br>• Harder to find<br>• Less evidence for vetting |
| Small | Lead Exposure Elimination Project | <3 yrs | <$0.5M /yr | • Wide range of orgs to choose from (strong change of finding neglected ones)<br>• Less likely to have unnecessary overheads<br>• Fast to pivot (low bureaucracy) | • Relatively risky (vulnerable to hitting roadblocks or early successes not being replicable) |
| Medium | Family Empowerment Media | <10 yrs | <$10M /yr | • Established track records<br>• Attractive balance of reward and risk | • Funding is more replaceable |
| Large | Oxfam, AMF | 10+ yrs | >$10M /yr | • Established track records<br>• Can absorb large amounts of funding | • Generally (but not always!) less cost-effective than smaller orgs |
| All sizes, i.e., don't specialize | n/a | n/a | n/a | • Able to choose the best opportunities across all charity types<br>• Most appropriate in small cause areas / targeted geographies with fewer total opportunities | • Difficult to build vetting systems that scale appropriately with the size of the grant and availability of evidence |

# 6.5. Identifying funding gaps

Foundations that aim to maximize their positive impact should avoid funding areas that have ample funding already and instead aim their funding where the gaps are. This increases the likelihood that the activities they fund would not have happened without their support.

While funding gaps are a common topic in the nonprofit sector, the discussion is often oversimplified, only focusing on broad cause areas. Claims like "global poverty has a funding gap" or "global poverty does not have a funding gap" are too broad and can lead to a lot of confusion about the state of funding. Strong charities commonly receive no funding despite a consensus that the given area is "funding-flooded." At Charity Entrepreneurship, we work with early-stage charities and have gained a nuanced understanding of where these specific gaps exist.

One place where funding gaps can exist within cause areas that are considered to be well-funded overall is at the sub-cause level. For example, some areas of global poverty (like hospital funding) tend to have very few funding gaps, while others (like neglected tropical diseases) have many. There are also gaps at the intervention level. Corporate campaigns in animal welfare might be well-funded, while at the same time, funding in vegan outreach might be quite limited (even when factoring in any differences in estimated cost-effectiveness).

There are several other, more subtle places where funding gaps appear, even within cause areas considered well-funded: gaps by organization size/maturity, gaps by values/worldview, and gaps by geography.

## Gaps by organization size and maturity

A factor not often talked about is that the size (and correlating factors like age) of an organization can be just as influential to funding availability as the cause or intervention area. For example, there are areas with large governmental funders who only consider organizations of a certain size and age or have requirements that would be near impossible for a smaller organization to fulfill. Governments are not the only entities with these restrictions – some big funders are uniquely keen on very large megaprojects. But of course, relatively few of these projects are launched from scratch. The vast majority of projects slowly build up resources and capacity.

To take global poverty as an example, GiveWell is typically looking for organizations that can absorb considerable amounts of funding in the near future (e.g. $10 million per year or more). This strategy is well thought-out. GiveWell wants to move a huge amount of funding and only has time to evaluate a certain number of organizations to the depth they require to recommend them. Although this strategy makes sense in GiveWell's case, it can have a strange effect on the ecosystem. A donor might not realize that a charity has only been ruled out due to its size and that they are actually very cost-effective. Being ruled out by GiveWell does not necessarily mean that they are not a strong project; new organizations that have not yet gotten onto that larger scale may have cost-effective projects left on the table, unfunded, that would potentially have a huge impact.

If you look at the funding available to the cause area of global poverty, you can clearly see the problem:

| Cause area | Seed (<$500k, 2 yrs) | | Small/medium (<$10M, 2-5 yrs) | | Large ($10M+) | |
|---|---|---|---|---|---|---|
| Global poverty | Limited | ◖ | Middling | ◑ | Very Strong | ● |
| Farmed animal welfare | Middling | ◑ | Strong | ◕ | Middling | ◑ |

Global poverty is a good example of an area with highly differentiated funding availability depending on organization size. Even in an area with funding overhangs, there are thus often highly promising projects with limited funding.

This funding gap makes for an exciting opportunity for funders. In the current landscape, a strong base of seed funders means animal welfare charities will likely have an easier time building from the ground up than global poverty charities. Providing the balance to a cause area like global poverty still lacking in seed funding could be catalytic to get highly effective organizations to the size they need to be to access other pools of support. There could even be opportunities with higher impact per dollar compared to the well-known impacts of larger-scale organizations. Finding cause areas with a gap could thus be a way for a smaller foundation to have a huge impact. Other cause areas may receive less funding overall but are more balanced across organizational size, as is the case with animal welfare.

## Gaps by values and worldviews

Another often overlooked factor is the diversity of funders in a given space. Funders will have different views and intuitions; one funder with $10 million per year of available funding would almost definitely make different calls from 10 funders with $1 million each. Doing good is messy; intelligent and reasonable people can disagree on the most impactful thing to do. Every funder has a certain worldview, as well as logistical and ethical assumptions (whether stated or not) that affect their donations. Sometimes an organization will be extremely clear on which areas they cover and which they do not (GiveWell does a good job of this); a lot more commonly, they will not, and most people who are not specialists in that cause area will not know about the gaps. Let's look at the same funding chart, with an estimated number of unique funders with different effectiveness-focused worldviews added in brackets to each cell. Unsurprisingly, areas with more limited funding will generally tend to have fewer differentiated funders. More surprisingly, an area can have a very large volume of total funding but relatively few unique effectiveness-minded actors making funding decisions. Although animal organizations might have an easier time scaling up, they may run into a different problem once they are large. If they have a different view or opinion than one of the relatively few big funders, that could dramatically impact their available funding. Global poverty, on the other hand, has a pretty healthy funding ecosystem at a higher scale. Diverse funding sources also make an ecosystem less likely to be affected by a historical fluke (e.g. if Open Philanthropy is the only/main actor in a space and recommends two areas but only finds a program officer for one of them, this could majorly affect the funding in the space as a whole).

| Cause area | Seed (<$500k, 2 yrs) | Small/medium (<$10M, 2-5 yrs) | Large ($10M+) |
|---|---|---|---|
| Global poverty | Limited (~1-3) | Middling (~1-3) | Very Strong (10+) |
| Farmed animal welfare | Middling (~2-5) | Strong (~3-5) | Middling (~1-3) |

Here is the current funding landscape (as of July 2023) as we perceive it at Charity Entrepreneurship by cause area, organization size, and worldview diversity. While it may not be a precise analysis, it gives some interesting insight:

| Cause area | Seed (<$500k, 2 yrs) | Small/medium (<$10M, 2-5 yrs) | Large ($10M+) |
|---|---|---|---|
| Global poverty | Limited (~1-3) | Middling (~1-3) | Very Strong (10+) |
| Farmed animal welfare | Middling (~2-5) | Strong (~3-5) | Middling (~1-3) |
| Artificial intelligence | Strong (~3-5) | Strong (~1-3) | Strong (~1-3) |
| Long-termist EA community building | Strong (~1-2) | Very strong (~2-3) | Very strong (~2-3) |
| Near-termist EA community building | Middling (~2-5) | Middling (~1-3) | Limited (~1) |
| Mental health | Limited (~1-3) | Middling (~1-3) | Middling (~2-5) |
| Family planning | Limited (~1-3) | Strong (~3-5) | Very Strong (10+) |
| Wild animal suffering | Middling (~1-3) | Middling (~1-3) | Limited (~1-3) |
| Biorisk | Middling (~1-3) | Strong (~3-5) | Middling (~1-3) |
| Climate | Middling (~1-3) | Strong (~3-5) | Very Strong (3-5) |
| Broad policy | Limited (~1-3) | Middling (~1-3) | Middling (~1-3) |

## Gaps by geography

Geography is another factor to consider when looking for funding gaps to fill. There is one type of geographic gap that is quite well-understood these days and a few that get less attention. Let's start with the former:

**Low-and middle-income countries are underfunded** relative to high-income countries because (a) they have more severe problems to solve,[111] (b) they have less wealthy governments who can spend fewer resources on solving them, and (c) the founders of philanthropic foundations come disproportionately from wealthy countries and many of these foundations choose to prioritize giving locally over giving to those who need it most.

This issue is increasingly well-known, and yet funders from wealthy countries continue to fund local organizations. They often believe they have good reasons to do so; for example, they might point out that they understand the local problems better than remote ones or how local institutions work better. This may be true, but in our experience, it's often overblown for three reasons: Firstly, people understand the problems in their local area less well than they tend to believe. For example, the context that I might have on homelessness from living in a city with a high homeless population is still pretty limited, even if the issue is more salient. Secondly, local knowledge is more generalizable than many expect. For example, a charity we incubated that works on lead policy initiatives in Africa found a lot of similarities when dealing with regulatory departments across a wide number of countries. Finally, building sufficient expertise in another geography is less of a barrier than people imagine, and other benefits of low-and middle-income countries (like orders of magnitude higher cost-effectiveness) justify the investment in building expertise.

Meanwhile, funders are biased locally because their network tends to be mostly local. So they come across more potential grantees locally (especially when they don't have open applications). As a result, a project headquartered in London, UK, will generally be able to access far more funding than the same project based out of Abuja, Nigeria. Funders should be conscious of this bias and actively try to adjust to it.

There are also some less frequently discussed types of geographical funding gaps:

1. **Gaps driven by cultural barriers:** Relatively separate media and legal landscapes in China lead to limited understanding by foreign funders, especially those from North America and Europe. Also, foreign donors may be treated with skepticism by local organizations and may have a harder time working with the local government. For this reason, ambitious impact-

---

[111] There are of course exceptions, for example high-income countries tend to consume more animal products and so often have far larger scale issues in terms of farmed animal welfare.

focused funders from China and its neighbors may have a unique opportunity to fill a relative gap.

2. **Gaps when considering the trajectory of different issues:** Certain issues might not be huge in an area right now but have growing burdens, e.g. factory farming in Africa or lifestyle diseases like diabetes (and relevant interventions like sugar taxes) in India.

3. **Gaps driven by an undeveloped nonprofit ecosystem:** There's a chicken-and-egg dilemma when it comes to funders and implementers in a region. If there are few established implementing actors in a region, there will be few funders familiar enough with the region and confident enough in the local actors to fund interventions there. With few funders, new organizations can't establish themselves, and existing ones struggle to scale or survive (as seen with farmed animal welfare funding in Asia). A foundation can help end this vicious cycle by having the risk appetite to fund the most promising organizations in a region (even if they are at an earlier stage) and publicly stating their interest in funding new projects in that region.

---

It is relatively uncommon to consider funding gaps at this level of granularity, but we think it presents a unique opportunity for new foundations who are choosing their scope. Identifying and meeting a previously overlooked need could considerably multiply a foundation's counterfactual impact.

## Words of warning on mission creep

There will always be a new idea, trend, or possibility on the horizon, and one of the strengths of a foundation, especially newer ones, is being able to pivot quickly. However, a common failure mode shared by both foundations and charities is where their original goal and mission get diluted as they slowly get broader and broader. The sad fact of limited time and resources means that an hour or a dollar spent in one place can not be spent in another. But usually, one activity will clearly be the more cost-effective, impactful one, so that is where it should go.

Psychologically, adding an area to your portfolio will always feel easier than taking one away. But building in systems such that you remain focused will greatly increase your overall impact. For example, a good rule of thumb for a large range of foundations is to have a policy of only focusing on, at most, three main focus areas. This means if a new area that seems considerably more promising than others arrives, you have to pick an area to remove your focus from.

Many advisors, employees, and friends will suggest new areas. Considering them can be worthwhile, but you should look at a new area with a high degree of skepticism (particularly if you put a lot of time into selecting the first areas you worked on). Suppose you used a formal evaluation system when setting your first areas. In that case, new areas should go through that exact same process. There are great and not-yet-discovered cause areas, but they are rare; for every one of them, there will be 10 that seem exciting on the surface but, upon deeper review, are weaker. Your benchmark for new areas or wings for your foundation should be that they have an exceedingly good chance of overperforming your current areas to make it worth all the costs of switching, re-orienting, and building up expertise and connections anew.

# 7. Structure

The second key decision to make when setting up a foundation is how to structure it. How should you organize your resources to have as much impact as possible within your chosen scope? There are three types of resources you'll need to bring to bear:

**Wealth**
..the money to be deployed

- What guardrails should you have on the rate at which you spend the funds?
- In general, will you lean towards spending sooner or later?
- How much will you spend on grantmaking staff vs. grants themselves?

**Wisdom**
..the good judgment to decide how to use it

- How will you acquire wisdom, i.e. to what extent will you build it personally, hire it, or access it through a network of advisors?
- How will you build feedback loops into your grantmaking?
- How will you ensure you put your wisdom into practice?

**Work**
..the labor to operate the foundation

- To what extent should you contribute your own labor?
- How many hires should you make, and for what roles?
- How will you structure your team?

# 7.1. Wealth

Compared to other NGO structures, foundations have the unique situation of not having to acquire wealth to operate. Although some foundations also receive donations, the vast majority are grantmaking-only. However, they still have important questions to answer regarding how to manage this wealth. Some of these questions are similar to those faced by implementing charities, for example, when to spend and how much to spend on staff vs. programs.

## 7.1.1. Spend-down rate

Every foundation has to consider the timeframe over which they'll spend down their pool funding. In some cases, there will be a practical ceiling on the spending rate (for example, it could be constrained by the rate at which assets can be liquidated). In many cases, foundations will also set a floor on how fast to spend-down for legal or personal reasons relating to the founder.

There is a legal minimum spend-down rate for private foundations in many countries.[112] This base amount needs to be granted year to year, and many countries also have overhead rules; e.g. if a program staff is hired, their costs cannot be more than 10%-20% of total spending. The most widespread legal minimum is the 5% spend-down rate for US private foundations. Canada has a similar rule but for 3%, and the UK tends to be concerned if an organization's spending goes below 6% for a

---

[112] Alana Petraske, "Comparing foundation minimum distribution in the US, Canada, and the UK", WithersWorldwide, 2nd Feb, 2022, accessed Feb. 20, 2023

number of years. These requirements stipulate a minimum spend amount without considering that the foundation's assets (which are typically invested) generally increase in value, sometimes by more than is spent each year. This allows foundations, if they so choose, to exist perpetually, and some of the largest foundations have far outlived their founders. Historically, hitting this legal minimum and existing in perpetuity was a fairly common foundation strategy but is less common with newer foundations. The Rockefeller Foundation is an example of a foundation that uses this minimal spend-down approach.

A large number of foundations aim to spend down their funding within a predetermined time frame, like within the founders' lifetime. This system makes a lot of sense if the founder wants to be highly involved in the foundation's activities. The Gates Foundation is an example of a foundation that uses the time-based approach, with a requirement that the endowment be fully deployed within 20 years of the end of the founders' lives.

But beyond these constraints, a debate rages between those who believe that foundations should aim to deploy all of their funding as quickly as possible and those who believe they should invest their principal in spending in the future (and a spectrum of opinions between). This debate hinges on three factors:

1. Will spending a dollar yield higher marginal cost-effectiveness now or in the future?
2. Will you be able to spend more money now or in the future?
3. Are the indirect effects better from spending now or later?

These empirical questions are, in principle, answerable; however, they are not simple to answer. We won't be able to explore their full depth in one short chapter, but we can lay out the key considerations and explain why we lean towards spending earlier rather than later.

## When will your marginal cost-effectiveness be higher?

If you had the option of giving a dollar now vs. giving a dollar later, you should decide based on when you have the better marginal impact per dollar. That depends on the availability of cost-effective interventions vs. the availability of funding for those interventions and on your ability to make good decisions about which problems are important and which interventions are most cost-effective.

## Availability of cost-effective interventions

Will the world have more room for improvement at a low cost in the future than it does today? Or, put another way: will the marginal cost-effectiveness curve be 'lower' and 'wider' in the future?

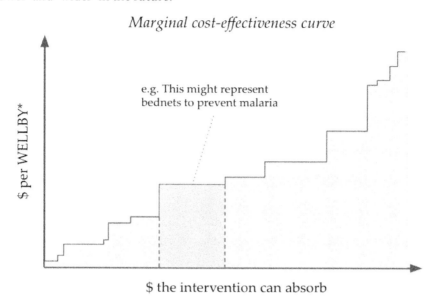

* This type of curve applies for any impact metric – WELLBYs used for illustrative purposes

This depends on a number of factors:

1. **Progress improving the world:** If humanity successfully deploys resources today to fix problems, then today's 'low-hanging fruit' will already have been picked in the future (i.e. the leftmost opportunities on the cost curve will already have been taken). One clear example of this is that extreme poverty is thankfully trending downwards globally.[113] This pushes us towards spending now. That being said, new problems may arise in the future, which means lower-cost opportunities are available to have an impact. However, it will often be cheaper still to prevent those new problems from arising.
2. **When we have more 'leverage' over the future:** In many cases, it will be cheaper to prevent a problem from emerging or stop it before it gets out of hand than waiting to address it later. We have a unique opportunity today

---

[113] Our World in Data, "Share of Population Living in Extreme Poverty," accessed Feb. 20, 2023

to spend our resources in this kind of preventative fashion. For example, preventing factory farming in countries where animals are still farmed more traditionally may be highly cost-effective. However, it will also be too early to mitigate many future problems because we're often clueless as to what consequences our current actions will have far into the future. As such, the direction this factor pushes us in will very much depend on the case at hand.

3. **Technological progress:** Future technology will make it possible to solve problems in ways that aren't available to us today, in some cases at far lower costs. For example, new vaccines or gene drive technology may make it far cheaper to prevent certain diseases, like malaria. This will create new interventions on the left of the cost curve and push down the cost of existing interventions.

4. **Intervention discovery:** The interventions that we have for tackling a given problem are the product of the technology available and the ideas we've come up with and tested for using that technology to solve the problem. Evidence-based philanthropy is still early in its lifecycle. So, even holding technology constant, there is a lot of progress to be expected in discovering new cost-effective interventions on the left side of the cost curve. For example, progress in understanding mental health could help us use existing technology to improve it far more cost-effectively.

5. **Execution capabilities within the nonprofit sector:** We're not only early in our collective journey of discovering cost-effective interventions but also early in our journey of building expertise in executing those interventions as efficiently as possible. Independently of the factors above, we should expect the cost of each step in the cost curve to come down over time. For example, it's only fairly recently that effectiveness-focused charities began being launched to advocate for specific health policies. Over time, they will accumulate learnings about which tactics are most effective and how to operate efficiently. In case it wasn't hard enough to figure out how these factors play out in general, one also needs to consider how they play out differently for different cause areas.

### *Supply of funding for those interventions*

Will the world have more available funding targeted at the most cost-effective interventions in the future? The greater the available funding pool, the lower the marginal impact of your donations (see the figure below – 'willingness to donate' captures both the amount of philanthropic funding available and the fact that effectiveness-focused funders have benchmarks of cost-effectiveness below which they will not spend).

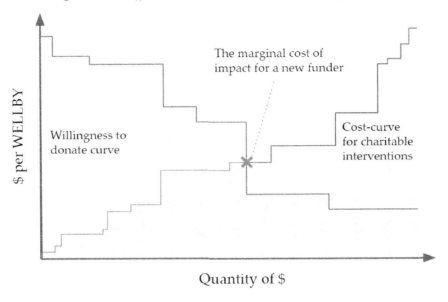

*Marginal cost-effectiveness curve meets funding supply curve*

The future state of this funding supply curve depends on the **growth of effectiveness-focused donations**: In the future, do we expect philanthropic donations to grow? There is good evidence suggesting that total donations are correlated both with GDP and inequality,[114] the former of which has trended upwards for most of human history[115] and the latter of which is more variable but has trended upwards in many of the countries that donate the most (like the U.S and U.K) over the past 50 years.[116] There is also the possible impact of moral progress (if it occurs) on the number and generosity of donors. Based on these factors, we'd bet on total donations growing in the future.

---

[114] Citi Global Perspectives & Solutions, "Philanthropy and the Global Economy: Opportunities in a World of Transition", Citi IGC, Nov. 17, 2021, accessed Feb. 20, 2023
[115] Max Roser, "Economic Growth," Our World In Data, 2015, accessed Feb. 20, 2023, https://ourworldindata.org/economic-growth
[116] Max Roser, Esteban Ortiz-Ospina, "Income Inequality," Our World In Data, last modified Oct. 2016, accessed Feb. 20, 2023, https://ourworldindata.org/income-inequality

But the average amount of consideration given to the cost-effectiveness of donations is pretty low in most cause areas. Only the proportion of total donations allocated to the most cost-effective interventions is relevant for the 'spend now vs. later' debate. Do we expect this proportion to grow over time? There are reasons to believe it will, such as progress made in the global health and development cause area. But this is hardly a sure thing, as other philanthropic trends focus less on cost-effectiveness than other values like justice or sustainability.

It's difficult to reach a robust conclusion on the likely trajectory of the funding supply curve. Out of the funders we have spoken to so far, the prevailing belief is that the funding will expand, which pushes us towards spending now vs. later.

### *Your ability to make good grantmaking decisions*

Will you be able to make better grantmaking decisions now or in the future? This depends on:

1.  **Ethical progress:** Will humanity get better at ethics, leading to better decisions about which problems are important to solve?
2.  **Epistemological progress:** Will humanity develop better methods for deciding what is cost-effective, or reach better conclusions about which of the methods already available to us are best?
3.  **Scientific progress:** Will humanity improve the size and quality of the empirical evidence base for deciding what is and isn't cost-effective?
4.  **Personal grantmaking progress:** Will you become better as an individual at making decisions, either when grantmaking or leading a grantmaking organization?

These considerations broadly point towards us making better grantmaking decisions in the future; however, the best way to make personal progress on grantmaking is through practice, so we advise beginning to make grants as soon as possible.

## When will you be able to spend more?

Having laid out the factors determining whether you can spend a dollar more cost-effectively today or in the future, the next question is: When will you be able to donate the most dollars? Typically, the backbone of the belief that we should 'be patient' and donate later is the notion that by investing the money today, you will end up donating more in the future. But it is not as clear as it may initially seem that this is the case.

### Return on investment, adjusted for inflation

It is fairly uncontroversial that on a long enough timeline, barring any societal collapse, investments will earn a return that exceeds inflation. While the S&P 500 has had an inflation-adjusted annualized return of ~7% since its inception in 1926, not all markets have fared so well, and some have completely ceased to exist. Credit Suisse recently attempted to adjust the global equity returns figure to consider selection bias and concluded that there was an annualized real return of ~5% from 1900 to 2019.[117] At this growth rate, an invested funding pool doubles every 14 years.

But before tallying this as a win for the case for spending later, it's worth digging a bit deeper than a simple base rate. Do you expect the period you might postpone giving (e.g. the next 20 years) to match this base rate? Or do you have reason to believe that the risk of investment collapse or hyper inflation is unusually high?

### Willingness and ability to donate

You know that you're willing to donate significant funds to improve the world today, have the good health to work on deploying the funding, and/or the ability to attract talented people to deploy it for you. But the future is less certain. People's values change over time (and not always for the better), health can take unexpected turns, and organizations can find themselves unable to attract talent the way they once could. In our experience, people structurally underestimate the size of this risk. Taking all these factors into consideration usually leads to a significantly lower growth rate in forecast future donations and may even lead one to expect future donations to be lower than they are today.

A common rebuttal to this point is that you can simply put your money into a fund that is legally compelled to disburse funds to the charitable sector. This is good practice, but as we know, there is a huge difference between giving and giving effectively. One can propose tactics to mitigate the risk that your future self is less motivated by effectiveness than your current self; for example, you could design the fund such that its decisions must be approved by a board. But this board is made up of people who are equally vulnerable to value drift. We're yet to see a surefire solution to this problem.

---

[117] SjirH, "The case for investing to give later", EA Forum, July 20, 2020, accessed Feb. 20, 2023

In addition to the risk that you are no longer willing to give, there is the risk that you may become unable to. This could be because you lose control over your fortune, for example. There is also the special case of existential risks. If some threat, like a large-scale nuclear war, a man-made pathogen, or an asteroid, ends humanity, it will be too late to spend our resources to improve the world. The non-zero chance of such an outcome should lead you to discount your estimates of how much you can donate in the future by investing to give.

## When are the indirect effects of spending better?

So far, we have discussed the considerations determining whether you will have a higher direct impact through donations now or in the future. But there are significant indirect effects to consider as well.

### *Norm setting and effects on reputation*

Deciding to spend later normalizes this decision within the philanthropic sector. You may think this is a good thing because you think the facts are such that more philanthropists should take this path. However, even if it *is* the right path for you, that is likely not the case for many other philanthropists. It is human nature to want to keep our money for ourselves; even someone who has decided to give it away will have some hesitancy about it at the back of their mind. When a philanthropist decides to give later, it leaves the option open of not giving at all, which makes giving later so enticing. This is usually entirely subconscious, which is why it is so dangerous for giving later to become the norm. Those most receptive to arguments advocating giving later are usually the ones who are most at risk of changing their mind and not giving as much, or at all, later down the line.

On the other hand, when individuals publicly and rapidly donate large amounts of their wealth to effective causes, it may encourage other individuals to give larger portions of their wealth more effectively.

### *The opportunity cost of grantmaking talent*

The longer you take to deploy a certain pool of philanthropic funding, the longer you occupy talented people who would otherwise be doing valuable work. The amount of labor you use for grantmaking is proportional to how much you spend, so spending slower does mean using less labor. But it is not a linear relationship (as discussed in Spending on Staff vs. Granting, 7.1.2.). A minimum amount of labor is required to keep the lights on at a foundation.

### Impact on your foundation's organizational culture

Aggressive spend-down aspirations can contribute to a higher general sense of urgency in the foundation. It also tends to encourage shorter feedback loops, higher risk tolerance levels, and bigger bets. Depending on the type of culture you would like to promote in your organization, this could increase or decrease the attractiveness of a rapid spend-down.

### Second-order benefits compound over time

In the same way financial investments today can yield future returns, so can investments in impact today. For example, curing a person of blindness today allows them to use their improved health to earn more money earlier in their lives than they otherwise would or to make further investments into their health, like through exercise. Their children may grow up happier, and so on. Or, as another example, recipients of cash transfers might use them to replace thatched roofs with metal ones or kerosene lamps with solar-powered ones, generating cost savings that represent a far higher return on investment than you could expect to earn on financial investments.[118] It's unsurprising that people who have the most basic problems could achieve a higher return by spending your money on simple solutions than you could by investing it.

All three of these other considerations point towards spending sooner rather than later.

————————

**In summary**, the decision between spending now vs. later is not an easy one. We do not have conclusive evidence in one direction or the other. However, our assessment of the factors above leads us to lean towards most foundations giving sooner rather than later. We also believe that practice is key whether you plan to do most of your giving now or in the future. As such, we recommend that you begin your grantmaking journey as soon as possible. Start with smaller "learning grants" and then ramp up your spending over time according to your strategy on giving now vs. later.

---

[118] One might protest that these benefits should already be captured in our marginal cost-effectiveness curve. But very few cost-effectiveness analyses today capture the full range of benefits to the beneficiary (for example, because they use DALYs and only focus on health, vs. income or happiness), let alone benefits to others (e.g. to family members, communities, or animals), and let alone the long-term benefits (i.e. over decades or even generations).

# 7.1.2. Choosing your giving vehicle: to DAF or not to DAF

A major decision any funder must make is which legal structure to use for their philanthropic activities. Although "foundation" is a commonly-used term for any philanthropic entity, in reality, the "donor-advised fund," or DAF for short, is a much more common choice for funders today. Legally incorporated private foundations, once the only option for philanthropists, are becoming increasingly uncommon. Because each country has variations on each of these structures, we will not go into too much detail on this decision but provide brief pros and cons of each vehicle.

## The Foundation

A favorite of major funders of the past, the foundation still has a lot of name recognition as the "gold standard" philanthropic vehicle. Carnegie, Rockefeller, and Gates are all private foundations. The main benefit of foundations is that they are independent non-profit organizations built to meet your philanthropic needs. This means you can use them to employ grantmaking staff if you'd like, or to house non-grantmaking activities, like program execution. You also have total control over how the foundation's assets are invested.

But being your own non-profit organization comes with costs. Firstly, foundations are time-consuming and require legal advice to set up. Secondly, they come with responsibilities. In most jurisdictions, foundations are required to publish who they've given grants to and how much. They are also often legally required to give a certain percentage of their total funds anually – in the US, it is 5%. While this is a downside in that it is a restriction, it can, in fact, be an excellent forcing function to ensure that you actually get the intended donations into the hands of organizations rather than just sitting in the foundation itself, helping no one.

Foundations tend to be a better fit for donors who want to give away larger amounts of money (e.g. $5M annually) over a longer period because having total control over how the assets are invested becomes more important. Similarly, a larger asset base makes it easier to justify the upfront effort to establish the organization.

## The Donor Advised Fund

The fastest growing philanthropic entity, DAFs are not independent organizations, but instead are housed within a larger, pre-existing entity (usually a bank, with Fidelity being the largest DAF sponsor in the US). This brings two significant benefits. The first is that DAFs are 'plug and play': You can quickly and easily set one up and disburse funds to grantees within days, relying on the DAF sponsor's existing infrastructure to give instead of having to do the admin in-house. The trade-off, of course, is that you lose all the flexibility of being your own independent organization. You will be subject to any limitations imposed by the DAF sponsor regarding how the assets can be invested (for instance, a sponsor bank may only allow you to invest using them as an intermediary) or what types of organizations you can give grants to. It may also be more difficult to hire grantmaking staff or structure your board as you'd like.

The second benefit is that DAFs have no mandatory annual donation. But this benefit also entails a risk: Many donors make a big donation to their DAF, receive their tax deduction, and never disburse the funds from it. If you do choose a DAF as your vehicle, we recommend setting an internal yearly minimum requirement so you don't fall into this all-too-common trap.

Monetary gifts to both DAFs and foundations are tax-deductible in most geographies and will not incur any further taxes while they await disbursement.

## Giving Personally

The last option is to simply give from your own bank account. This choice is preferred by funders who want to be able to give to for-profits, individuals, political organizations, or other entities that are difficult to donate to from a DAF or foundation[119]. This may be a good option for the right donor, but for most, there are some major downsides to consider. Once funds are placed in a DAF or foundation, you get immediate tax benefits from the donation and are never taxed on the gains going forward. Over time, keeping intended donations outside of a philanthropic entity can seriously dilute the overall amount of money you can donate over your lifetime.

---

[119] While it is technically possible to donate to a for-profit entity from a DAF or foundation through a PRI (Program Related Investment), it is much easier to do so from a personal account.

Additionally, with DAFs and foundations, you can make the donation at a time best for your tax situation and later make a donation from the entity at the best time for the organizations you are donating to. Another major consideration is the real possibility of value drift. We change a lot over our life. And as long as that money stays in your bank account, it can be used for a mid-life crisis just as easily as it can be donated to effective charities.

## Summary

We recommend the donor-advised fund for the small-to-medium-sized funder who is not hiring staff. Beginning a philanthropic journey can be psychologically difficult, so it is better to lessen the number of hoops you have to jump through on your road to impact. Suppose you are giving large amounts annually, running your own operational programs, and hiring program staff. In that case, the private foundation may be a better option for you. And if your comparative advantage is funding unique and diverse types of organizations – from for-profits to political campaigns – then your donations may be best kept in your own bank account.

| Benefit | Foundation | DAF | Personal giving |
|---|---|---|---|
| Minimum annual donation | Yes | No | No |
| Protection against value drift | Most | Some | None |
| Flexibility in who you can donate to | Some | Least | Most |
| Ease of set up and administration | Involved | Very easy | No set up |
| Optimal tax benefits | Yes | Yes | No |
| Optimal control over asset investments | Yes | No | Yes |

For simplicity's sake, in this handbook, we have chosen to use the term "foundation" to refer to all of the above-mentioned philanthropic entities. Don't get distracted by the use of this term – as you read, feel free to substitute the giving vehicle of your choosing.

## 7.1.3. Spending on staff vs. grants

Every foundation has one major cost: the grants it is making. The second highest expense is almost always the staff cost: Vetting opportunities takes time, and once that exceeds the founder's availability, it starts costing money to hire that time. So how much time (and therefore money) should you spend on grantmaking relative to your spending on the grants themselves?

***Spending on staff should scale with money moved.***

It is uncontroversial that larger grants deserve more scrutiny and vetting than smaller grants. The greater the stakes in a decision, the greater the appropriate level of rigor. Yet, in practice, many grantmakers use the same process with the same level of rigor for all the grants they consider. And even when this principle of greater scrutiny for larger grants is applied, it's applied inconsistently by different grantmakers for understandable reasons: If you are giving $10 million across a whole year, it can seem worth putting a huge amount of time into vetting a $5 million grant. Conversely, if you are giving away $500 million, a $5 million grant might seem like a small investment. As a result, across the philanthropic space, the time allocated to grants of the same size varies dramatically. Ideally, funders would be more consistent with one another in terms of how their investment in vetting scales with grant size. As a starting point, we'd like to see all funders apply some degree of scaling and for funders to aspire to be more consistent collectively. But how should vetting scale with grant size?

***Scaling should be less than linear.***

Whilst more hours should be allocated to assess larger grants, we suspect it should scale less than linearly.

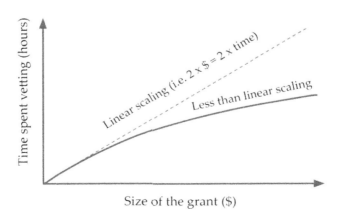

This is for two main reasons:

- Firstly, fixed costs are involved in vetting grants, like the time taken to read applications or do a back-of-the-envelope calculation to sense-check a cost-effectiveness analysis. These costs don't scale with grant size, so doubling the grant size won't cause a doubling of resources spent on vetting.
- Secondly, there are limits to what can be learned with additional time spent vetting, so spending more time has diminishing returns once you approach the limit of the available relevant evidence. As a result, doubling the grant size won't cause a doubling of resources spent on vetting.

So perhaps, rather than increasing vetting resources 10x each time the grant size increases by 10x, vetting resources should increase closer to 5x instead.

### *A broader scope requires more time spent vetting per dollar.*

Another factor to consider is that the more diverse the pool of grants a foundation considers, the more hours they'll need to spend vetting to achieve the same level of rigor. This is because there is less generalizable knowledge between different cause areas, interventions, or organizations. For example, a foundation specializing in policy interventions will accumulate knowledge about what types of tactics do and don't work, how to model the cost-effectiveness of policy advocacy, and so on. As a result, they'll be able to vet an additional policy grant to a high standard far more efficiently than they'd be able to vet a direct-delivery intervention.

## Spending on staff vs. grants in practice

Looking at the table of real-world foundations and their estimated spending on grantmaking staff versus the grants themselves (page 248), we can see how this plays out in practice. Firstly, we can see that the number of hours spent per grant generally increase with grant size, which is what we'd hope to see. But is it increasing in the way we'd like to see – less than linearly? Let's look at a specific example: Givewell's average grant size is ~23x larger than Open Philanthropy's, and the hours spent vetting each grant is ~15x higher. Looks good, right? At first, but less so once we consider grant diversity. GiveWell's grant diversity is extremely low: Not only do they only look at classes of intervention (direct delivery) within one cause area (global health and development), but they tend to focus on just a handful of organizations that they've looked at in detail for years. Meanwhile, Open Philanthropy looks at an extremely diverse pool of grants. Once we factor in how much extra time it would take them to build the expertise and stay up to date with such a vast scope, the number of dollars Open Philanthropy disburses per hour of vetting is arguably too high.

Another factor that makes it difficult to compare real-world examples is that not all vetting hours are of equal quality. For example, we suspect that the average large U.S. foundation program officer is not using the best practices in systematic vetting. So the amount of rigor per hour of their vetting is lower than, say, D-Prize or Open Philanthropy.

## Our recommendation

Based on the considerations above, we recommend the rough rule of thumb of half-linear scaling (e.g. hours needed = 0.5 * vetting hours for a grant), assuming that your foundation has already invested enough time to build the necessary expertise in your focus area. It's hard to point to specific foundations as a reference point of what 'good' looks like. We're fairly confident, though, that GiveWell isn't investing too little in vetting, and the average U.S. foundation isn't investing enough.

Estimates of some real world foundations' spending of dollars vs. time on grantmaking

| | Average grant size | Annual grants given | Grants considered* | Grant diversity | Vetting staff equivalent | Vetting hours per grant considered* | Ratio ($/hr) |
|---|---|---|---|---|---|---|---|
| **D-Prize** | $10k | $0.34M | 70 | Medium | ~2.5 FTE (4,500 hrs) | ~65 hrs (2 wks full time) | $160 |
| **EA Animal Welfare Fund** | $75k | $4.5M | 120 | Low | ~0.5 FTE (900 hrs) | ~8 hours (0.2 wks full time) | $10,000 |
| **Avg. large US foundation program officer** | $90k | $6.5M | 72 | - | 1 FTE (1800 hrs) | ~25 hours (0.7 wks full time) | $3,600 |
| **Charity Entrepreneurship** | $100k | $1M | 15 | Very high | ~5 FTE (9,000 hrs) | ~600 hrs (16 wks full time) | $170 |
| **Woodleigh Impact** | $200k | $1M | 10 | Medium | ~1.5 FTE (2,700 hrs) | ~270 hrs (7 wks full time) | $740 |
| **Open Philanthropy farm animal welfare** | $560k | $50M | 90 | Low | ~10 FTE (18,000 hrs) | ~200 hours (5 wks full time) | $2,800 |
| **Open Philanthropy overall (excl. GiveWell)** | $1,200k | $300M | 500 | Very high | ~80 FTE (144,000 hr) | ~300 hours (8 wks full time) | $4,200 |
| **GiveWell** | $28,000k | $500M | 20 | Very low | ~50 FTE (90,000 hrs) | ~4500 hours (120 wks full time) | $6,200 |

*Here we mean grants seriously considered (vetted in full depth) vs. applications received (many of which will be quickly ruled out)*

Numbers are estimated based on publicly available information in early 2023, except the average large US foundation program officer, which is based on Powell, A., Seldon, W., & Sahni, N. (2019). Reimagining Institutional Philanthropy. Stanford Social Innovation Review

## 7.1.4. Summary

- Foundations have three key decisions to make regarding how they deploy their wealth: Spend-down rate (i.e. when to spend), which giving vehicle to choose from, and how much to spend on grantmaking staff vs. grants themselves.
- Minimum spend-down: Many foundations have a minimum spend-down rate due to legal requirements (e.g. a minimum of 5% per year in the U.S.) or an internal goal (e.g. to spend all of the funds within the founder's lifetime).
- Spend-down strategy: Beyond the minimum spend-down, foundations disagree on the extent to which they should deploy their funding as quickly as possible versus investing it to spend in the future. This debate hinges on three factors:
  1. When will your marginal cost-effectiveness be higher?
  2. When will you be able to spend more?
  3. Are the indirect effects better from spending now or later?

(1) When your marginal cost-effectiveness is higher depends on:

  a. The trend in the availability of cost-effective interventions:
       i. We may make progress on fixing problems (see the decline in global poverty, for example) such that the marginal cost to make further progress goes up.
       ii. We may have more leverage over the future now, e.g. stopping factory farming in some countries before it takes off.
       iii. Technological progress may make interventions more cost-effective in the future.
       iv. Better interventions may be discovered in the future.
       v. The nonprofit sector may get more efficient at executing interventions in the future.

  b. Global trends in philanthropic funding (will funding continue to grow with the global economy? How will the share of philanthropic funding deployed based on cost-effectiveness change over time?)

c. Whether we improve our ability to make grantmaking decisions, personally or as a society, over time.

(2) When you choose to spend more depends on your expected return on investment (adjusted for inflation) and the risk of losing the motivation or ability to donate in the future.

(3) Spending down quickly may have positive indirect effects like (a) setting a norm that wealthy individuals give larger proportions of their wealth and give more effectively; (b) minimizing the amount of time that talented grantmakers are working at your foundation when they could be having an impact elsewhere; (c) creating a fast-paced organizational culture.

- Foundations in many countries can choose between giving from their own bank account, starting a private foundation, or starting a donor-advised fund. The best choice of legal structure will vary depending on your needs and desires as a funder, and each has its own advantages and disadvantages.
- When it comes to spending on grantmaking staff (i.e. salaries) vs. grants themselves:
    - o Larger grants are worth more scrutiny, so time spent vetting (and therefore, money spent on grantmaking staff) should scale with grant size.
    - o Scaling should be less than linear due to fixed time investments (e.g. reading a proposal takes a similar amount of time no matter the grant size) and diminishing returns on vetting (the 1000th hour of research on a topic changes the picture less than the 10th hour).
    - o A broader scope will need more time spent vetting per dollar because you need to pay the fixed cost of building expertise in an area multiple times for each area in the scope.
    - o We recommend the rough rule of thumb of half-linear scaling (e.g. hours needed = 0.5 * vetting hours for a grant).

# 7.2. Wisdom

All the wealth in the world is useless if you don't know how to spend it wisely. Although this book will arm you with some tools to make better decisions, theoretical knowledge of how to make decisions is no substitute for years of experience, subject-matter expertise, or a holistic understanding of how different concepts and systems fit together.

When it comes to acquiring the wisdom your foundation will need, there are three options: acquiring it personally, hiring it, or accessing outside wisdom via a network of advisors. How to hire will be discussed at length in Part C of this book, so this chapter will focus on the other options. Don't forget, you not only need to possess wisdom, you need to apply it too. Consistently applying wisdom is no trivial matter, and it is often much more difficult than simply acquiring it theoretically.

## 7.2.1. Acquiring wisdom personally

Building the wisdom necessary to be a great grantmaker is no small feat: It takes a lot of time and energy, a growth mindset, a broad understanding of your scope, mastery of the decision-making tools in your toolkit, and crucially, it requires feedback loops so you can determine whether you're on the right track.

### Investing the time and energy

Properly vetting potential grant recipients takes time, and getting better at making grantmaking decisions takes a lot of practice. Be realistic about the time you are going to put into the project. If it's very limited, then your personal wisdom as a grantmaker will be too. You'll need to hire others and spend your time focusing on a few important decisions that you can give adequate attention to instead of being involved in a huge number of decisions at a shallow level.

It can be very rewarding to make running a foundation your full-time or part-time job rather than a hobby you put a couple of hours into per week. Not only will it allow you to build the personal wisdom to make far better grantmaking decisions, but it will also give you the opportunity to learn about some of the world's most important issues and to see firsthand how your values are being put into practice at your foundation.

## Bringing a growth mindset

Practice is only valuable if you have a genuine desire to grow and improve. One prerequisite for bringing a growth mindset to your grantmaking is acknowledging that you have something to learn in the first place. In our experience, this is not an issue for most beginner grantmakers. Rather, the issue many face is that they're hesitant to start making grants because they're uncomfortable that their decisions probably won't be excellent immediately. We've seen many aspiring grantmakers put off making their first grant for years. We think this is typically a mistake. If you're to become an excellent grantmaker, it's important to put aside your pride and start making small grants, even if they turn out to be imperfect. What you learn from this process will make these imperfections well worth it in the long run. While you should be careful not to do harm with your grantmaking, you don't need to aspire to never make mistakes. Even great grantmakers make mistakes – what separates them from the rest and *makes* them great is that they set up systems to notice and learn from those mistakes.

## Developing a broad understanding

Broadly knowledgeable people make better grantmakers because their decisions are based on a more complete and accurate model of the world and they can connect the dots between disparate domains to generate new insights or ideas. These abilities do not always come naturally, and although grantmaking skills have similarities with other skills, like investing, you will find that most of the required skills need to be learned fresh. Many of the best grantmakers are voracious readers and learners; reading several books that disagree with each other is one of the best ways to learn and gain a deep understanding of a topic.

Some tips for developing a broad understanding:

## 1) Reading diverse sources

This is something we all know that we should do. But in practice, we often overlook valuable sources because we dismiss the perspectives of those who don't share our goals or those who aren't 'insiders' on the topic.

For example, consider these relevant sources of content on farmed animal welfare:

- **Animal welfare advocates:** This includes anything from books like *The Animal Activist's Handbook* to podcasts interviewing the leaders of prominent animal welfare organizations like The Humane League and the publications of organizations like Animal Ask. This makes up most of what most people who are interested in improving animal welfare read. While this may well be the most important content, it can give a fairly shallow understanding of the world by itself.

- **Animal husbandry:** Farm workers may not see improving animal welfare as their number one priority, but because they work so closely with the animals, there is a lot to learn from all of their written content. For example, what specific situations that happen on a farm stress out the animals? How do different breeds respond to different environmental conditions? What do farm animals tend to do when given high levels of freedom?

- **Outsiders:** Most of the world, of course, falls outside of these first two groups. People outside of the animal advocacy and animal husbandry camps produce a lot of useful content that can be directly applied to helping animals; for example, an economist analyzing the elasticity of demand for meat or a futurist talking about what they expect the future of farming to be (unsurprisingly, their predictions tend to be quite different from animal activists').

Reading from each of these sources can provide a broader understanding of farmed animal welfare than just focusing on the views of animal advocates. When building your knowledge on your foundation's focus area, ask yourself what perspectives you might be missing, and seek those out.

## 2) Seeing the context directly

Witnessing it firsthand is another way to get a broad understanding of a topic.

This principle applies to understanding a problem you're trying to solve and its potential solutions. For example, to understand the problem of farmed animal suffering, visiting a farm (or preferably, a few farms) can paint a more complete picture. By witnessing each step of the work done on multiple farms, you can start to get more of a sense of what really happens there, contrary to the carefully curated versions in content that argues for or against the status quo.

The same principle applies to organizations you're considering funding or working with. For example, one of this book's co-authors founded a charity working on global health issues, which involved working with a number of partner organizations to deliver an intervention. He made an effort to speak to employees at every level of these partner organizations, which often yielded very different results. In one case, he talked to the CEO, manager, a field manager, a head surveyor, and a standard surveyor: As he got closer to where the work was being done, he got more and more accurate (and often negative) information.

This work is time-consuming, but we believe it's very valuable, particularly early in the process of understanding your foundation's scope. And it will pay dividends by improving your ability to make impactful grants and giving you new ideas currently being neglected in the sector. But it's also important to remember that the picture you get from the individual experience will be incomplete and likely not representative.

### 3) Taking steps to increase your absorption

If you're anything like this book's co-authors, you find it increasingly difficult to remember what you once learned. We can't offer you a silver bullet for this challenge, but we have two suggestions that may be helpful in the context of grantmaking:

**Explain what you've learned to others:** There is considerable evidence that the best way to retain information and improve understanding of materials is to explain it to others.[120] Moreover, sharing a piece of advice you were given that you accept as correct creates a sense of accountability to the person you shared it with, so that you act on the advice. Specifically, we recommend summarizing books you've read, site visits you've conducted, and conversations with advisors, experts, or other organizations and sharing these summaries with your program officers. That way, you'll increase your absorption and propagate knowledge through your organization.

---

[120] D. R. Johnson et al., "Cooperative Learning Methods: A Meta-Analysis" University of Minnesota, (January 1, 2012).

Similarly, you could present your learnings to a funding circle, positively influencing the thinking of your peers.

**Learning with a specific application in mind:** We expect that reflecting on how the information you're learning could be applied in practice will better enable you to integrate the lessons into your grantmaking. For example, you could imagine how a lesson applies to grants you're currently considering, to projects you've funded in the past, or even to a set of mock grant proposals.

## Mastering the decision-making tools

This handbook explores some of the decision-making tools you'll need to be an effective grantmaker. But (and this will come as no surprise) reading about the tools is insufficient. You will need to put in the hours practicing them. A great way to start is to come up with practice projects and have a peer, co-founder, or mentor give you feedback on your work. For example, you could practice making WFMs, or spend some time applying rational thinking to a hypothetical problem. Another option is to apply to participate in our Grantmaking Program. But ultimately, most of your practice hours will come from applying the tools when assessing real potential grants.

## Establishing feedback loops

*Sarah had passed all the tests and had been told this was the final one – the test that would determine whether she would be allowed to survive. Her alien captors had been strict but not unkind. They always made the rules very clear, and the tests all seemed achievable. This time they led her into a large room with a table at its center. The challenge was explained to her: She was to build the best bowl she could. But there was a catch. There always was a catch with the aliens. She had to build it out of an alien substance that was a lot like clay but was completely transparent. This was not glass, which can bend light and distort what you see while looking through it; it was more like working with air. The aliens gave Sarah some of the substance to handle. She could feel it - it was cold to the touch - but she could not see any sign of it.*

*The aliens explained that she was not allowed to mix or sprinkle other materials on top of it to make it more visible; she would have to work with it as was. Finally, she was told she would have a week to make the bowl, the quality of which would determine if she lived or died. It seemed like a strange test. The other tasks ranged from solving math problems to explaining biological phenomena. Sarah figured that, like the others, this test would have some intellectual component to it. The aliens pulled a sheet from atop* the desk on the left side of the room to reveal a heaving pile of 'earth clay' that Sarah could use to build an understanding of the alien substance by comparison. They assured her there was an equal-sized pile of the invisible substance on the desk on the opposite side of the room, although the two substances were not to be mixed.

Sarah thought back to her pottery class in high school, where the teacher had told them a story about a class he had once taught: He had split the class into two halves. One half was instructed to spend the term studying, planning, designing, and eventually creating a single perfect bowl which would be judged at the end of the term to determine the grade for the entire class. The other half was given a different goal: make as many bowls as possible. Their grade would be determined by the number of bowls with unique designs they made, although they were also welcome to have their best bowl judged for a bonus mark. Both halves of the class worked hard. The first half poured time and energy into research, planning, and designing, while the second half of the class got straight to work. They initially made simple and imperfect bowls but slowly gained the skills to create more varied and complex designs. At the end of the class year, both halves entered their bowls for professional judgment. The answer was unanimous: the best bowls had come from the students focusing on creating the highest number of bowls. The practice they had gained turned out to be more important than the theoretical knowledge or the planning the other group had accumulated and conducted. The point of the teacher's story was clear: To make the best bowl, the winning strategy was to aim to make many different bowls instead of one perfect one.

Simple enough advice to follow when you can see the bowls you are working on, Sarah thought to herself. She could make 100 invisible bowls, but she could not tell if they had holes in them or were completely misshapen. She sunk her hand through each of the substances feeling their differences. The 'invisiclay' was ever so slightly heavier and slightly stickier, but the differences were very minor. Sarah sat down to make her first bowl. She tried to recall her lessons, but they were many years ago, and she hadn't been a particularly attentive pottery student. She worked the invisible clay into something she guessed was half decent and put it to the side. She wished she could see her work! Then a thought occurred to her: She had seven days. What if she spent the first four working with regular clay, building up her skills by making many visible bowls. Of course, none of them would be the bowl she would be judged on, but at least she could tell whether what she was doing was working and make adjustments to her technique as needed. She grabbed some clay from the desk on the left side of the room and brought it over to the table at the center that had become her workspace. She tried to replicate her *first bowl using the same half-remembered lessons from her pottery class. The result was horrifying. It was misshapen and far too shallow - almost unrecognizable as a bowl. She looked over to where she had placed the invisible bowl, wondering if it was as bad as this result!*

*Clay in hand, with her life depending on it, Sarah made bowl after bowl. Days passed, and she got better and better. She had become faster and more accurate than she thought she'd be able to in a week. By the end of day three, she started closing her eyes while working with the visible clay. She decided for the next few days, she would spend half her time making visible bowls with her eyes closed and the other half making invisible bowls. Then on the final day, feeling nervous but not entirely hopeless, she sat down to create one final bowl, all out of invisible clay. Sarah's hands and mind were exhausted when the aliens came in to inspect. They produced a small vial of white sparkling material and sprinkled it over Sarah's bowl. The sparkles stuck to the bowl as they fell, gradually revealing their form. It was pretty good. Not the best bowl she had made, but the skills she had developed over the course of the week had clearly paid off. The aliens looked at each other, nodded, and then told Sarah she was free to go.*

Grantmaking can be a lot like Sarah's predicament, but with even less friendly forces (like poverty and disease) playing the role of the aliens. It will be very hard to assess the success of many of the grants you will consider making. But building strong feedback loops is absolutely crucial for you to improve as a grantmaker.

To this end, we recommend:
1. Prioritizing grant applications with strong measurement and evaluation plans even more highly than you would otherwise (especially early on in your grantmaking journey).
2. Conducting regular, systematic internal reviews of your past grants.
3. Seeking external reviews of your past grants.
4. Making testable predictions related to your grantmaking (e.g. 70% chance Charity X will make an agreement with Institution Y within three years). Another source of objective feedback on the accuracy of your decision-

making is participation in forecasting competitions (e.g. Metaculus) and prediction markets (e.g. Manifold Markets)

5.  If your foundation aims to have significant indirect impact, e.g. through thought leadership or active grantmaking, then you should build in monitoring and evaluation for this as well.

We discussed monitoring and evaluation for foundations in more detail in Chapter 5.2.4.

# 7.2.2. Accessing wisdom through advisors

It's impossible to personally gain all the advice you'll need, and inefficient to hire it all.[121] This is where advisors come in as an efficient way to plug the gaps. For many entrepreneurs, some of their advisors will also offer encouragement and emotional support, something to keep in mind as you craft your network of advisors and mentors.

## What types of advisors you want

Your advisors should bring wisdom complementary to you and your team. Often, the first impulse is to ask the wisest decision-makers in your network to be your advisors and call it a day. The problem is that people's networks are often skewed towards people with similar backgrounds, which may not provide the complementary perspectives you need. This is not to say that you shouldn't draw upon your network – rather, do so consciously and make sure your final set of advisors covers all your bases.

## Testing advisors

Some things sound like great advice initially but don't stand under scrutiny. Trivial things like whether we heard the advice on a sunny day, whether it rhymed, or whether it was written in a clear or messy font can influence how likely we are to believe something, regardless of the real strength of the advice. Whilst having a good

---

[121] It's inefficient because (a) sometimes you'll want to access more wisdom but not more 'work' (labor) so you'll have to hire more staff than you need, (b) sometimes the people who have the wisdom you need are willing to share it, but aren't willing or aren't a good fit to work at your foundation. Therefore having to acquire wisdom and work as a package deal introduces inefficiencies.

KEY DECISIONS FOR NEW FOUNDATIONS

vetting system for your advisors goes a long way to ensuring that the advice you receive is generally of high quality (see Part C); ideally, you want to test and track as much of the advice you receive as possible, to see whose advice proves correct the most often and in which domains. Ongoing tracking also allows you to ensure that the quality of the advice you receive remains high over time.

Let's review four possible ways to test advice, borrowing many concepts from our rationality and science chapters.

### Get advice where you already know the answer

When talking to a new advisor, one way to get a sense of the quality of their advice is to ask about one topic you know well for every three topics you know little about. If they give wise advice in the field you know well, you can have more confidence in the wisdom of their advice in other domains.

### Get advice that is falsifiable

Although broad advice can be helpful, getting more specific numbers, probabilities, and predictions allows you to test wisdom much more objectively. For an example of what these kinds of predictions might look like, consider those made by GiveWell for their recent grants to Fortify Health.[122] If their mental model of Fortify Health is accurate, you would expect 80% of their predictions with 80% confidence to be correct, 20% of their predictions with 20% confidence to be correct, and so on.

| Confidence | Prediction | By time |
|---|---|---|
| 50% | Fortify Health has successfully signed agreements with at least 29 open market mills total by year 1 | July 2023 |
| 50% | Fortify Health has successfully signed agreements with at least 52 open market mills total by year 2 | July 2024 |
| 50% | Fortify Health has successfully signed agreements with at least 83 open market mills total by year 3 | July 2025 |
| 70% | Fortify Health has successfully signed agreements with at least 1 mill producing for schools total by Year 1 | July 2023 |

[122] GiveWell, "Fortify Health – Support for Expansion," Dec. 2021, accessed Feb. 20, 2023

| 60% | Fortify Health has successfully signed agreements with at least 8 mills producing for schools total by Year 1 | July 2024 |
|---|---|---|
| 50% | Fortify Health has successfully signed agreements with at least 14 mills producing for schools total by Year 1 | July 2025 |
| 20% | Fortify Health has successfully signed agreements to partner with at least one mill producing for the public distribution system total by Year 4 | July 2026 |
| 20% | Fortify Health has successfully signed agreements to partner with at least one mill producing for the public distribution system total by Year 5 | July 2027 |
| 85% | Laboratory tests from random samples of atta produced by Fortify Health's partner mills do not fall more than 1 mg below the target (21.25 mg of iron per kg of wheat flour) in more than 25% of cases | July 2025 |

Getting advice at this level of specificity is hard. But you can record down even approximate guesses and check back on them later. For example, questions like "will GiveWell be able to fill its top charities' room for funding next year" are concrete enough to assess and allow you to get a read on someone's prediction skills in that area. Asking experts and advisors to frame their advice in the form of falsifiable or bet-like terms also tends to make their advice more honest and carefully considered.

### *Test out lessons in a smaller or easier arena*

When a high-stakes piece of advice is given, it's worth trying to see if a small step can be taken to test it out as a way of dipping your toes in the water. For example, when Charity Entrepreneurship was considering the advice to incubate policy startups, we were able to get an early answer to the question, "Can two talented but inexperienced altruists make a difference in policy?" before making very large investments or changes to our operating model. All it took was a $70,000 grant to two co-founders to try their hand with a relatively narrow and tractable goal (regulating lead paint) to give us enough evidence to have more confidence in longer timeline projects (e.g. tobacco taxation).

### *Look for disconfirming evidence*

A simple but highly effective way of testing out advice is just looking hard for disconfirming evidence. Is there a three-hour piece of research you could do that would give you a better sense of the evidence? Or if there isn't, have you heard the best arguments against the advice? Try to think through who is the most informed person you know who disagrees with it, and talk to them about it. One simple practice you could employ would be to fact-check the first three surprising or unintuitive claims they make.

# 7.2.3. Applying wisdom

A lesson has little to no value if you don't put it into practice. For example, suppose you learn that exercising makes you happier and increases your lifespan. If you don't exercise as a result of this learning, then it didn't do much good for you. In fact, it might have made you feel stressed about what you aren't doing, which decreases your happiness and lifespan! This is not to say that unapplied knowledge is always useless. For example, learning things can act like exercise for your mind, increasing your ability to learn other things quickly. Overall, however, most of the value of learning something comes from its application.

The same applies to learning about how to do good in the world. For example, the tools we discuss in this handbook can be excellent aids in decision-making, but knowing about them does not mean you'll use them. Similarly, you can get great advice from someone, but it will have no impact if it does not make its way into practice (an aspect few advisors can help with).

We recommend three tactics to maximize the use you get out of your wisdom:

1. Build it into your processes
2. Teach it to others to create social pressure
3. Cross-apply it from one domain to another

**Building wisdom into your processes:** One best practice for putting wisdom into practice is using checklists and rubrics[123] to build it into your processes. For example, many grantmakers know that a sound theory of change should be a

---

[123] Rubrics are like checklists, but instead of simply ticking an item off, the degree to which each item has been accounted for is given a number or qualitative assessment.

prerequisite for any charitable project seeking funding.[124] But grantmakers often fail to check this before making their funding decision. If this is a part of a checklist of actions before signing off on funding; or better yet, if there's a rubric for assessing theories of change in your grant assessment process, this lesson is far more likely to be applied. This idea is quite intuitive, but there's also some empirical evidence that it's effective: Checklists have been found to improve doctor and nurse performance.[125] Rubrics for teachers to use when marking students' work have been found to be one of the highest-impact ways of improving school performance.[126] Using a rubric for basically every process can lead to far higher performance; it forces you to apply the best advice you've received and assess things consistently.

**Teach it to others to create social pressure:** As mentioned previously, considerable evidence shows that the best way to retain information and improve understanding of materials is to explain it to others.[127] But more importantly, to help with the goal of putting our wisdom into practice, sharing a lesson with someone and endorsing it as correct creates a sense of accountability to the person you shared it with so that you act according to the lesson.

**Cross-apply what you've learned from one domain to another:** This tactic is less about forcing yourself to act according to your wisdom and more about squeezing as much value out of your wisdom as possible. Cross-applying advice and wisdom from one domain to another can be quite hard. But if successful, it can multiply the value derived from a given piece of information. In fact, this is where some of the most novel and game-changing ideas come from. One tactic to find ways to cross-apply lessons is to consider parallels between different areas. Many people who work in one area have a habit of thinking their area is entirely unique when there are inevitably many parallels with other domains. One of the most helpful things a grantmaker who works across multiple areas can do is to notice these parallels and then bring applicable lessons from one area to another. However, one does need to be mindful of the risk of generalizing a piece of information to a context where it

---

[124] We discuss why in Chapter 8.1.1 on theories of change.

[125] Atul Gawande, *The Checklist Manifesto: How to Get Things Right*, Picador, 2011

[126] Sebastian Waack, "Hattie Effect Size List - 256 Influences Related To Achievement," Visible Learning, Oct. 27, 2015, accessed Feb. 20, 2023, http://visible-learning.org/hattie-ranking-influences-effect-sizes-learning-achievement/.

[127] D. R. Johnson et al., "Cooperative Learning Methods: A Meta-Analysis.," University of Minnesota (January 1, 2012).

doesn't actually apply (a common mistake when using the scientific method as a decision-making tool).

With these lessons in mind, you should be able to source, validate, absorb, apply, and cross-apply the wisdom required to run a truly impactful foundation.

## 7.2.4. Summary

- Wisdom in grantmaking can be acquired personally, it can be hired, and/or can be accessed via a network of advisors.
- Acquiring it personally takes time and energy, and a growth mindset. As you go down this path, we recommend the following:
    - o Developing a broad understanding by reading from a diverse range of sources, including conflicting viewpoints, and witnessing the context firsthand instead of relying entirely on desk research.
    - o Master the decision-making tools through intentional practice.
    - o Build strong feedback loops so you can assess the success of your grants.
- Your advisors should be complementary and have broad coverage of the areas you need to understand, especially gaps in your own knowledge. To decide who to trust, test their advice by:
    - o Asking for advice on something where you already know the answer – you'll know immediately if it is accurate.
    - o Getting advice that's falsifiable. This way, you can check back to see if the advisor's opinion was accurate.
    - o Testing out their advice where the stakes are low.
- Make sure to actually apply the wisdom you gain! It's pointless unless you put it to good use.
    - o Build it into your processes (e.g. with checklists and rubrics).
    - o Teach it to others to give yourself a sense of accountability to practice what you preach.
    - o Look for creative opportunities to cross-apply what you've learnt from one domain to another.

# 7.3. Work

The final resource your foundation will need is work (i.e. labor). Where will you source it from? How much of your own labor should you contribute? How should you structure your team?

## 7.3.1. Founder involvement in decision-making

*The staff fidgeted nervously around the table. Their boss was due... well, 45 minutes ago. Franklin had never been the 'on time' type. He had innumerable hobbies that took up his attention. It had been difficult to fit this meeting into his schedule in the first place; he had been persuaded to squeeze it between his meditation retreat and his trip to Fiji. Franklin was a charismatic actor who had leveraged his success to start a charitable foundation and had been its very first donor. The problem was that he was not really a great fit to be the head of an organization. The fact that he was 45 minutes late was a surprise to no one; the foundation often seemed like his 11th priority. He would pop in to make big decisions that often made huge pivots in direction and then disappear on unrelated trips or take on other projects. Ultimately though, he was the one supplying the money, and his word was law.*

*Finally, Franklin and his entourage appeared in the doorway, and the staff breathed a collective sigh of relief. Four department heads had promising projects they wanted to pitch, but no grants would be made without his approval. It all came down to 10 minutes to pitch their best and hope that Franklin liked them.*

*The head of the health department was up first. She knew her challenge was to make the projects interesting enough; Franklin was a bit of a novelty junky and got bored easily. He did not like funding the same sorts of things again and again. She started with what she hoped would be a safe one, a renewed grant to the Johns Hopkins Health Center for Research. They were doing cutting-edge research to stop the next pandemic. She pulled up their logo and a short description of their top four projects (she had found one slide was the best format for Franklin). As soon as he saw the logo, he made up his mind: "Pass on research organizations this time," he said flatly. "What, why?" the department head asked, trying not to let her disappointment show too much. "I read a newspaper article about how most research does not replicate and have lost some trust in the system." "But... but..." She knew the article he was talking about. It was focused on psychological research, and even then, it did not suggest not doing research. But she could see by the look in his eyes that the call was already made. She looked around, and although her colleagues were sympathetic to her experience (similar things had, of course, happened to them), they were also a bit pleased as it left more money for their departments. This was going to be a long meeting.*

*Three hours later, it was all over. Franklin had met a founder who he had liked at a conference, so one of the biggest grants was going to her organization. The other large grant was going to a new charity that had barely made the list in terms of impact, but he loved the sound of it. The staff tried to reassure themselves that if it wasn't for them, the grants would have been chosen even more randomly, so they were at least having some impact. And just like that, Franklin left the office for a month in Fiji.*

In the world of foundations, it can sadly be too common to observe hundreds of hours of excellent research go down the drain because of a founder's whims or preferences... decision-making power is often in the same hands as the money. A big question to consider as one of the first people involved or as the founder of a foundation is: What should your personal role be? What level of time investment do you want to put in, and what does that look like when setting up the organization?

At the end of the day, you want a great grantmaker to make the key decisions for your organization. If you want that to happen, **there are really only two options: become a great grantmaker, or hire and defer to a great grantmaker**. In the previous chapter, we discussed how you can build the wisdom to become a great grantmaker. But is that for you? You may have the intelligence and the ability to learn things quickly, but do you have the time and energy to dedicate to it? If you don't, you'll need to hire someone else to lead.

Suppose you've decided to hire someone else to be the grantmaking lead or executive director. The next challenge is striking the right balance between setting their direction and deferring to their judgment. This might sound trivial, but ceding control over something very important to you is harder than most people expect! In fact, the challenge of deferring just the right amount applies to all team members, not just in the scenario where you've hired someone else to lead the grantmaking.

Getting this wrong has real costs too. In the Franklin example at the start of this chapter, he trusted his quick evaluation more than the output of many staff hours going into the project. This either suggests he does not trust enough to defer or needs to hire stronger staff. When this happens, the foundation has wasted the grantmaker's time working on an evaluation that would never move the needle. Not only is this wasting a valuable resource, but it damages the team morale and culture. And most importantly, it means sub-optimal grantmaking decisions are being made because they're being made by a founder who doesn't have the time to evaluate them in sufficient depth – after all, that's why they hired a team in the first place!

Trusting your team enough to defer generally requires the following elements:

- Confidence in the vetting systems you used to hire them *(See Part C)*
- Trust that they have internalized your foundation's core values and scope *(It's worth vetting applicants for this and investing time regularly to ensure the team is aligned on this)*
- Your acknowledgment that decisions will be better if you leverage the time and expertise of others (*This is often the sticking point. Remember: Nobody can make the best decision on every possible grant – we all have weaknesses, blind spots, and limited time*).

Cultivate these elements, and you should have a team you feel comfortable deferring to, even on important decisions. Trust your team, and you will be able to accomplish far more.

## 7.3.2. Team structure

So far, we've just discussed foundation leadership. At first, your foundation's leader (whether you or someone else) may take on all the tasks necessary to achieve the organization's goals. But once the target for annual grants reaches a certain amount, you'll find that the bottleneck is the number of hours at your disposal to find and vet high-quality projects. Hiring and deferring to staff can be justifiable with as little as $250k spending a year, but it becomes essential once about $5m is starting to be distributed.

### Options for structuring the team

Suppose you have chosen one type of intervention across five cause areas. Next, you have to start looking for grantees, vetting them, and supporting the progress of these grantees. How should you go about doing this?

For early hires, generalists should be preferred over specialists. However, having a team of generalists where everyone does everything is not an optimal structure long-term. Over time, you should look to carve out specialized roles. While there are many different ways to structure a team within an impactful foundation, the two most common roles within grantmaking institutions are program officers and grants managers.

- Program officers are typically responsible for managing a topic area or portfolio within the foundation, with responsibilities such as:
  - Building expertise (by conducting research and analysis into the topic area and engaging with experts and other organizations in the field to stay up to date with the latest developments)
  - Sourcing opportunities (by participating in conferences and networking events to stay connected with the broader community)
  - Evaluating opportunities (by reviewing grant proposals and conducting due diligence on potential grantees)
  - Managing grantee relationships (by checking in regularly, providing support as needed, and monitoring progress)
- Grants managers are more focused on the logistical and administrative aspects of the grantmaking process, with responsibilities such as:
  - Administrating the grantmaking process (by coordinating the internal grant workflow – from grant leads to initial vetting to due

diligence and finally decision-making – as well as making the process more efficient and keeping clear records of the process)

- o Managing disbursements (by creating grant agreements and processing grant payments whilst ensuring the foundation's expenditure is within budget)
- o Tracking grantee milestones and outcomes (by liaising with grantees to gather their reporting and other necessary information)

One officer or even the funder can successfully navigate both roles for a small foundation. However, as grantmaking gets more involved and the amounts given grow larger, it becomes increasingly necessary to create tracks for these complementary specialties: program area expertise and back-of-house operations support. These positions require different skill sets, and when looking for potential hires, you should take this into account.

They are also by no means the only way to carve up a foundation's activities into distinct roles. Foundation teams (especially large ones) can be structured in a wide variety of ways through specialization along one or both of two dimensions:

- Subject area, i.e. the subject matter of the grant, including the problem, the interventions to address it, and the landscape of funders and actors that surround it
- Function, i.e. a step in the grantmaking process, from lead sourcing to vetting/grant evaluation to post-grant support

Consider Open Philanthropy as an example. They have program officers specializing either in one of their specific cause areas (e.g. South Asian air quality) or in one of the broader focus areas that each cause area falls within (e.g. Global health and well-being). These officers are tasked with building a strong network and forming high-trust relationships with the best-informed people in the field.[128] Open Philanthropy believes that specializing by subject area is important when using a hits-based grantmaking strategy (a topic covered in the following chapter), as it equips grantmakers with the ability to identify opportunities that are high-risk and neglected by other funders but still very promising in expectation. These program officers are

---

[128] Holden Karnofsky, "Choosing focus areas and hiring program staff", Open Philanthropy, July 9, 2015, accessed Feb. 20, 2023, https://www.openphilanthropy.org/research/key-questions-about-philanthropy-part-2-choosing-focus-areas-and-hiring-program-staff/

less specialized in the function dimension (i.e. they don't specialize in just one out of generating, vetting, and following up on grantees).

However, Open Philanthropy also has research analysts who specialize both by subject area and function: For example, one might specialize in the subject of global health and well-being and the function of researching new cause areas to focus on within it. Another might specialize in the subject of immigration and the function of conducting research to inform the foundation's view on key questions like "Does immigration reduce pay or employment for local workers?".

Open Philanthropy also has some roles which work across subject areas, like the Grant Management team of ~10 who take care of grant processing and operations – functions that benefit less from subject matter specialization. Having this team allows the program officers and research analysts to focus on building specialized expertise in their subject areas.

## Be careful not to hire too much or too quickly

While we worry that many foundations don't have enough staff to give sufficient rigor to their grantmaking decisions, hiring employees (outside of your grants) is one of the most expensive things you will do as an organization and is quite costly to reverse. For this reason, it's worth putting some time into calculating the expected benefits of hiring and what structure you plan to incorporate your hires into. Will more grants be processed, for example? Will you be able to research grants more rigorously? On top of the time and financial cost of hiring and onboarding staff, it can also make it harder to make big changes to your foundation's scope, structure, ways of working, and culture. It might make sense to hold off if:

- ... your strategy, structure, and scope are still very much up in the air. Things will always change, but you should at least have an outline of your key areas. This is common in other fields as well - Y Combinator, for example, discourages hiring during the three-month accelerator program, as any activity other than finding product-market fit would be a distraction. It is not uncommon for a foundation to make an earlier hire that results in them strongly committing to a cause area that they likely would not have done without hiring an advocate for the area so early.
- ... you can outsource a specific task that could be better done by a temporary contractor/freelancer. For example, for reviewing expenses and adding them to bookkeeping software, hiring a part-time contractor or freelancer on a

platform such as Upwork might make more sense until you have enough regular tasks for a full-time operations hire. Registration of your foundation is a great example of a task that should be outsourced instead of hired for.

- ... you have not been able to define a clear job profile for your first hire. Without a clear role, it will be difficult to identify the best candidate. Whilst it's advisable to hire generalists early on, and it makes sense that your first few hires will take on a wide range of tasks, don't expect someone to be a superb researcher for three months and then switch to the completely different profile of a highly flexible operations generalist. You are setting yourself and your employee up for failure if you want a superman or woman that ticks all the boxes.

## 7.3.3 Summary

- Key decisions about foundation structure include who to employ, how much of the work to do yourself, and how to structure the team you have.
- If you want to make grant-making decisions yourself, you must build wisdom (as discussed in the previous chapter).
- If you want to defer the decision-making, you need to ensure you have the following:
    - A great vetting system for your hiring process (See Part C of this book).
    - Trust that your hires have internalized your foundation's core values and scope.
    - Acceptance that grantmaking decisions will be better if you leverage the time and expertise of others.
- When structuring your team, hire generalists first and specialists later. Specialization can occur along two dimensions: subject area and function.
- Hire slowly. Hiring is expensive, and getting it right the first time is very valuable. Hold off from hiring if:
    - You have no direction yet on strategy, structure, and scope.
    - What you're hiring for could be cost-effectively outsourced.
    - You're not yet able to define the role clearly enough to find the right candidate for it.

# 8. Strategy

Once you've set your foundation's scope and chosen its structure, the next step will be to define the strategy your foundation will use to achieve its fundamental goals. We will start this section by discussing three strategic questions that will be valuable to consider early in your journey:

1. Evidence vs. hits-based giving strategy?
2. Active vs. passive grantmaking?
3. Open vs. closed application process?

We will then discuss three more factors to consider to ensure your foundation is reaching its impact potential:

1. Whether and how to create leverage
2. Thinking about your giving in terms of counterfactuals
3. Neglected grantmaking strategies that could be a good fit for you

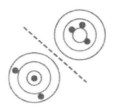

# 8.1. Evidence vs. hits-based grantmaking

Deciding what type of giving strategy to adopt is one of the most important decisions you will make when starting a new foundation. There are currently two rival approaches among philanthropists seeking to maximize their impact:
- Evidence-based giving (championed by organizations like GiveWell)
- Hits-based giving (championed by organizations like Open Philanthropy)

Let's look at both strategies in more detail.

## 8.1.1. Overview of evidence-based giving

Evidence-based giving involves funding projects that fulfill two conditions:
- The strongest possible evidence to suggest that they have a large positive impact per funding dollar
- The ability to absorb more funding at this level of cost-effectiveness

For example, GiveWell funds the distribution of long-lasting insecticide-treated nets (LLINs). This intervention for preventing malaria is backed by over 20 randomized controlled trials. It has been formally recommended by the World Health Organization. Specifically, GiveWell chooses to fund the Against Malaria Foundation (AMF), which has a strong monitoring and evaluation process, is transparent, and sufficiently funding-constrained. This allows funders to estimate with a high degree of confidence that further donations will fund distributions of nets for ~$5 each, saving lives for an average cost of ~$4,500 each.[129]

There are parallels between the evidence-based strategy in philanthropy and the value investing strategy in for-profit investment:

| | Evidence-based giving | Value investing |
| --- | --- | --- |
| Risk profile | Low | Low |
| Notable players | GiveWell, The Life You Can Save | Warren Buffett (Berkshire Hathaway), Michael Burry (Scion Capital) |
| Priorities when choosing projects | **1.** Interventions that increase welfare according to scientific research, which is generalizable to other contexts (e.g. in other countries; at scale) | **1.** Proven business models in comparable markets (e.g. comparable countries or industries) |
| | **2.** Established organizations with a track record of executing these interventions at high cost-effectiveness | **2.** Businesses with a strong leadership team and strong fundamentals |
| | **3.** Organizations that have room to deploy more funding at a similar cost-effectiveness | **3.** Businesses that are undervalued and/or could profitably deploy more capital |

---

[129] GiveWell, "Against Malaria Foundation," Dec. 2022, accessed Feb. 20, 2023, https://www.givewell.org/charities/amf

## 8.1.2. Overview of hits-based giving

Hits-based giving involves funding a portfolio of projects that fulfills the following two conditions:

- A relatively low probability of success, but...
- Successful projects generate a truly massive impact - enough to offset the lack of impact from unsuccessful ones, resulting in a high average impact per dollar.

For example, The Rockefeller Foundation funded research into agricultural productivity, a key enabler for the "Green Revolution," which is claimed to have saved more than a billion people from starvation.[130] If this were the only impact achieved from the total $17 billion in cumulative donations from the foundation, it would still have achieved a cost-effectiveness of less than $20 per life saved - several hundred times more cost-effective than the best high-evidence interventions available today.

The rationale for the hits-based approach is as follows: The giving opportunities with the strongest evidence base will generally already be well-funded by rational philanthropists and so will be least constrained by access to funds. The low-hanging fruit will already have been picked, and new funders will experience diminishing returns. Conversely, promising projects in fields with limited empirical research (e.g. wild animal welfare) or where it's hard to measure impact (e.g. government advocacy) will likely have the hardest time accessing funding. As such, funding these projects can have a large counterfactual impact on whether they survive or scale. If this is the case, the funder that enabled a project to survive or scale is responsible not just for the good done directly by spending the money on the intervention but also for much of the cumulative good done by the project over its entire lifespan.

There are parallels between the hits-based strategy in philanthropy and the venture capital strategy in for-profit investment:

---

[130] University of Minnesota, "The Man Who Saved a Billion Lives," Aug. 12, 2020, accessed Feb. 20, 2023, https://twin-cities.umn.edu/news-events/man-who-saved-billion-lives.

| | Hits-based giving | Venture capital |
|---|---|---|
| Risk profile | High | High |
| Notable players | Open Philanthropy, EA Funds | Sequoia Capital (early funding for Apple, Google, YouTube, Airbnb, but also many failed projects we never hear about) |
| Priorities when choosing projects | **1.** Each grant has the potential to result in cost-effective impact <u>at scale</u> such that it can more than offset the cost of grants to unimpactful projects | **1.** Each investment in the fund has the potential to turn out profitable and scalable enough to generate a return that could offset the failure of every other investment in the fund |
| Bonus points for... | **2.** Projects that contradict conventional wisdom or expert opinion but still have a strong impact in expectation, as these have the greatest potential to be truly transformative | **2.** Projects that address needs that consumers don't realize they have yet, as these have the greatest potential to disrupt entire industries and generate massive returns |
| | **3.** Projects that are particularly dependent on your grant to survive or scale, as the counterfactual impact of funding them includes much of the project's cumulative impact over its lifespan | **3.** Projects that are particularly dependent on your funding to survive, so you can negotiate higher equity for your investment |

Hits-based giving does not entail choosing projects at random with no regard for empirical evidence. Rather, it involves relying more heavily on heuristics and triangulating multiple weaker forms of evidence. To ensure that chosen projects truly do have enormous impact potential and to maximize the percentage of projects that are "hits," funding decision-makers or their trusted advisors need a deep understanding of the area that the project is in, including any evidence which does exist, and of the key players in that area (organizations, thought-leaders, funders).

This is analogous to how venture capital firms often have specialist fund managers for investments in specific regions, industries, or business models.

If you're considering a hits-based strategy, it's crucial to account for three things:

## 1) Risk ≠ uncertainty

In both the for-profit and nonprofit sectors, hits-based strategies are high-risk. They involve taking actions where there is a considerable chance of undesirable outcomes (the donation has no or negative impact, or the investment loses value) but where it's possible to form an evidence-based view on the range of possible outcomes and the probability that each eventuates. This is like betting $10 on the roll of a six–sided die where you will win $100 if you roll a 1 – you are more likely than not to lose your bet. But you can be confident that the overall expected return of the bet is positive and that the more bets you make, the greater the chance you will come out ahead.

Uncertainty is when the range of possible outcomes and the probability that each eventuates is not or cannot be known with any degree of confidence. This is like betting $10 on the roll of a die with an unknown number of sides, where you win a mystery prize if you roll a 1 – you have no reason to believe that the expected return of the bet is positive.

If a venture capital firm made all its investments with no justified confidence in the scale of the potential upside and the probability of success, it would soon go out of business. Betting millions on decisions made with that low degree of uncertainty is not good business. On the other hand, taking calculated risks where the evidence suggests that the scale of potential upsides justifies the low, *known* probability of success can be very good business indeed.

***The takeaway:*** Don't mistake your uncertainty for taking calculated risks.[131]

## 2) There is a natural bias towards a hits-based strategy

It is far easier to convince yourself a pet project could be a hit than to prove it's impactful with strong evidence. As a funder, you're likely to come across many novel opportunities that it's easy to get excited about funding. Meanwhile, you'll probably

---

[131] To be clear, taking risk involves uncertainty in the sense that which outcome will eventuate is unknown. But it doesn't necessarily involve the range of possible outcomes, or their probability distribution being unknown. That's the distinction we're trying to make.

never come across an excellent evidence-based opportunity that doesn't require spending a lot of effort validating the evidence base.[132]

***The takeaway:*** When justifying a grant as part of a hits-based approach, be careful that you aren't simply doing so because the evidence is hard, and the knowledge that 'hits-based strategies can work' can be used to give yourself permission to take that approach, whether it's right for your organization or not. Both hits-based and evidence-based giving are hard – if hits-based giving feels easy, you may be fooling yourself.

## 3) The funding landscape for some types of hits is relatively crowded

Hits are likely to be early-stage, innovative projects. Some forms of innovation are very popular, such as technological innovation (e.g. a mental health app for depression). In fact, given the number of new foundations whose funding comes from tech entrepreneurs, the bias towards technological solutions is perhaps stronger than ever. As a result, funding for technological innovation is relatively abundant. This makes the job of foundations looking for tech-based hits much harder, as it's harder to find potentially transformative projects that wouldn't have been funded otherwise.

On the other hand, other forms of innovation are far more neglected. For example, the fields of social innovation (e.g. a program that uses the influence of community leaders to increase vaccination uptake) or legal innovation (e.g. environmental personhood, analogous to corporate personhood, as a tool for addressing issues like climate change), are far less trendy than technological innovation. Moral innovation (e.g. an intervention that improves the welfare of insects) is even more neglected.

***The takeaway:*** When deciding whether your foundation has a comparative advantage in hits-based grantmaking, consider whether the types of potential hits you'd be excited about and well-equipped to evaluate are based on crowded or neglected forms of innovation.

---

[132] In fact, the best evidence-based opportunities are likely to be especially effortful to identify: Given two interventions with the same cost-effectiveness, the intervention with the more complicated or controversial evidence base is more likely to be neglected by funders. Therefore, under an evidence-based strategy, the greatest counterfactual impact will likely come from funding interventions that require a lot of evidence-vetting efforts.

## Example: Charity Entrepreneurship

Where does Charity Entrepreneurship sit on the hits-based vs. evidence-based spectrum? Charity Entrepreneurship's incubation program model combines both spectrums. We use an evidence-based approach regarding our choice of cause areas and charity ideas and a hits-based approach in that each charity we incubate has a relatively low probability of being extremely successful (as is the nature of start-ups) but a large expected impact for those charities that do succeed. Meanwhile, the track record of our incubated charities to date, combined with the evidence that these charities would not have been founded without us (or at least not as soon or as well), serves as a strong evidence base for the impactfulness of CE as an organization. Therefore, you could say:

- **Charity Entrepreneurship** invests its time in an evidence-based fashion (researching, recommending, and incubating charity ideas with the strongest possible evidence to suggest that they have a large positive impact per funding dollar).
- **CE's funders** are making an evidence-based investment because they fund work that has, on aggregate, reliably been highly cost-effective and impactful.
- **CE's Seed Network** (which funds incubated charities) makes a hits-based investment when deciding which new charities to fund.

## 8.1.3. Which strategy is better?

### Empirical evidence

Unfortunately, there is very limited empirical evidence available today. However, our team attempted to empirically compare the expected value of hits vs. evidence-based giving by estimating historical hit rates and trying to quantify some of their outcomes. We tried a few different approaches for this, all of which had problems. Ultimately, we settled on looking at the track record of one specific type of hit in a highly quantified area. Specifically, we went with the discovery of new vaccinations, which some of our team has existing experience with, having founded a charity to increase vaccination uptake in India. This approach allowed us to make a fairly high-quality estimate of the cost-effectiveness of historically funded vaccination research, which was eventually developed into a large research project completed by Rethink Priorities (see footnote for a link to the results).[133]

Even this method is far from perfect: It pertains to one type of cause area/intervention and does not necessarily tell us about the relative effectiveness of hits-based vs. evidence-based strategies in general by itself. But we can construct a thought experiment to draw general conclusions about hits-based vs. evidence-based strategies from this data point and to update our prior views on the relative attractiveness of these strategies. Before reading further, note down your beliefs about the following:

- **Hit magnitude for infectious disease**: How much more cost-effective would you expect the best "hits" in the cause area of infectious disease to be than the best evidence-based funding opportunities – 2x, 20x, 200x?
- **Hit magnitude for one of your priority cause areas**: How much more cost-effective would you expect the best 'hits' in one of your foundation's priority cause areas (e.g. mental health) to be than the best evidence-based funding opportunities – 2x, 20x, 200x?
- **Hit rate**: What would you expect your foundation's success rate would be in betting on hits – 1 in 10? 1 in 100?

---

[133]Peter Wildeford, "Cost-Effectiveness of Vaccines: Appendices and Endnotes," May 8, 2018, accessed Feb. 20, 2023, https://forum.effectivealtruism.org/posts/4FDYHJpgcbpZAawRz/cost-effectiveness-of-vaccines-appendices-and-endnotes

(Note that for a hits-based approach to be more cost-effective than evidence-based alternatives, the cost-effectiveness multiplier of the best hits multiplied by your hit rate would need to be greater than 1).

Our findings in the infectious disease cause area were quite surprising. In short, we found that different efforts to discover new vaccines ranged from far less cost-effective than AMF (one of the most cost-effective, evidence-based charities available today) to less than 2x AMF's cost-effectiveness at best. So unless your expected success rate in betting on hits is greater than 50%, or one hit for every two grants (an extremely high bar), a hits-based approach to infectious disease looks less cost-effective than donating to AMF. Does learning that the hit magnitude for infectious disease is only ~2x make you less confident in your expected hit magnitude for your priority cause areas? If so, with your original hit rate estimate, does a hits-based approach to your priority cause areas still look exciting?

For us, this research updated our thinking about hits-based giving pretty negatively. Although we would like to see a lot more evidence on this topic, this information seems compelling enough evidence to be cautious with hits-based giving.

## Theoretical arguments

Some argue that we should expect a hits-based strategy to have a higher impact on average because, in the for-profit space, according to some, venture capital investing sees a higher rate of return than value investing, particularly when comparing the most successful practitioners of each approach. However, some key differences between hits-based giving and venture capital investing mean that we can't expect things to play out the same way:

- **For-profit has bounded downside risk**: At most, for-profit investors can lose 100% of their investment. When your goal is to do the most good, you can do worse than zero good - you can actively do harm.
- **Replaceability doesn't matter in for-profit investing**: In for-profit investing, it doesn't matter whether someone else would have invested in the high-return project had you not invested - all that matters is whether you got to invest. When your goal is to do the most good, you have to achieve something harder and more unlikely than just picking the "hit" - you need to pick "hits" that would not have been able to become "hits" had you decided not to fund them.

## General weaknesses to understand

The relative weaknesses of each strategy include:

- **Evidence-based giving neglects areas that are inherently hard to measure**, e.g. policy interventions, macro-economic interventions, and interventions that aim to improve the far future.
- **Hits-based giving is more vulnerable to bias and conflicts of interest** because the decision-making process is more subjective and harder to audit.
- **Hits-based giving risks doing significant harm**, e.g. by funding AI-safety research that accidentally accelerates the development of dangerous general AI.

## Foundation-dependent considerations

**An evidence-based strategy may be more appropriate for foundations that:**

- **Are particularly sensitive to reputational risk**: Foundations who are under a lot of public scrutiny or with ties to political figures may prefer to adopt evidence-based giving and avoid hits-based giving because they can't risk being seen to support projects that (a) are controversial, (b) are supported by limited evidence or vague reasoning, or (c) end up having no impact, or even causing harm.
- **Require unanimous support from many stakeholders for funding decisions:** It is relatively easy to achieve consensus when decisions are informed by a strong evidence base. In contrast, decisions to invest more speculatively in projects with limited evidence that contradict conventional wisdom or expert opinion are unlikely to be agreed upon by more than one or two stakeholders. As such, foundations that attempt a hits-based giving strategy whilst requiring many stakeholders to sign off on each funding decision are unlikely to fund many projects and are particularly unlikely to fund the most counter-intuitive but ultimately transformational projects.
- **Think that the world is relatively uncertain, and it's hard to identify hits**: This is a matter of your foundation's worldview. Do you believe your foundation can identify hits at a high enough frequency? You might be comfortable taking calculated risks, but do you believe your foundation can calculate those risks accurately enough?

The first two of these characteristics are more typical of governments and public foundation charities that distribute public donations than of private foundations.

**Meanwhile, a hits-based strategy may be more appropriate for foundations that:**

- **Possess a comparative advantage in discovering promising projects due to their network**: Some foundations occupy a niche in which they are uniquely well-connected, or they have a large enough team or a strong enough brand to have an especially broad overview of the existing funding opportunities. These foundations will be particularly well-positioned to discover the most promising projects, so they are more likely to be in a good position to find particularly high-magnitude hits that would otherwise not have been found.

- **Have a comparative advantage in determining whether and how likely projects could be a "hit"** due to access to subject-matter expertise: When a foundation has specific subject-matter expertise, has the ability to hire particularly good subject-matter experts, or has a network of trusted subject-matter experts to consult, it can make unusually good assessments of the likely impact of projects in the absence of strong evidence, as well as of their likelihood. Foundations like this will likely be better positioned to have particularly high hit rates.

## Conclusion: A path forward amid uncertainty

**When it comes to doing good, it makes sense to be risk neutral:** In the context of personal prosperity, money has diminishing returns as you move along the scale from impoverished to trillionaire. As such, it's arguably appropriate to be somewhat risk averse, choosing not to risk everything on a bet, even with a strong expected return. This logic does not apply in the context of improving well-being, where a unit of well-being is worth the same amount regardless. As such, hits-based giving, being a high-risk, high-return strategy, shouldn't count against it. All that should matter is the expected impact of a hits-based strategy vs. the expected impact of an evidence-based strategy for your foundation.

**When weighing up the empirical and theoretical evidence**, the answer to the question of whether hits-based or evidence-based giving is better overall remains undecided. As such, it is best to arm oneself with an understanding of the relative strengths/weaknesses of each strategy in general and then to focus on whichever strategy is a better fit for your particular type and structure of foundation, cause area, potential comparative advantages, expertise and ability, network, epistemic beliefs about the world and feedback loops, worries about biases and downside risks, and general appetite for risk.

In sum: Be clear and intentional about where you stand on the issues discussed in this section, calculate the expected impact for your case, discuss it with trusted advisors, make a decision, and keep evaluating how it goes.

## 8.1.4. Summary

- Evidence-based giving means funding projects that are backed by the strongest possible evidence of being the most cost-effective at the margin:
    - o It often neglects areas that are inherently hard to measure, e.g. policy interventions, macro-economic interventions, and interventions that aim to improve the far future.
    - o It is easier to achieve consensus on decisions with this type of giving if you require it from your stakeholders.

It is a great strategy for foundations particularly sensitive to reputational risk.

- Hits-based giving means funding projects with a low probability of success but with the potential for extremely high levels of impact, such that the "hits" more than offset the lack of impact from the majority of projects that fail:
    - o Remember that risk ≠ uncertainty. Using hits-based giving correctly means taking calculated risks and informed bets, not loose speculation.
    - o Beware the natural bias towards hits-based giving: It allows one to justify giving to something emotionally appealing by claiming its plausibly extremely high upside.
    - o It has the potential to do serious harm, e.g. by funding AI-safety research which accidentally ends up accelerating the development of dangerous general AI.
    - o It's more vulnerable to bias and conflicts of interest because decision-making is more subjective and harder to audit.

It is a great strategy for foundations with a comparative advantage at discovering hits that others miss, for instance, because of a particularly strong and differentiated network or unique expertise.

- Although there is limited empirical evidence on which approach has the better track record, CE's best research suggests that hits-based giving has performed worse on average.
- Some claim that, in theory, we should expect a hits-based strategy to have a higher impact on average, based on trends in the for-profit investment world. However, the nonprofit sector has relevant differences:

- o For-profits can, at worst, lose their investment. Nonprofits have the potential to do actual harm.
- o For-profits don't have to worry about replaceability (i.e. whether someone else would otherwise have invested in the hit) to be successful with this strategy. Nonprofits have the harder job of being the funder that the project wouldn't have become a hit without.

# 8.2. Active vs. passive grantmaking

Some foundations like to be deeply involved in the operations and decision-making of their grantees. In contrast, others see their role as providing funding to talented implementers and otherwise staying out of the way. This first approach is generally called 'active' grantmaking, and the latter is called 'passive' grantmaking.

It's common for funders to feel that implementing charities owe major donors influence over their decisions. In our opinion, what's more important than any obligations that charitable funders and implementers have to one another is that *both* have to make the decisions that lead to the best outcomes for the charity's beneficiaries. After all, impact is the point of charity, to begin with! Therefore, the question is, what's best for beneficiaries – for your foundation to be an active or passive grantmaker?

First things first, it's important to understand that this framing is misleading because it's actually impossible to be completely passive as a grantmaker: You could try by only giving anonymous, unconditional donations, but still – the decisions to fund some things and to not fund others creates incentives for implementers. In this way, funders always wield influence over what gets implemented. It's unavoidable. So the question isn't *whether* to be active at all as a grantmaker but *how* active to be.

To this end, we will look at a few ways that you can have more than the minimum amount of influence over what gets implemented as a funder and why you might want to do so:

| Ways to be more 'active' | Reasons to be more 'active' |
|---|---|
| Using soft power to influence grantee decisions | Your foundation has strong decision-making abilities or complementary expertise that could improve decision-making |
| Giving restricted funding (conditional grants) to limit what activities you support | You're supportive of some but not all of the programs your grantees are considering |
| Employing tactics that cause new projects to come into existence | Within your foundation's scope, the availability of projects to fund is a major bottleneck |

We'll discuss the why, how, and limitations of each. A general theme is that the more well-respected your foundation is as a thought leader, the more it will be able to influence the decisions of implementers without resorting to more coercive tactics. If you are perceived as overpowering, and implementers disagree with your views, it can strain your relationships with your grantees.

# 8.2.1. Influencing grantee decisions with soft power

Simply letting grantees know what you'd like to see them focus on and how you'd like them to operate differently can significantly impact their decisions. This could be because they respect your foundation's judgment, because you provide them with compelling evidence and arguments, or simply because they want you to be pleased enough with their performance to keep funding them. This final reason is a cause for caution – relationships based on coercion rather than mutual respect are seldom healthy and are generally short-lived.

### Why you might want to use soft power

There are two good reasons you might want to exert influence in this way:

1. Comparative advantages: If you have complementary expertise or decision-making skills that grantees would benefit from, you may want your input to be included in decisions.

2. Disagreement about direction: If you think the grantee is on the wrong track, you may want to influence them in a better direction.

## Comparative advantages

This is when you think you have complementary abilities such that a decision would be better if it had your influence or if it was deferred to you entirely. These comparative advantages could be a matter of general ability or something more specialized.

### *General ability*

There will be some areas where even a relatively uninformed grantmaker would be the better decision-maker (e.g. when considering what other funders might think of an idea) and some areas where a recipient will almost definitely be more informed (e.g. specific details of operations). But despite this, it can still be the case that either the grantmaker or the grantee has better decision-making abilities in general due to their relative experience, knowledge, intelligence, and focus on impact. Four combinations can occur with different levels of decision-making ability:

## Grantmaker ability

| | Low | High |
|---|---|---|
| **High** | **Common**, as grantmakers have a broader view and **less deep knowledge** in any given area **than specialized charities**<br><br>e.g., new grantmaker donating to a GiveWell top charity | **Rare**. Generally the **grantmaker cedes operational control to the charity**, but makes their **criteria for ongoing support explicit**<br><br>e.g., GiveWell donating to a GiveWell top charity |
| **Low** | **Most common**, due to **poor feedback loops** in charity & grantmaking. **Difficult for either party to make strong decisions**.<br><br>e.g., new grantmaker donating to a struggling charity | **Grantmaker should take more control**. Generally occurs in new cause areas / interventions, or with low charity competition<br><br>e.g., a talented grantmaker donating to the best charity in a nascent area |

*Charity ability*

Although it can be flattering to think that you are a high-ability grantmaking organization in your space, it's a question that every funder needs to consider truthfully if they want to have the most impact possible. Some questions to ask yourself or others about your grantmaking:

- How much time have you spent in the relevant space? How much knowledge, experience, and understanding of context do you have?
- Would an independent effectiveness-oriented actor think your organization is more informed than the charity?
- Has your organization made and tracked historical predictions that match reality more closely than the charities it has supported?
- Do other funders look to you for guidance or use your writing/ideas as a resource?

### Specialized ability

It's far more common for a grantmaker to have a comparative advantage in making certain kinds of decisions relative to their grantees than for them to be more capable in general. Perhaps your foundation has seen many other grantees try something similar to what a charity is considering and has gleaned some lessons about what works and what doesn't. Perhaps one of your grantmakers is an expert on a niche topic at the heart of the charity's intervention (e.g. the epidemiology of malaria) or on a broad topic with general implications for the intervention (e.g. the economic impact of aid on local markets). Perhaps your foundation is more informed on how to interpret or design scientific studies than the implementing charity, or maybe you've spent hundreds more hours creating cost-effectiveness analyses than they have. These highly plausible scenarios may cause you to want to influence some of your recipient's decisions.

## Disagreement about direction

Comparative advantages aside, when you think the charity is going in the wrong direction, you might be more vocal with them to try to change their mind. There are three main causes of disagreement about direction:

### 1. Different amounts of emphasis placed on impact

The most common goal divergence is when a charity does not have impact as a major focus and the grantmaker wants them to move impact up the queue of their priorities. It is tricky to make this happen. Ultimately, without a huge time investment, it's very hard to check how much impact a charity is having, particularly if the charity has an incentive to deceive to get more funding.

This is a fairly intractable issue. Foundations are best off avoiding this scenario by clearly signaling to potential grantees that maximizing impact is your top priority and backing this up with a good vetting process to catch people who are 'talking the talk' without planning on 'walking the walk.'

### 2. Different ideas about what impact means

What if both actors are impact-focused yet still have some ethical disagreements about what should count as impact and what altruists' goals should be? This can happen – many ethical questions remain open and are debated even among highly-informed thinkers. For example, how one is willing to make tradeoffs between saving lives and improving lives depends on highly speculative or subjective views on ethical questions.

As with the first cause of disagreement, this is fairly intractable, and so again, prevention is the best tactic. Good vetting systems will help mitigate this risk.

### 3. Differences in opinion about the facts

The other cause of disagreement can be differences in opinion about the facts. Unlike ethics, these sorts of differences can be tested. "Are government or corporate campaigns better for getting a policy implemented?" is a question with an objective answer (even if it's not known by both parties). This makes these kinds of disagreements more tractable: A lot of these differences can be resolved by asking falsifiable questions that could be determined by research or time, allowing you and the charity to come to an agreement. However, it will take time to get an answer, and you may disagree about what approach to default to in the short term.

## How to use soft power

It's hard to avoid using soft power to some degree. But transparency about how you plan to engage with your grantees will help prevent conflict.

- Clearly and publicly communicate your strengths so grantees know when to call on you for advice.
- Set expectations upfront about the areas where you'd like to have your input properly considered (even if not ultimately incorporated) before providing funding.

- Express your willingness to have regular advisory calls or join the board (but it's important that this is optional and only if they see it as beneficial. Funding contingent on board seats can be a waste of time for both you and the nonprofit if you are on different pages).

## Limitations: You may not have any soft power, and if you do, it's a finite resource

In many cases, your soft power will be limited. For your foundation to actually have soft power over a recipient, you'll need one or more of the following conditions to be met:

- They find your evidence and reasoning compelling enough to change their mind
- They respect your judgment in this area enough to defer to you even when they disagree
- They need you for future funding, so your approval is important to them

Even when you have soft power, it's crucial to use it in moderation. Working with dozens of charity entrepreneurs taught us that they highly value their autonomy. If your influence is more coercive than advisory, your relationship will deteriorate quickly. You have limited social capital – choose your battles wisely.

# 8.2.2. Restricted funding

Funding restrictions are when a donation is contingent on certain conditions, such as how the recipient will use the funds or their operations and trajectory more broadly.

## Why you might want to restrict funding

Many charities work on a huge number of topics and issues; a grantmaker will rarely think every program the charity works on is equally impactful. A common and seemingly simple solution is to give restricted funding to a portion of the charitable organization's work.

## How to use funding restrictions

### *Hard vs. soft restrictions*

The first thing to consider is that restrictions can range greatly in terms of how hard or soft they are.

A hard restriction might look like, "This $100k grant is only for your work in Uganda." A hard restriction is clear and often legally built into the grant that is made. Hard restrictions are very common in government funding and rare with high-net-worth individuals. They are sometimes used by foundations and mid-size grantmakers.

A soft restriction might sound more like, "We are most excited about your work in Uganda and are giving this funding to support that." Often, soft restrictions will have social expectations rather than legal ones.

Another class of restrictions is unstated restrictions. Some of these are pretty obvious; e.g. you do not expect the charity to radically change its mission and strategy overnight. Some, however, can be a little less clear. Do you expect them to check in with you? Are there implicit targets they have mentioned before that you expect them to hit now that you have given the grant? It's good to try to have as few unclear, unstated restrictions as possible. It is better to have them written up somewhere, even if they seem obvious.

### *Three types of hard restrictions*

Let's consider some times when restrictions are commonly used and might make sense.

### Cause area restrictions

Many NGOs work on a wide number of cause areas (for example, CE might incubate charities across poverty, mental health, and animal issues). And your foundation might be focused on some, but not all, of these cause areas. Suppose you were excited about CE's human-focused work but not its animal-focused work. In that case, trying to fill that gap and leaving another donor to cover the animal side of things might make a lot of sense. Cause area restrictions can be some of the cleanest restrictions, particularly if a program has a separate staff or team working on different areas.

### Intervention restrictions

This same situation can occur for intervention areas within a cause area. Perhaps Oxfam has 100 human-focused programs. But if you think their malaria control initiative is uniquely impactful, you might want to restrict your funding to that cause or intervention area. This can get a bit harder than cause area restrictions, as the lines internally might not be as clear to the organization, and many costs will cross-cut (e.g. the operations team). It might be the best option to fund very large NGOs.

### Execution restrictions

Another possible restriction could be in terms of execution, e.g. a certain geographic restriction or a certain requirement to hit a given target. These are the restrictions one has to be more careful with. If it's a mutual goal that the charity might have set internally in any case, it can be a good fit. If it's pulling in a different direction, however, then at best, it puts strain on the relationship, and at worse, it incentivizes gaming (see next chapter).

## Limitations: There are many ways to get around restrictions

Restrictions come with some major risks. This can include animosity between the charity and grantmaker, suboptimal decisions being made, and gaming of restrictions.

Let's talk about some ways to game restrictions; this is important to be aware of to understand why even restrictions that make sense to you might miss their mark.

Ultimately, if a grantmaker wants to restrict funding and a charity wants to avoid that restriction, there are many ways to work around it. There are many well-known tricks that charities can use to get around restrictions. We are going to talk about five common ones. Not all of these are done deliberately or with the hope of misleading a funder. But they are natural and common reactions to restricted-funding grants. For each of these examples, we will imagine a theoretical charity that has program A (a high-impact program that you, as a grantmaker, are excited to fund) and program B (a bad program that you think is a waste of funding but the charity is convinced is worth doing).

### 1) Moving flexible funding from other funders

The simplest way to move around a restriction is to move other funding. If the charity aims to raise $500k for each program and a grantmaker makes a large donation to program A, virtually every charity will move its unrestricted funding over to program B to try to hit both goals. It is quite easy to do this if the charity has a sufficient amount of unrestricted funding.

### 2) *Moving fundraising capacity to the under-supported project*

Even if a charity receives no unrestricted funding (very rare), it is very easy to move flexible staff capacity to end up hitting all goals. For example, a full-time fundraising staff or Executive Director's fundraising time will naturally move to the areas they have gaps for. If a donor funds program A, more effort will be put into fundraising for program B. Fundraising and senior staff are typically not tightly connected to a single sub-area of the charity.

### 3) *Creative accounting.*

There are many defensible ways to allocate costs across different projects/teams within an organization's budget. This is especially true of support costs, like office costs, the salary costs of leaders, IT, and HR costs. This means that organizations can often allocate more of the costs of under-supported activities to better-funded projects or teams, such that donors who provide restricted funding may end up funding activities outside those restrictions due to creative accounting. For example, suppose a charity runs two programs that deliver medicines to rural communities. But a funder provides a grant that is restricted to just one program. The charity might choose to allocate 100% of the cost of purchasing the delivery trucks to the program with the restricted funding and then use the delivery trucks across both programs.

## 8.2.3. Initiating new projects

Instead of looking for existing projects, funders can also be the impetus for new projects starting. This is a fairly involved and challenging area to work in as it requires both fleshing out cause areas and ideas and undertaking actions to counterfactually get more great projects started in that space.

### Why you might want to initiate projects

You might want to do this if you see a neglected issue or cause area with few existing projects working on it. This might sound like an uncommon scenario, but it's really quite common. As we've discussed, there are many important problems and even more possible solutions to consider – other actors haven't considered them all. Moreover, where there is no funding, there will be no projects. Often, it takes a funder making their intention to fund an area known for implementers to start giving it serious thought. The lack of implementing organizations in an area doesn't mean a lack of appetite to work in that area if funding exists.

In the same way that we believe that founding a new effective charity or foundation (instead of just working for one) can be an extremely impactful choice, we also believe that funding the creation of a new project is a very promising option.

## How to initiate projects

Here are four relatively direct ways of getting projects started in a given area:

### 1. Requests For Proposals (RFPs)

One way to do this is by creating a request for proposals (RFP). This is basically a write-up for a particular project with a grant sum attached to it. The idea of RFPs is to encourage interest in an area and find an actor who would be keen to conduct the project. RFPs are very common by government actors and somewhat common with very large foundations. However, they risk attracting "mercenary NGOs" who are motivated by growth and will go wherever the funding is. The issue with this is that these NGOs will be happy to use every cent of funding available rather than aiming for maximum impact at minimum cost. For this reason, RFPs should be used carefully.

### 2. Open application rounds for new projects

Another approach is to run an open grant application round where you specifically ask for new projects addressing a specific problem or using a specific type of approach. The advantage of this is that you can be less prescriptive on the solution you're looking for, leading to more diverse ideas for solutions. It will also make it harder for mercenary NGOs because it requires applicants to better understand the field.

### 3. Prizes and competitions

Another way to encourage interest is to create a prize or competition to encourage a number of actors to work in a space. This works well when outcomes are verifiable, and there might be benefits of many different groups simultaneously working on the same question. Often the prize has to be considerably larger than the cost of running an RFP, as each competition actor only has a fraction of a chance of winning and thus will only do it if the rewards are proportionally large. It also requires considerable staff time or volunteer time to evaluate the entrances (much like an open grant application, which we will cover in part IV). That being said, this can be a highly useful tool for idea generation or for getting a wide range of angles on a topic and drawing interest from people who otherwise would not consider an area.

### 4. Playing an incubator role within the ecosystem

Many highly promising areas are capped, not by a lack of talent or funding, but by would-be project founders not knowing how to get started. Sometimes providing a bit of guidance and a clear path for project founders is all that is needed to overcome this constraint. This is one of the areas we focus on in the Charity Entrepreneurship Incubation Program. We spend thousands of research hours each year to find the best ideas for new charities and help them get started.[134]

## Limitations

We have learned many lessons from running our incubation program about what is and isn't important for incentivising the creation of new projects. These lessons may also apply in the context of incentivising existing projects to scale or improve.

### 1. Potential founders look at past success and support of other projects

Quite sensibly, most people considering founding a new project will look at the track record of previous projects tackling the same issue. It doesn't matter how impactful a project idea may be; if 50 previous projects fail, it is unlikely to be founded or funded. One of the biggest draws of the Charity Entrepreneurship program as a founding and funding opportunity is the progress and success of previously founded charities under its mentorship. This is true of other incubator programs too. You can insist all day long that a particular area has huge theoretical potential. But if a knowledgeable person can see the graveyard of failed and rejected projects around it, they will certainly proceed cautiously. Conversely, projects progressing and succeeding in an area will encourage a closer look from potential founders (and funders). Often this can lead to a ramping up of talent in an area with a couple of *pretty* good projects, leading to enough proof of concept for a *great* project to get started.

---

[134] You can read more about our research process and methodology, in any given year, on our website: https://www.charityentrepreneurship.com/research

## 2. Entrepreneurs desire autonomy

"Looking for an entrepreneur who will do whatever I say." This is the implication of a lot of job ads and projects we see. If you are to appeal to entrepreneurs, you must recognize that autonomy is a huge priority for most. They are not looking for your average job or a 'boss.' If we at Charity Entrepreneurship were to mandate that our staff be included on the board of every project in our program, we would see a big drop in attendance. If we were to micro-manage projects by providing the logos and names instead of just the broad strokes of the intervention, it would be a huge turnoff for most people. Why? Because a huge part of the appeal of entrepreneurship as a career is the ownership of the project. People with a truly entrepreneurial spirit would rather run their projects than just be hired to do all the work, even if the salary is considerably lower.

This is particularly important in areas limited by entrepreneurial talent and not funding. You need to put the entrepreneurs first when considering making a project happen. Sometimes that means supporting a project that not all other funders are 100% sold on in the early stage and giving the project space to prove itself. For more on how to find these kinds of projects, see part IV on vetting.

## 3. We need to ensure we are removing barriers, not creating them

A lot of organizations unwittingly create more barriers than they remove. Imagine I am a large funder; most would think I am clearly someone removing barriers to projects getting started. But what if the only way to get funding from me is to meet me in person? Is that removing or creating a barrier to projects getting funded? What if other funders move out of the space, assuming I am covering it? Am I funding a wide enough range of projects to allow some to have success, even if not all of them do? Many barriers are actually less obvious than they initially seem, and sometimes funders unintentionally create more barriers than they solve.

In our experience, these factors deserve serious consideration. It is crucial to consider what helps projects get started and what inhibits them if we aim to start as many high-impact charities as possible. While good intentions are admirable, to be effective, we need to be ruthless with our ideas and approaches. Skepticism can have negative connotations, but it is an underrated quality to possess when figuring out the best way to approach an issue. Suppose we can review our methods with a healthy dose of skepticism and a little humility. In that case, we will likely experience more success in our endeavors.

## 8.2.4. Summary

- Grantmakers operate on a spectrum between 'active' grantmaking (where they're deeply involved in the operations and decision-making of their grantees) and 'passive' grantmaking (where funders provide money to talented implementers and otherwise stay out of the way).
- The mere act of deciding who to fund has some influence on grantee decisions, so the question isn't whether to be active or not but how active to be.
- Ways to be more 'active' include:
1. Using soft power to influence grantee decisions.
    - o This can make sense when grantees could benefit from your foundation's decision-making abilities or complementary expertise.
    - o Soft power is a finite resource to be used judiciously.
2. Giving 'restricted funding' (i.e. conditional grants) to limit what activities you support.
    - o This can make sense when you're supportive of some but not all of the programs grantees are considering.
    - o This tactic has limited effectiveness because there are so many ways that grantees can work around restrictions.
3. Employing tactics that cause new projects to exist.
    - o This can make sense when the availability of projects to fund is a major bottleneck within your scope.
    - o Tactics include requests for proposals, open application rounds, prizes/competitions, and playing an incubator role in the ecosystem (like Charity Entrepreneurship).

# 8.3. Open vs. closed application process

Another key strategic decision for your foundation is whether your grant-sourcing process should be open or closed. That is to say, do you source opportunities using an open application process to the public, or do you source opportunities through your network?

Open application processes could involve a general application form or a request for proposals that is open and advertised to the public. Closed application processes could involve inviting members of the foundation's network to make a general application or respond to a private request for proposals, or receiving referrals for good projects or people through network members. There are advantages and disadvantages to each grant-sourcing approach, and ultimately, it is likely that your grantmaking will incorporate elements of both open and closed grant-sourcing. However, we believe there is a lot of value in some degree of open sourcing, provided the foundation can vet a potentially high volume of applications. Let's take a deeper look at why.

## 8.3.1. Relative advantages

Many foundations default to the type of application process they find most convenient, without considering their relative advantages and disadvantages.

| | Open process | Closed process |
|---|---|---|
| Main capacity required from foundation | Effective outreach strategy for sourcing candidates<br><br>**Time-efficient vetting system** | **Strong, differentiated network** or outreach capability to source competitive candidates with the best in an open process.<br><br>Effective enough vetting system and **discipline not to grant if below a certain benchmark** |
| Resource intensity | **High** (Foundations: assessing applications;<br>Unsuccessful applicants: writing applications) | **Lower/flexible** (as much networking and outreach as the foundation would like) |
| Opportunity pool | **Large** and **diverse** | **Small** and **narrow** |
| Risk of bias | **Lower** | **Higher** |
| Systematic | **More** | **Typically less** – effort is needed to make more systematic |

Most foundations today source opportunities via a closed approach. Meanwhile, in our experience, roughly 20% of charities tend to make up roughly 80% of the attendees at major conferences and networking events. As a result, the average foundation using a closed applications approach will likely end up granting to these particularly well-networked 20% of charities. For these foundations, the impact of their granting is lower: If they hadn't donated to one of these particularly well-networked charities, someone else probably would have. So in closed grant sourcing, impact is only high for foundations with a differentiated network who can find opportunities that wouldn't have been funded otherwise.

Foundations considering an open grant sourcing approach, on the other hand, should consider whether this has a strong impact given their scope. Suppose a foundation runs an open process that seeks grant applications within the same scope (cause area, location, org size, etc.). In that case, the best applications in your process may have otherwise been funded by the other foundations' processes. In open grant sourcing, the counterfactual impact is highest when the foundation's scope doesn't completely overlap with another organization, especially if they also have a well-run open application process.

## 8.3.2. Real-world examples

### Open: EA Funds

EA Funds invites anyone to apply for funding who thinks their project could be highly impactful and cost-effective within the scope of one of their four funds.

| Fund | Focuses on... | Usually supports... | Decided using... |
|---|---|---|---|
| Global health and development fund | Funding outstanding, evidence-based opportunities to provide better access to healthcare & economic development where it's needed most | Established organizations | Scientific evidence and fund managers' judgment |
| Animal welfare fund | Funding organizations and projects that will help alleviate the suffering of millions or billions of animals | Early-stage & established organizations | Organizational track record and fund managers' judgment |
| Long-term future fund | Funding to people or projects that aim to improve the long-term future, such as by reducing risks from artificial intelligence and engineered pandemics | Individuals & organizations (includes speculative opportunities) | Fund managers' judgment |
| Effective Altruism infrastructure fund | Funding to organizations or people that aim to grow or improve the effective altruism community | Organizations and early-stage projects (includes speculative opportunities) | Fund managers' judgment |

Despite being open, they don't put many resources into advertising themselves. This is perhaps because, without much active promotion, they receive several hundred applications per year. To minimize the resource intensity associated with processing applications:

a.  They try to be crystal clear about the scope of projects they fund, going as far as to make applicants tick a box confirming that they have read and understood the scope. This saves the time of applicants who aren't a good fit and saves fund managers' time processing applications. At the same time, they avoid being overly narrow or prescriptive in their stated scope because "having too-prescriptive rules could lead to grant applicants (intentionally or unintentionally) modifying their applications to game the system by conforming to what they expect fund managers will be more likely to recommend grants to, rather than applying for the thing that they actually care about."[135]

b.  They set a limit of 5000 characters for the initial application and recommend that applicants use far below this, spending just 1-2 hours on the application.

c.  They have applicants fill out a prescriptive application form rather than writing a document they can structure however they like. This makes it faster to systematically compare applicants.

d.  They have created a help center on their website with answers to frequently asked questions to reduce the administrative burden.

## Closed: Mulago Foundation

The Mulago Foundation has no channel for members of the public to apply for funding: "We don't take proposals. Proposals are a hassle for all concerned and rarely give us the information we need. We source through our own network and ask our own questions".[136] It has taken them time to build a portfolio of recipient organizations through this grant-sourcing process, which is inherently less scalable than EA Funds' open application process. However, they have managed to amass over 70 recipient organizations in which they have enough confidence to invest in long term. They also run several fellowship programs which aim to find leaders with

---

[135] EA Funds, "Scope and Limitations of EA Funds," accessed Feb. 20, 2023, https://funds.effectivealtruism.org/scope-and-limitations

[136] The Mulago Foundation, "How We Fund," accessed Feb. 20, 2023, https://www.mulagofoundation.org/how-we-fund

promising solutions that Mulago can help to design and scale. Similarly, these fellowships have no open application process, with participants headhunted by Mulago staff or referred by their network.

## A bit of both: Unorthodox Philanthropy

As the name suggests, Unorthodox Philanthropy (UP) does things a bit differently than most foundations. Firstly, their grantmaking process is structured as a series of experiments that they're using to determine the best way to operate. Secondly, they run funding rounds (which they call "searches") focused on topics like 'endgames with finite capital' and 'extraordinary leaders transforming a field' rather than focusing on specific cause areas or types of interventions.

Their creativity has thus far allowed them to identify and support some great opportunities before other foundations. For example, the winner of their first search was GiveDirectly, which gives unconditional cash transfers – a relatively controversial idea in 2010. GiveDirectly is now seen by many as *the* intervention to beat in the global health and development space.

Due to their approach being experimental by nature, where UP sits on the open/closed grantmaking spectrum has changed over time:

- Their first search was structured as a winner-takes-all competition, with applicants competing for a single grant prize.
- Their second search was structured as a more typical open application process, in which they received 1000 submissions, of which they shortlisted 150 and awarded grants to 18. They noticed that most applications came from their existing networks, suggesting that their open application approach was not delivering on its supposed comparative advantage of generating a broader pool of opportunities than a closed system. Going forward, they resolved to invest more energy in reaching out to communities that do not already have the ear of private philanthropists.
- Their third search, which was focused on the COVID response, was closed in nature. They sourced grants from their network to respond rapidly to a time-sensitive problem.
- UP's latest search is experimenting with a nomination process instead of individuals applying on their own behalf.

Experimenting in your grantmaking takes effort, making it more difficult to build expertise in any approach. It does, however, have the potential to be extremely beneficial; it could help you to figure out the best approach for *you*, rather than just picking one and hoping for the best.

# 8.4. Creating leverage

In the context of grantmaking, leverage is when the donor is able to give $X to a cause in such a way that the recipient ends up receiving *more* than $X, adding a multiplier to your impact. Broadly, you can divide the tactics for creating leverage into two categories: Those that leverage the people inside your personal network and those that leverage the people outside of it. In this chapter, we'll discuss both and some of the options to consider within each category.

Of course, the additional funds recipients receive through leverage must come from somewhere. They're still costs to someone. But this is still a positive thing so long as the ways those funds are now being spent generate more benefits for the world than they would have otherwise.

## 8.4.1. Leveraging your personal network

Early on in our effective giving journeys, most of us realize the value of convincing others to support the most cost-effective charities in the most important cause areas: We reason, "If I cause just one other person similar to me to donate effectively, then I've doubled my impact!" This is a hugely important realization and one which may apply to you even more than others, given that those who are in a position to be starting a foundation often have other people in their personal networks with significant resources that they could use to do good (e.g. your family, friends, colleagues or other philanthropists).

However, the repercussions of this realization can prove fatal to many of your social relationships if you become the philanthropic equivalent of a religious evangelist, verbally assaulting everyone you know with arguments for focusing less on charity overhead ratios, measuring things in disability-adjusted-life-years, and for the sentience of chickens. Please, don't take this route. Instead, keep in mind these tips for influencing your personal network's philanthropy for the better:

## 1. Be humble and listen

When spreading the word about effective giving, people commonly make the mistake of speaking like they have all the answers already, when of course, we're all very uncertain and just trying to figure things out. It's important to remember to be humble and to listen to the person you're speaking to. Many of the people in your life will have been around longer than you have, and all of them will have learned relevant lessons that you haven't. Asking for their views on things can be both a great way to learn and to start a longer conversation; when someone feels heard, they are often more willing to listen in turn. Another common mistake people make when spreading the word about effective giving is speaking with a superior tone. The basic principles of giving effectively may be so obvious to you now. But it's important to remember that you once didn't know these principles either. The fact that you happened to have stumbled upon them before someone else is not reason to act superior.

## 2. Focus on sympathetic people first

For some, the effectiveness mindset just "clicks." For these people, when they first read a book about effective giving, like *Doing Good Better* or *The Life You Can Save*, it feels like the answer to a question they didn't even know they were asking. In your network, some people like this may be just waiting to be discovered. Focusing your efforts on these folks first will have a higher success rate and be more time efficient than trying to convince random members of your network. One way to identify them is to send around some gentle emails. These emails could go something like this: "I am so excited. I just found this great new resource called GiveWell – here's their website!" This alone may be enough to rouse someone's interest. If they engage, you can send them deeper resources like the Giving What We Can pledge or maybe even buy them a copy of the CE Foundation Handbook. You may also have a pretty good sense of who in your network will be most sympathetic to effective giving just by thinking about what you know about their personality and interests.

### 3. Put things in their language

Some readers may come from communities that place a strong emphasis on helping others. For those of you in this position, it helps to frame your conversations on effective giving in terms of the ways of helping others they already believe in. By doing this, effective giving can be a way to build on, rather than replace, their current efforts. For instance, if they give to the local homeless shelter every year, then there is a good chance they will be open to giving to people suffering from extreme poverty in low-income countries. If they give or volunteer at a local animal shelter, odds are they would be open to funding an organization that works on factory farming. This approach may seem obvious, but people often neglect to think about people's interests strategically, instead resorting to a one-size fits all case for effective giving. Focus on the listener's existing passions, and you will get much further with them.

These tips are cross-applicable, but there are some tips that are more useful in specific situations, such as talking to family or others who already identify as philanthropists.

## Having a positive influence on your family foundation

Some readers will have families who are starting or already have a family foundation or donor-advised fund. People in this situation have a great head start since they can skip the difficult step of actually convincing people to give away money. It may sound simple, but one of the most effective ways to influence a family giving vehicle over the long term is just to show up and express interest. For many philanthropic families, it can be difficult to get the next generation to engage with philanthropy at the level of their parents and grandparents. If you express true, genuine, and sustained interest in the operation of your family's foundation, you may find that you are given increasing levels of responsibility within a surprisingly quick period of time. If you have the means to support yourself, you could even volunteer full-time for the foundation, filling in any gaps in their operations. If you approach this opportunity enthusiastically, not trying to manipulate or convince anyone, you could have real grantmaking power in your hands before long.

Sometimes family members can seem so far from an effectiveness mindset as to be utterly hopeless. Remember, though, that family relationships are inherently long-term, so there's no pressure to convince anyone in a hurry. In fact, if you try to rush the process, it can come across like a sales pitch, and you can turn your family away from effective giving. Instead, if you prioritize respectful, open communication with your relatives, there's no telling how much they may change over the course of a few years.

Remember that guilt and obligation are dangerous motivators to use for positive action. When people are confronted with uncomfortable facts, they often simply turn the other way, or they take action but aren't motivated to do so long-term. Focusing instead on the opportunity people have to improve people's lives, and the joy that brings, is a more reliable way to motivate others to engage and to give.

Holidays are especially good times to engage with your family about giving effectively. Many cultures have a holiday, like Thanksgiving in the US, with a strong emphasis on gratitude. This type of holiday presents an excellent opportunity to talk about those with less and how we can best help them. Most cultures also have a holiday that involves gift giving — maybe this year, for Christmas or Chinese New Year, you could give your family members a donation to an effective charity in an area they care about or ask for a donation to one of your top nonprofits.

One way to increase your chances of getting your family to buy into effective giving is to become the "family expert" on a specific topic. Note that while this strategy can prove highly effective, it is very dependent on the individual culture of your family. Some families think highly of the opinions of their own family members. In others, it doesn't matter if you have a PhD - you will always be the baby. Assuming your family is open to taking your guidance, pick an important topic that you and your family are interested in and dedicate a significant amount of time to learning as much as possible about it. You could then position yourself as a resource to your family when it comes time for them to give. For example, if your family already donates to transmissible disease nonprofits abroad, there is a very good opportunity for you to become the "family expert" on the topic and provide them a real service.

## Influencing other philanthropists

Another fantastic opportunity for leverage is the larger philanthropic community. While "mainstream" philanthropy has accomplished many incredible things, "effectiveness" in how we conceive it is still a relatively foreign concept. As a funder, you will have unparalleled access to the often secretive world of philanthropists. Most countries have their own philanthropic networks, communities, and organizations where philanthropists gather to discuss their giving (an example of this is the National Center for Family Philanthropy in the US). Several are also global in scope, such as The Philanthropy Workshop or Nexus Global. If you engage with these communities, you will be pleasantly surprised to find a group of generous, well-intentioned people open to all types of discussions. So, engage with them! You may make new connections and inspire someone to start giving with effectiveness in mind.

For highly motivated readers to leverage their position as philanthropists, you could also consider setting up a philanthropic advising practice. Philanthropic advising is a relatively new concept in the world of philanthropy. But it is growing increasingly common for philanthropists to reach out for help and guidance before giving. It doesn't take a lot of time to set up a 'side hustle' as a philanthropic advisor, and a very limited number of 'effectiveness-minded' advisors are on offer. As the demand for advisors with this skill set grows, this could become a unique opportunity for greater leverage and career capital.

## 8.4.2. Leveraging the broader community

Whilst your network may be full of people with lots of resources who might be receptive to the idea that we should use our resources to help others as much as possible, not everyone has this opportunity to the same extent. And no matter how large your network's resources are, there are even more resources outside of your network than within it. After all, there are all of the philanthropists you haven't met, millions of individual donors who give over $300 billion a year in U.S alone, and governments who collectively command tens of trillions of dollars. How might your foundation influence each of these groups to use their resources for the better?

### Philanthropists outside your network: Leverage through signaling and thought leadership

The grants you make can create leverage via philanthropists you've never heard of, let alone met. For example, you could make a modest but highly conspicuous donation to a promising and neglected opportunity. This brings the opportunity to the attention of other potential funders and signals the quality of the opportunity. The strength of this signal depends on your reputation as a grantmaker (or sometimes just on your reputation in general). For example, GiveWell's endorsement in the form of a small donation to a charity carries huge weight and would influence other foundations and individuals to donate there as well. The same can happen for endorsements from authors, professors, or others who are seen as good decision-makers.

Foundations can significantly amplify their long-term impact by fostering a reputation as a strong grantmaker or knowledgeable specialist in a particular field, which can then be used to create leverage through thought leadership. To aid in building this reputation, young foundations can engage in the public grantmaking discourse (e.g. the Happier Lives Institute's well-received critique of GiveWell's deworming cost-effectiveness analysis).[137] Transparency regarding your grantmaking process and individual grant decisions (e.g. publishing reasoning on your website) is also a valuable way to build trust.

## Individuals donors: Leverage through matching campaigns

One popular way to leverage individual donors is through matching campaigns. These involve a funder committing to match or even double the donations made to a nominated recipient within a specific timeframe. The appeal for donors is that for each dollar they donate, two or even three dollars will go to the charity. The appeal for the funder running the campaign is attracting more donations to a worthy recipient, either shifting those donations away from less worthy opportunities or, even better, causing donors to give away more than they would have otherwise. This can either be used by the funder to direct a larger total amount of funds to the matching recipient or to direct a fixed amount of funds to the recipient at a lower cost to the funder, allowing them to deploy the savings on other grants.

But do matching campaigns actually increase donations relative to crowdfunding a grant without matching? In addition to common anecdotal evidence from fundraisers for the effectiveness of matching campaigns, a J-PAL study in the United States found that merely announcing that matching funds are available increased charities' revenue per solicitation by 19%.[138] Meanwhile, contrary to conventional wisdom, they found that matching ratios above 1:1 saw no additional impact on donations.

---

[137] Joel McGuire, Samuel Dupret and Michael Plant, "Deworming and decay: replicating GiveWell's cost-effectiveness analysis", Happier Lives Institute, July 25, 2022, accessed Feb. 20, 2023, https://www.happierlivesinstitute.org/report/deworming-and-decay/

[138] Dean Karlan and John A. List, "Does Price Matter in Charitable Giving? Evidence from a Large-Scale Natural Field Experiment," The American Economic Review 97, no. 5 (November 1, 2007): 1774–93, accessed Feb. 20, 2023, https://doi.org/10.1257/aer.97.5.1774.

From a funder's perspective, running a matching campaign is a fairly low-risk tactic to achieve leverage on their donations. From a participant in the matching campaign's perspective, things look a bit different. Participants in the matching campaign must ask themselves, "If I donate $10 as part of this campaign, how much more will the organization counterfactually receive than if I hadn't donated?" Ideally, for a 1:1 matching campaign, the answer is $20 - $10 from you and $10 from the matcher. This is known as a counterfactual match. However, sometimes matchers have a floor for how much they want the charity to receive, and they plan to top-up any shortfall from the matching campaign. In this case, participants in the campaign aren't actually causing the charity to receive more funds; they're just saving the foundation money. Even when the foundation commits to not provide any top-up funding, making the donation match more legitimate, the amount raised in the matching campaign may influence how much they donate to the charity in the future. As such, matching campaign participants need to look carefully at what the matcher is committing to and discount the impact of their match accordingly. It's in the interest of the philanthropic sector to maintain donor trust in the validity of matching campaigns by acting with integrity; however, this is rather seldomly adhered to in practice. The takeaway for those running matching campaigns is that it is important to think carefully about whether you provide counterfactual matching and communicate honestly to would-be participants. Recipient charities can also play a role in safeguarding the integrity of matching campaigns by committing to not accept top-up funding, returning anything beyond the crowdsourced donations and agreed matching amount.

## Governments: Leverage through partnerships, policy, and underutilized programs

*Partnerships:* Nonprofits can partner with governments to split the cost of interventions, particularly when the intervention is something the government would like to see rolled out but lacks the capability or budget to spearhead itself and when it's clear that the nonprofit sector would not be able to execute it without government support.

This can happen in the form of literal cost sharing. It can also happen through the nonprofit sector establishing a service that is then handed over to the government. As a funder, you could support a project or intervention during the proof of concept and scaling phase until it's mature enough to be adopted as a government program or service provider. This is the 'government adoption endgame.' A potentially surprising example of this is an education intervention that you'll be familiar with – kindergartens.[139] Kindergartens were first run by private charities, religious schools, and orphanages in the United States. Eventually, the government recognized the developmental benefits of this kind of early education and incorporated it into the structure of the public school system. Soon enough, the vast majority of kindergartens were government funded, no longer depending on charitable donors.

***Underutilized programs:*** Governments often commit to funding highly impactful activities, but they don't end up reaching their maximum committed funding because of other bottlenecks. By funding the removal of these bottlenecks, foundations can cause a lot more money to flow to highly impactful activities. For example, the Indian Government has large amounts of committed funding for infant vaccination programs; however, limited uptake constrains how much the government ends up spending on this highly impactful intervention. Charity Science Health and Suvita, two CE charities, stepped in to increase the uptake of infant vaccination programs through SMS reminders and community immunization ambassadors. This is an exciting opportunity for a funder who only needs to pay for the cost of the SMS reminders and recruit the ambassadors to unlock government funding for the vaccinations themselves.

***Policy:*** If successful, funding policy advocacy is perhaps the grant with the most leverage you can possibly make. In scenarios where you're aiming to change laws, all you need to do is fund the advocacy, and (hopefully) the government will fund the enforcement for as long as that law remains in effect. We can see this kind of leverage at play in several of the charity ideas that Charity Entrepreneurship has incubated, like banning lead paint (Lead Exposure Elimination Project) and banning the import of animal products that don't meet local welfare standards (Animal Policy International).

---

[139] Gugelev, A., & Stern, A, What's Your Endgame? Stanford Social Innovation Review, 13(1), 41–47. https://doi.org/10.48558/Q4SM-M719

### 8.4.3. Summary

- In the context of grantmaking, leverage is when giving $X results in the recipient receiving more than $X, adding a multiplier to your impact. This can be done by leveraging your personal network or the broader community.
- Convincing others in your personal network to give more effectively can be very impactful or very risky to your relationships. Best practices include:
  - Be humble and listen. Nobody likes being preached at.
  - Focus on sympathetic people first.
  - Put things in their language and in terms of what they already know they value.
- You can also influence the wider community beyond your personal network.
  - Philanthropists outside your network: Leverage through signaling and thought leadership.
  - Individuals donors: Leverage through matching campaigns,
  - Governments: Leverage through cost-sharing partnerships, policy advocacy, or removing bottlenecks to the uptake of underutilized programs.

# 8.5. Counterfactuals

## 8.5.1. Counterfactuals in funding decisions

The final step in defining a strong strategy for your foundation is to consider your counterfactual impact. In this handbook, we've mentioned counterfactual impact in passing several times. Now we will explore it in more detail.

Counterfactual thinking considers the hypothetical question of how things would have played out differently if something that happened in reality had not actually happened.

When thinking about making a positive impact on the world in a consequentialist fashion, most people take the consequences that follow from their actions at face value. For example, imagine a person named Tom trying to decide whether to have a positive impact by becoming a surgeon or by working in finance and donating to effective global health charities: A heart surgeon's impact appears to be saving the lives of each patient, while a donor to the Against Malaria Foundation appears to have the impact of saving one life from malaria per ~$5,000 donated.

Thinking counterfactually about impact, Tom would ask: if Tom does not study medicine, will the patients die? Probably not. Studying medicine is highly competitive, and if Tom doesn't do it, another person just as capable would probably take his place. On the other hand, if Tom had not donated to the Against Malaria Foundation, would the beneficiaries have been prevented from dying of malaria? Considering that AMF still has a sizable funding gap, the answer to this question is probably not. To be more certain that he will actually save a life, Tom should donate to AMF. Thinking about impact in terms of what would have happened otherwise generally leads one to apply a discount to their estimate of how much impact their actions will actually generate. However, it is a far more consequential and realistic picture of the impact of your actions.

In the context of grantmaking, there are many counterfactual questions to consider, but two stick out:

1. If I don't fund this grant, will someone else fund it anyway?
2. If this grant application is not funded, how will the recipient's impact differ?

Let's look at these questions in more detail, with an example.

Imagine a young global health charity with two proposed programs designed to combat parasitic worm infections in children: one program distributes deworming medication in schools and is highly impactful; the other aims to educate families on how to avoid infection and is ineffective. Suppose the charity is applying for a grant to fund the highly impactful program.

## (1) If I don't fund this grant, will someone else fund it anyway?

- In some cases, the grant applicant plans to apply to a number of foundations and government schemes, and their application will be attractive to many of these potential funders. In this case, if you choose not to fund the grant, the grant will probably be funded anyway, significantly discounting the impact of your funding decision.
- In other cases, the grant application will not be attractive or in scope for most funders in the landscape, or the applicant lacks the confidence/network/resources to pursue funding from other sources. In this case, if you choose not to fund the grant, it probably won't get funded at all, meaning deciding to fund it has a significant counterfactual impact.

## (2) If this grant application doesn't get funded, how will the recipient's impact be different?

- In some cases, if a grant application doesn't get funded, the applicant will move their budget around between programs so that they can still execute the program the application was for. If our example charity did this, the impactful program would still be funded, and the ineffective one would not be. In this case, the grant being funded has little to no counterfactual impact.

- On the other hand, in many cases, a specific grant not being funded means a specific program is not being executed or being executed on a smaller scale. In this case, there is significant counterfactual impact from the grant being funded.
- Moreover, for small/early organizations, not receiving funding for a particular grant could be the difference between continuing to operate or shutting down. In this case, the counterfactual impact of funding the grant is not just the additional medication distribution that the grant pays for - it is also the lifetime impact the organization might achieve by continuing to operate.

As a grantmaker, you need to consider the likelihood of these kinds of scenarios when deciding whether to fund a grant. It helps to have a strong understanding of the landscape and your competitive advantage as a funder: Who are the other funders who are likely to fund similar projects to you? What types of projects are particularly attractive or unattractive to them? How do your capabilities (e.g. network, subject matter expertise) overlap, and how do they differ? How do your values, worldviews, and approaches to vetting differ, and where might they result in gaps? What types of projects tend to be neglected by funders? As a result, what types of projects are you uniquely qualified to discover and vet?

Figuring out counterfactual impact precisely is actually very difficult. A decision to do or not do something has cascading effects, like how dropping a pebble in a lake sends rings propagating across the lake's surface. So far, we have just discussed the first of these rings. Let's go further out:

Consider a promising grant application you choose to fund but which would have been funded by another foundation if you hadn't funded it. The first level of counterfactual thinking would suggest that you achieved no real impact by funding the grant. But because you funded the grant, you displaced another foundation who will now probably spend that money elsewhere. If that other foundation is effective at grantmaking, they will probably fund another strong opportunity with that funding, which may displace another foundation's funding. This process can continue, with the consequences of your decision to fund a promising grant rippling out across the funding landscape. The implication is that when thinking counterfactually, you shouldn't completely discount the impact of funding projects that would have been funded otherwise. You also shouldn't apply zero discounting to the impact of funding projects that wouldn't have been funded otherwise.

When it comes to applying counterfactual thinking in the real world, some strange scenarios arise which can easily lead to incorrect appraisals of one's impact. For example, if only 90% of the funding needed to start a project has been raised, does donating the last 10% mean you should get full credit for the project or 10% of the credit? Counting the full impact seems sensible using counterfactual thinking, but it will lead to double counting between different organizations (the foundation that donated 90% is unlikely to take 0% credit for the organization's founding). Dividing impact proportionally can make sense in some cases, but it can result in leverage not being accurately taken into account. A possible way to solve these decisions is using a formal methodology, like a Shapley value.[140] But a simpler heuristic might be to hold your counterfactual views lightly and fund the best projects you can, even if there is some concern that other funders would support them.

In the end, when the goal is positive impact, all that matters is that charity funders collectively find and fund the best opportunities. A way to help make this happen is by increasing donor coordination so that funders make better decisions collectively.

## 8.5.2. Donor coordination and funding circles

### What does an ideal funding landscape look like?

The funding landscapes in most cause areas leave plenty of room for improvement. Funders don't tend to have a deep awareness of each other, information sharing is limited, and great organizations often fall through the cracks. A far more ideal structure would be one with a clear pathway for organizations to scale up, moving from smaller funders to larger ones. A diverse range of informed funders would share notes and information with each other. This would enable them to notice the gaps between them and avoid missed opportunities. Shared information and perspective would hopefully mean their scopes would overlap somewhat so that high-impact organizations in their cause area would always get the necessary funding. One structure that does these things well is funding circles.

---

[140] The Shapley value is a solution concept used in game theory that involves fairly distributing both gains and costs to several actors working in coalition. Game theory is when two or more players or factors are involved in a strategy to achieve a desired outcome or payoff.

## What is a funding circle?

A funding circle is a collaboration between a number of funders who typically target a certain cause area. For example, The Mental Health Funding Circle is a group of funders keen to support projects in the cause area of mental health. These funders range fairly dramatically in size, and many of them support other cause areas as well. Meeting together as a group can allow the network members to research, find opportunities more effectively, and generally coordinate with each other. This reduces the risk of double-funding or missing promising opportunities. Another example of a funding circle is Big Bang Philanthropy.

## How funding circles can increase impact

Funding circles can be a powerful way to leverage and coordinate multiple funders with common interests. Often, a cause area will have a number of funders. But between closed application rounds, unclear standards, and disjointed networks, the funding is not organized as well as it could be.

Having different funder views is really important for a good funding ecosystem. But a funding circle has the added massive benefit of having a centralized point of contact. This means that organizations can apply as if applying to a single large funder but gain exposure to several potential funders. The structure also means that if one member of the network discovers a promising opportunity, but it falls outside of their scope, the communication channels are open and ready for them to pass the project on to a grantmaker who is a better fit.

## How to structure a funding circle

A few things are needed for a funding circle:

1. Criteria for joining
2. Grantmaking process
3. Staffing plan

Let's look at each of these in more detail:

1) First, you need the criteria for a funder to join a donor circle. An interest in the cause area and a minimum donation amount are two of the most common criteria. Farmed Animal Funders require a minimum of $250,000 anually to be donated to farm animal issues. The minimum does not need to be as high as this; a funding circle

could easily be made with five donors aiming to donate $100,000 each to the topic area.

2) The second thing you need is a default grant-making process or at least a default application process. Many funding processes are 'closed' (see Chapter 8.3) and require a ton of effort spent networking for an organization to break into them. Funding circles can save the non-profit sector resources by offering a more open pathway that involves less time wasted on networking and more time spent improving the world. Many of the funders in a circle will be interested in the same initial information (e.g. a short description of the project, external reviews conducted on it, and the CVs of the founders) and then have more specific questions relevant only to themselves. It would therefore be mutually beneficial to sync up the early stages of the process. For example, a funding circle's first round of an open application might consist of a one-page write-up of the idea, one CV from each founder or a one-pager on the team, and links to deeper external reviews or other published information. Each interested funder could then take a deeper look into a proposal by asking specific questions to see how well the project fits into their view of impact.

3) The final structure a funding circle needs is staffing. Do the funders want to organize the structure themselves, or do they want to hire a shared program officer? Some circles have a small team that does research, vetting, and coordination. Most large funding circles could benefit from one FTE staff to vet the first stage of applications. They would then pass on applications to the different funders according to their fit. Beyond that, they could generally facilitate information sharing. If we use our previous example of five funders spending $100,000 each, then a $50,000 staff member would represent a solid ratio of 10% total spend on vetting and coordination. One full-time program officer could typically process hundreds of applications and dive deeper into a few dozen.

## How to start a funding circle

If you are a funder looking to initiate a funding circle, the first step is to connect with other funders in your cause area. This could happen at events, via your network, at a conference, or during an education program. Once the funding circle is established and other foundations have a public way to join, the network will increase in size over time. One person with time and two people with funding can be all that is required to start the process of getting a circle going. CE has helped set up some funding circles in the past and might expand to more cause areas in the future.

## Tips for running a funder circle

Keep the group highly aligned/focused. Most of the funding circles we know that have struggled have typically done so because they got too large and viewpoints across funders had too wide a range. This can cause the group to lose focus, and the members feel less connected to each other. Starting small with people who are very likely to trust each other's recommendations will lead to the group having many of the benefits but far less administration or politics, as well as keeping its focus sharper. A rule of thumb is that once your circle is bigger than can be reasonably handled on a video call (e.g. more than 10), it might be worth splitting it into subgroups (e.g. low-income-country mental health and high-income-country mental health).

Another challenging scenario for funding circles is when participants try to optimize for their individual impact by not funding anything that they think would otherwise be funded by other participants. This can result in projects that multiple participants think are worthy of funding not receiving what they need because each participant is waiting for the other to provide the funding. This now looks the same as uncoordinated funders outside of a funding circle! To avoid this, participants must adopt the goal of maximizing the funding circle's impact instead of maximizing their individual impact. After all, what matters is the impact, not who created it. When multiple participants think a project is worthy of funding, they should work out a way to split the donation between them fairly.

It can also be easy for the members of a funding circle to lose touch with one another. Pick your communication medium carefully (e.g. Slack, email, monthly meetings, etc.), stick to it, and take responsibility for keeping it alive.

## 8.5.3. Summary

- Counterfactuals refer to hypothetical scenarios of what might have occurred if certain conditions had been different. There are two main questions about counterfactuals that are very significant for a foundation's impact:
    1. If I don't fund this grant, will someone else fund it anyway? *If so, the impact of funding the grant is significantly lower.*
    2. If this grant application doesn't get funded, how will the recipient's impact be different? *If they can reallocate existing funds to carry out the intervention, then the impact of funding the grant is relatively low. If they are dependent on the grant to carry out the intervention, then the impact is relatively high. If receiving the grant could determine whether the organization can continue to operate or is forced to shut down, the impact could be especially high.*
- When thinking through these counterfactual scenarios, it helps to have a strong understanding of the landscape and your competitive advantage as a funder (e.g. who are the other funders likely to fund similar projects to you? What types of projects are particularly attractive or unattractive to them? How do your capabilities overlap, and how do they differ? What types of projects are you uniquely qualified to discover and vet?)
- Starting or joining a funding circle (where grantmakers collectively source, vet, and fund grant opportunities) is an effective tactic for managing counterfactuals: In a funding circle, grantmakers can coordinate so that their collective funds are distributed efficiently:
    o They can ensure that no promising opportunity goes underfunded (as it might if uncoordinated donors each assumed someone else would fund it)
    o They can ensure that no opportunity gets over-funded (as it might if uncoordinated donors each assumed no one else would fund it)
    o Funding circles combine the coordination benefits and outreach efficiency of one centralized funder with the worldview diversification benefits of many decentralized funders.

# 8.6. Neglected strategies

So far, our approach to grantmaking strategy has been to disaggregate grantmaking models into a number of independent strategic 'settings.' Foundations can then build their bottom-up operating model by choosing settings that suit their strengths and limitations while filling a gap in the funding landscape. Another way to look at grantmaking strategy is to think top-down, looking at gaps in the landscape and considering which operating models could fill them. In this chapter, we look at some promising ideas for foundation operating models that could be highly impactful and drive innovation in the grantmaking community.

## 8.6.1. Specializing in M&E

Monitoring and evaluation (M&E) is a best practice in the nonprofit sector, which we discussed in depth in Chapter 5.2. Although many foundations have some M&E standards for organizations they fund, very few make this their comparative advantage. A foundation with field-leading requirements and vetting regarding M&E could be highly impactful. An even more neglected approach is being willing to fund charities to conduct more rigorous M&E of their operations than they would have been able to otherwise (e.g. funding a randomized controlled trial).

### Why is this promising?

A foundation giving a grant is seen as endorsing the recipient organization, and in some cases, foundations defer quite heavily to others they know do their homework. For this reason, building a reputation as a foundation with a strong focus on M&E

could increase the extent to which your grants influence other funders' decisions. Even if it costs a large proportion of total spending, the information provided could benefit the broader foundation community. Meanwhile, more foundations focusing on this capability would set valuable norms in the nonprofit space. For example, if charities know that foundations have very high standards regarding M&E, they would invest more effort to get this right.

## Why is this neglected?

One potential reason this function is neglected is "the tragedy of the commons," where the benefits in terms of impact per dollar spent don't incur directly to the foundation that invests in the M&E. Thus, no one feels responsible for stepping up.

## Who does this suit?

This could be a great fit for a foundation that wants a high degree of evidence for their grants (as opposed to taking a hits-based strategy), wants to bring more of their high standards to a certain cause area or other scopes, and is willing to hire a team of skilled experts to build it out.

# 8.6.2. Funding primary research

We discussed being willing to fund research into the effectiveness of a specific charity in the previously neglected strategy, but what about funding primary research more generally? Firstly, a foundation could fund replication studies in areas where the field relies on just one study that is not strong or generalizable enough to give us a high degree of confidence. For example, they could try replicating the study by Miguel and Kremer on the relationship between deworming and increased income, which is the foundation of GiveWell's recommendation of four deworming charities.[141] Secondly, a foundation could fund studies on interventions with a promising theory of change but lack conclusive empirical evidence (e.g. the efficacy of different interventions to reduce meat consumption and/or increase veganism). Thirdly, a foundation could fund studies that don't test an intervention per se, but generate crucial contextual information for a cause area, for example, preference studies to

---

[141] GiveWell, "Combination Deworming (Mass Drug Administration Targeting Both Schistosomiasis and Soil-Transmitted Helminths)," accessed Feb. 20, 2023, https://www.givewell.org/international/technical/programs/deworming.

understand how important different factors are to animal welfare (e.g. not being in pain vs. thermal comfort vs. space to move around vs. enrichment to prevent boredom).

## Why is this promising?

This is a promising strategy because quality primary evidence is a bottleneck to doing good at the moment, especially in less established cause areas like animal welfare and biorisk. Relatively speaking, there are plenty of desktop researchers trying to analyze the primary evidence to figure out how to do the most good, plenty of implementers ready to do whatever the evidence says is most effective, and plenty of funders willing to fund the most effective projects – the limiting factor is often the primary evidence that fuels this ecosystem of effectiveness-minded altruists.

## Why is this neglected?

This approach is neglected because the cost-effectiveness looks poor on face value. Still, this shallow assessment misses something important: The most cost-effective, high-evidence interventions we know of today only look so cost-effective because someone else already paid the cost of generating the research. Now all that needs to be paid is the marginal cost to execute it. But the cost of primary research needs to be paid by someone if we're to discover other highly cost-effective interventions. When you make a more fair and complete comparison of the long-run cost of developing and executing two interventions, funding this primary research looks a lot more sensible.

## Who does this suit?

This suits foundations that understand research well enough to decide which grants will likely generate high-quality evidence that fills a knowledge gap. It also suits those willing to be the enablers of cost-effective giving without being able to claim a strong marginal cost-effectiveness themselves – in other words, it requires foundations to have a small ego.

## 8.6.3. GiveWell-style approach in a different area

### Why is this promising?

GiveWell has had a huge degree of success, both in directing money to fantastic areas and in shaping the culture of giving more broadly. However, it's often forgotten just how small an area they cover. Foundations could have a similar level of impact by applying similar methodologies to areas GiveWell has not worked in, for example, charities with <$1 million budget or charities that focus on health policy instead of on direct delivery health interventions. Foundations aren't dependent on funding from the general public, so they would be able to take more risks than GiveWell and move faster.

### Why is this neglected?

This model is neglected because emulating GiveWell is an intimidating challenge. However, suppose you consider their humble beginnings and set your short-term aspirations based on where GiveWell was able to get to in their first several years. In that case, it becomes a lot more approachable. Another reason this may be neglected is that people tend to assume that GiveWell's focus is where it is because they've already considered every alternative option in detail and ruled them out. But GiveWell never set out to be as comprehensive as that. Plenty of areas beyond their scope would greatly benefit from their rigorous approach.

### Who does this suit?

This could be a great fit for a foundation that really likes GiveWell's work but wants to create more impact than donating directly to them or whose most logical scope is in a different area to GiveWell.

## 8.6.4. Leveraging the power of competitions

Impact-focused competitions with prizes in the form of cash or opportunities are a great way to motivate a lot of activity in an area at a low cost. Recent examples include GiveWell's "Change Our Mind Contest" and OpenPhilanthropy's "Cause Exploration Prizes." When these competitions focus on generating ideas or proposing solutions, and when the submissions are made public, the world can benefit from many submissions even though only the winner gets funded. This is in contrast to an open grant application round (which could be thought of as a competition), where only the submissions that get funded have any impact.

We're yet to see an impact-focused foundation specializing in competitions. And there may be benefits in doing so—for example, expertise in running them well and sourcing more/better entries when the competition is run by an organization well known for running them.

## Why is this promising?

Competitions can have a large scope for counterfactual impact; they are a form of active grantmaking that can result in charities and projects getting created that otherwise would not be. They can also have the advantage of being more approachable to charity world outsiders, garnering interest from a broader range of people whose talent is not currently being harnessed by the charity sector. Specializing in competitions could allow a foundation to be highly impactful, even at relatively small staffing and funding levels (e.g. most of the examples we've seen cost less than $200,000).

Competitions can also create a lot of public interest and excitement for otherwise neglected issues. They can be an opportunity to make progress on topics the charity world has not considered, e.g. a prize for cost-effective ways to solve loneliness in South Korea.

We see competitions as more promising for generating ideas than motivating the execution of a specific existing idea. A competition to determine who will execute a specific existing idea is essentially a request for proposals, which runs the risk of attracting mercenary NGOs who aren't aligned with the goal of maximizing impact (discussed in Chapter 9.2.4).

## Why is this neglected?

There is no obvious reason this strategy is neglected.

## Who does this suit?

This could be a great fit for a smaller foundation that wants to get more leverage out of limited funding and that wants to be more creative and to identify and compare relatively diverse solutions to a problem.

## 8.6.5. Solving a narrow problem, globally

Some of the most impactful foundations have picked a very specific problem (e.g. Smallpox) instead of a broader cause area (e.g. Global health) and focused on that problem until it is solved.

### Why is this promising?

A problem like lead exposure or a disease like Guinea worm is of the scale that a single foundation with a sharp focus could ultimately solve the issue. In particular, solving the last 1% of the problem (e.g. curing the last case of Guinea worm) requires a degree of farsightedness and determination that is rare in the philanthropic world. Often, this foundation will need to motivate and coordinate other players in the space, as they won't be able to solve the problem unilaterally. It is rare for a foundation to cultivate this level of dedication and focus. But it can be extremely impactful: Permanently solving a problem means you can act once and continue to accrue impact forever as the cost the problem would have had on individuals and societies is saved, year after year. It also frees governments and NGOs to focus their time and money on solving other problems instead.

### Why is this neglected?

The level of focus required to execute this effectively is rare. When foundations do focus to this degree, they tend to focus on something hyperlocal (e.g. improving literacy in Washington) instead of solving a narrow global problem. However, this focus isn't necessarily difficult to cultivate – it simply requires a foundation to identify one problem to solve and double down on that.

### Who does this suit?

This could be a great fit for a foundation that expects to be around for a long time and wants to gain deep knowledge and expertise in a narrow area.

## 8.6.6. Focusing on overlooked talent

Typically, a foundation evaluates the grantee team, cause area, and intervention. However, it is possible to double down on one of these elements. For example, a foundation could focus on supporting talented teams, regardless of the cause area they are in. YCombinator and many other for-profit incubators have seen a great deal of success from focusing far more on the person than the specific idea. But what if you were focused on finding the best talent that others overlook, for example, those that don't have typically impressive credentials or track records?

## Why is this promising?

The kind of talent that gets into YCombinator, or that is typically supported by talent-focused funders, is what we would call "obvious talent;" they are people typically getting many job offers and opportunities due to their impressive track record and charisma. A new foundation could have a major impact by focusing on finding more overlooked talent. It could be supporting someone who is highly capable but introverted. Or someone doing great things but whose communication skills are foolishly written off because they have a strong accent.

## Why is this neglected?

Finding overlooked talent requires a willingness to go against the grain by not simply relying on traditional markers of impressiveness, like a strong charismatic presence or an impressive university degree. Finding hidden talent requires an uncommon degree of independent thinking as well as confidence in your ability to vet people.

## Who does this suit?

This could be a great fit for a founder interested in psychology who wants to dive deep into vetting people.

# 8.6.7. Focusing on the taboo

Focusing on areas that many find uncomfortable or controversial to talk or think about can be a creative way to fund impact.

## Why is this promising?

Certain areas look highly promising but receive limited attention because they relate to taboo or culturally difficult topics. For example, this applies to human waste management; photos of work in this area might not be the most exciting to put on your website, but that doesn't mean it's not an important area. The Gates

Foundation has not ignored this taboo and invested in efforts to reinvent the toilet to improve human health.[142] Another example of taboo topics are sexually transmitted infections, which are far more neglected than non-sexual health issues. Foundations are uniquely equipped to work on taboo topics as they don't need to appeal to the public for funding or appease voters.

## Why is this neglected?

Because the subject matter is taboo.

## Who does this suit?

This could be a great fit for a foundation that is willing to take on unsexy problems or risk being controversial.

# 8.6.8. Focusing on regranting networks

Using regranting networks involves deferring the decision-making for some of a foundation's funds to third parties who are not full-time grantmakers themselves - for example, Open Philanthropy ran their first major regranting program last year, giving $150 million to four other organizations to distribute.[143] Regranting can also be used to empower individuals (rather than organizations) to make grantmaking decisions.

## Why is this promising?

Not everyone who would make great funding decisions can become a full-time grantmaker. In fact, many who are best informed about the most promising funding-constrained opportunities in a field already have a full-time job working in that field. Re-granting allows foundations to empower those with the skills, but not the financial resources, to make impactful grants. This approach allows foundations to shift from vetting projects to vetting people who might be good regranters. This is a

---

[142] Doulaye Kone, "The future of sanitation: 10 years of reinventing the toilet", The Bill and Melinda Gates Foundation, July 29, 2021, accessed Feb. 20, 2023,
https://www.gatesfoundation.org/ideas/articles/sanitation-reinvent-toilet.
[143] Chris Smith, Emily Oehlsen, and Alexander Berger, "Announcing the awardees for our $150M Regranting Challenge," Jan. 12, 2023, accessed Feb. 20, 2023

different skill set, which will suit some foundations better than the standard approach of vetting projects.

## Why is this neglected?

Foundations can be hesitant to seemingly give up decision-making power. Instead, they should see re-granting as changing the type of decisions they make to better suit their strengths.

## Who does this suit?

This approach works best for foundations that have more money than they can grant out with their current staff and/or who know a number of people who have clever granting ideas but not the funds to support them. It also suits a foundation that has a comparative advantage in vetting people relative to vetting projects.

# 8.6.9. The 'Grim Reaper' foundation

In the for-profit world, an organization's customers are their source of revenue. If they aren't properly serving those customers, they won't generate enough revenue and will go out of business. The same is not true in the nonprofit sector – a charity's beneficiaries and funders are generally different groups. This means that a charity can continue to operate for years without doing a good job serving its beneficiaries as long as it's good enough at fundraising.

In theory, a charity's board has the power to decide to shut it down if it's ineffective. But in practice, this is uncommon for a number of reasons. For one, members of a charity's board often have encouraged people to fund the charity in the past. And they may worry that they'll lose face if they have to publicly admit that the charity they recommended funding isn't effective enough. Often, boards are structured such that the charity's founder is really calling the shots, and they'll be even more emotionally and reputationally invested in the charity's continued operations than the board. Finally, and sadly most commonly, many charities and funders aren't focused on having as much impact as possible. So the fact that the charity can still secure funding and the beneficiaries say a few positive things about it is reason enough to continue operation. No matter who is calling the shots, shutting down a charity is a hard decision to make – it involves putting all of the staff out of a job and telling the beneficiaries that they won't be receiving support anymore – so it's unsurprising that many organizations don't do it, even when they should.

A 'Grim Reaper' foundation aims to solve this problem by providing grants that enable underperforming charities to shut down. It might seem counterintuitive to give a grant to an underperforming charity. After all, the grant won't be funding impactful activities. But it may make sense if it frees up the resources the charity uses (funding and staff) to be deployed on more impactful projects. The foundation could work by offering to fund an independent evaluation of a charity, with the condition that if the charity doesn't perform to a certain level, it'll shut down, but the staff will receive a severance package to support themselves while they look for other work. The foundation could also play a supporting role in connecting the staff to more effective organizations looking for employees.

## Why is this promising?

This strategy is highly unconventional, but it aims to address an entirely neglected issue that will improve the effectiveness of resource distribution within the nonprofit sector.

## Why is this neglected?

This strategy is unprecedented, as far as we're aware. It may involve being a foundation that some charities treat with suspicion rather than warmth, and this will deter many foundations from choosing it.

## Who does this suit?

Like the "focusing on the taboo" strategy, this suits foundations that are willing to do controversial work and be "the bad guy." It also suits foundations particularly passionate about improving effectiveness norms in the nonprofit sector and stopping charitable resources from being wasted.

## 8.6.10. Summary

- Pursuing a neglected grantmaking strategy can allow a foundation to address a gap in the funding landscape and have a large impact.
- Specializing in M&E: Setting field-leading requirements with regard to M&E could raise standards in the nonprofit sector at large.
- Funding primary research: (1) You could fund replication studies in areas where the field relies on just one study that is not strong or generalizable enough; (2) You could fund studies on interventions that have a promising theory of change but lack conclusive empirical evidence; (3) You could fund studies generate crucial contextual information for a cause area, like preference studies to understand how important different factors are to animal welfare.
- GiveWell's approach in a different area: Applying GiveWell's high-rigor approach to another area (like charities that focus on health policy instead of the direct delivery of health interventions) could direct large amounts of money to more impactful charities and positively shape the culture of giving more broadly.
- Competitions: Awarding prizes for proposing new ideas and solutions is a highly cost-effective way to generate a lot of activity in an area: The world can benefit from many submissions even though only the winner gets funded.
- Solving a narrow problem globally: Leading efforts to permanently solve a relatively small problem like leaded paint or Guinea worm.
- Focusing on overlooked talent: Addressing underfunding of talented teams that lack conventionally prestigious credentials or track records.
- Focusing on the taboo: Addressing funding gaps in areas that many find uncomfortable or controversial to talk or think about.
- Focusing on regranting: By deferring grantmaking decisions to others, foundations can (a) leverage a comparative advantage in vetting people instead of vetting projects and (b) enable those with unique expertise to identify impactful grants (e.g. because they're working in the field) to make some grant decisions.
- The 'Grim Reaper' foundation: Providing independent evaluation to charities and funding grants for underperformers (who would otherwise limp along consuming nonprofit resources) to shut down.

## PART C

# Choosing who to hire and who to fund

Most investors spend a great deal of time and thought on where their money should go. They are unlikely to hand thousands of dollars to a budding entrepreneur just because they enjoy talking to them. And yet, this happens all the time in the nonprofit world; grantmakers end up funding projects just because they chatted with someone exciting at a conference. If they think about it, most people would agree that this is not a particularly good methodology for making funding decisions, in the same way that hiring someone without vetting them thoroughly is not the best practice.

When your goal is to improve the world as much as possible, running an effective foundation is fundamentally about making good decisions about who and what to support - whether that's grantees who you expect to design and execute promising projects or staff who will make many important decisions for your foundation. In setting up your vetting processes, you should use a process that will help you identify interventions, projects, and people that will give you the most bang for your buck – that is, improve the world the most per unit of resources invested.

Unfortunately, grantmaking is an area with relatively low levels of historical accountability or research on which tactics and processes work and which don't. There is considerable variance in how systematic grant decisions are. However, there is an adjacent area that deals with many of the same challenges, has lots of evidence on what does and doesn't work, and is easy to gain feedback on: hiring.

This part of the book is about creating and executing a highly impactful vetting process that can be used to vet in hiring, grantmaking, or finding advisors.

## The evidence on what works in predicting job performance

Unlike for vetting grant applications, there is a wealth of evidence on what works and what doesn't when it comes to vetting people for employment. This evidence can be used not just to inform your hiring process but also for your grant evaluation process. So let's dive right in:

A meta-analysis on individual differences in work performance estimates that "in low-complexity jobs, the top 1% averages 52% more (productivity) than the average employee. For medium-complexity jobs, this figure is 85%, and for high-complexity jobs, it is 127%," with some jobs, such as sales, having ratios that are even more skewed and not following a normal distribution.[144] This variation suggests that you can be quite a lot more productive if you hire the right people. Yet, most hiring decisions are made without an explicit process and on the basis of irrelevant factors. In the 1980s, it was common practice for firms to hire on the basis of "graphology," which purported to derive a person's traits from their handwriting.[145] We are not immune to making similar mistakes today (particularly in less evidence-based fields such as grant assessment), as it is now common for hirers to use various unscientific personality tests and compatibility metrics. Top-performing companies like Google once used quirky "brain teasers" as interview questions, only to find that they didn't end up predicting anything – although many hiring managers still use them.

Given the fact that so many organizations conduct essentially useless candidate processing, use caution when designing an application process. A badly designed one will trick you into thinking you are selecting the best candidates when, in reality, you are wasting their time and yours.

The most highly cited meta-analysis regarding which selection methods work is *F. Schmidt & J. Hunter's (1998) work*.[146] Schmidt recently published an updated meta-analysis (2016; less frequently cited).[147] These authors conclude that the best interview

---

[144] J.E. Hunter, F.L. Schmidt, & M.K. Judiesch, "Individual differences in output variability as a function of job complexity," Journal of Applied Psychology, 75(1), (1990): 28-42.

[145] Aaron, "Graphology as a Personnel Selection Method," EffortlessHR, May 5, 2017, accessed Feb. 20, 2023, https://www.effortlesshr.com/blog/graphology-as-a-personnel-selection-method/

[146] F. Schmidt and J. Hunter, "The validity and utility of selection methods in personnel psychology: Practical and theoretical implications of 85 years of research findings," Psychological Bulletin 124 (1998): 262-274.

[147] Frank Schmidt, "The Validity and Utility of Selection Methods in Personnel Psychology: Practical and Theoretical Implications of 100 Years of Research Findings," 2016

processes combine general mental ability tests with either work sample tests, structured interviews, or 'integrity tests' (which purport to measure ethical behavior like conscientiousness and the probability of counterproductive work behaviors like bickering). Of course, the exact way to test a skill will change depending on the role - you will test differently when hiring a carpenter versus a sales director. Schmidt and Hunter also found that education and experience matter less than you might think. Job experience hits sharply diminishing returns after five years. Additionally, reference letters tend not to matter much. This is the sort of evidence that allows us to start building an efficient vetting process that focuses on the factors that matter.

Of course, the science isn't perfect. It can fail to replicate or generalize (although common sense is a useful guide on this),[148] and the science is incomplete; the most promising techniques have not been scientifically tested yet. So consider scientific research as a guide and first step to prevent yourself from picking useless metrics or trying something completely untested. You can choose methods that are both backed by research, by rational analysis of our context, and by common sense.

## Four golden rules

From the literature and our considerable experience, we can pull out some characteristics that almost all vetting processes should conform to:

1.  **"Structured"** means that your process has a clear structure; steps are laid out and completed by applicants in a certain order.
2.  **"Systematic"** means that you are intentional about the purpose of every stage of your process and have clear rubrics for what constitutes a good submission for each step.
3.  **"Scientific"** means that you consult the available evidence on what works and what doesn't work and regularly assess the successes and failures of your process.
4.  **"Standardized"** means that the process is the same for every applicant. This allows for equal application of rigor to decide whether a grant applicant meets your bar or to compare different applicants to each other.

This section will help you identify a list of traits to vet for and to design a systematic process for vetting them.

---

[148] Jesse Singal, "Want To Know Whether A Psychology Study Will Replicate? Just Ask A Bunch Of People," Research Digest, Oct. 16, 2019

# 9. Selecting traits to look for

Before you can set up the bespoke stages of your vetting process, you need to clarify what the goal of your process is. In this chapter, we will first look at important traits for hires and then cross-apply these lessons to potential grantees. We will supplement these with specific research on the traits of successful project founders and leaders. There are lots of cross-applications between those who might be a good hire and those who might be a good leader for an organization.

Your organizational structure and the role you are hiring for will influence which key traits and skills you want to vet for. Some skills you should look for in almost every hire, while others might be less important, depending on the role.

Creating a list for the role you are hiring for can help anchor you throughout the process, create good test tasks and interview questions, and weigh them accordingly. It will also be the basis for writing a good job ad to find and attract the right candidates for a role (see the chapter on how to write a good job ad for applications below).

## 9.1. Selecting traits to vet for in hiring

### Generalists first, specialists later

If you are a new foundation or new to running large projects, it is easy to feel overwhelmed by the fact that you lack the expertise necessary for all the goals you wish to accomplish. Your first instinct might be to hire a specialist with a CV filled with years of experience and a technical background specializing in the area you're focusing on. They may have the connections and intuition you lack. However, it's worth keeping in mind that in small organizations with many diverse tasks, hiring generalists who are pretty good at everything may be more important than specialists who are really good at one specific thing (instead, get that specialist onto the advisory board). A specialist will also tend to lock you into a certain cause area, an action many early-stage foundations would prefer not to do. Hiring a generalist allows you to remain flexible and avoid finding yourself shorthanded when it comes to tasks outside of your employees' specialization. The ideal, of course, is a specialist who is also generally good at a large number of other things, but they are a rare find.

If you over-value specialization and experience, you will also have a smaller set of candidates to choose from (recall the research suggesting education and experience matter less than you might think!). If you decide that hiring a specialist is important, keep in mind that it can be tough to evaluate skill in an area where you may not be competent in yourself. You may need to consult someone you trust who is more skilled than you in that particular area for designing and evaluating test tasks and more technical interview questions. A member of your advisory board might be able to help.

## Mission alignment is more important than you think

In an early hire, we recommend prioritizing not only competence but also mission alignment. Remember that employees don't mindlessly execute instructions – they often make important decisions for the entire organization, often without your input or oversight. For example, suppose your hire doesn't particularly buy into the notion of measuring impact and ranking interventions according to cost-effectiveness. In that case, the organization as a whole will shift in that hire's direction. Whatever you envision your organization's core mission to be, there are certain roles where you want to hire people who "get it" and don't need to be convinced to buy in. Of course, this may be more important for some roles than others, e.g. a researcher who picks interventions to support needs to be more mission-aligned than, say, an operations generalist.

It's common for people to prioritize things other than maximizing impact, such as "growth" (commanding a bigger budget or hiring more people), because they are accustomed to the prestige signals and incentive structures of the corporate world and public sector (also present in much of the nonprofit world). We have found that however well-intentioned people are, if they are not accustomed to thinking about what it means to maximize impact, they will often want to maximize intermediate metrics that aren't directly tied to impact instead. Often they will expand the program to cover multiple interventions rather than focus on the most cost-effective one, or they'll be too quick to accept weak forms of evidence, such as one beneficiary's positive feedback, instead of being sufficiently skeptical. Sometimes a quick explanation will be enough to change a person's mind. But other times, these disagreements are deeper and more ingrained. Fields such as economic studies, medicine, and public health ascribe to values like impact and prioritization and can thus be good pools to hire from early on when it is extra important to find people who will make aligned decisions.

## Organization and team fit matter

You need to consider how each person's strengths, weaknesses, and personal quirks might interact with and complement your team and your organization. If all of your current staff struggle to give speeches or come across well in meetings, hiring someone charismatic could provide a huge advantage in representing the organization. Suppose your current staff tend to be too blunt and direct. In that case, hiring someone who struggles to accept criticism might exacerbate the problem.

Another thing we recommend is to always look for collaborative, low-drama personalities to join your team right from the start. It is hard to overstate the financial, time, and energy costs of interpersonal conflict or even just tensions on your team - someone may be brilliant and do great work by themselves. But if they don't mesh well with the team, both their work and your team's output will suffer.

## Conscientiousness almost always matters.

In the literature on job performance predictors, the "Big Five" personality dimensions (Extraversion, Emotional Stability, Agreeableness, Conscientiousness, and Openness to Experience) are correlated with certain job performance criteria across certain occupational groups. One standout factor is conscientiousness (being reliable, responsible, hard-working, goal-directed, disciplined, detail-oriented, thoughtful, and careful), which consistently correlates with high performance across a wide range of occupations.[149] Therefore, look for indicators of conscientiousness

---

[149]Murray Barrick, Michael Mount, "The Big Five Personality Dimensions and Job Performance: A Meta-Analysis," Personnel Psychology, Vol. 44, 1991, accessed Feb. 20, 2023, https://onlinelibrary.wiley.com/doi/10.1111/j.1744-6570.1991.tb00688.x.

## 346     SELECTING TRAITS TO LOOK FOR

across all roles and contexts. It is also a conveniently easy trait to test for, with 10 publicly available[150] multiple-choice questions doing the job well.

## Avoid the temptation to select traits that don't really matter

As a general rule, the more positive qualities we ask for, the fewer options we will have. Hence, it helps to think about which traits and skills are truly the most important for the position we are hiring for. Furthermore, if we are influenced by traits that don't really matter, we may miss out on the best person for the job. For example, charisma and English skills (assuming a role that doesn't directly involve those things) are traits that are irrelevant to every job and can easily bias an interview process. One of the best hires CE ever made was a candidate with dyslexia who had multiple typos in their cover letter[151] and might have been ruled out by many, even for a non-writing-focused role.

As always, we recommend making a spreadsheet to help ourselves reason through which criteria are important to us (like in our example below). Assigning values to qualitative judgments can help us to clarify our thinking.

| Role | Value alignment | Verbal ability | English skills | Organiza -tion skills | Charisma | Self- starter | Intervention/ country specific knowledge |
|---|---|---|---|---|---|---|---|
| Co-founder | 10 | 8 | 4 | 5 | 7 | 10 | 4 |
| Operations | 7 | 5 | 6 | 8 | 3 | 4 | 3 |
| Research | 8 | 9 | 4 | 3 | 4 | 6 | 7 |
| Program manager | 6 | 6 | 4 | 7 | 6 | 3 | 9 |
| Copy editor | 4 | 9 | 10 | 5 | 2 | 2 | 1 |

Some traits tend to be overrated or underrated relative to their difficulty in testing. Other traits are very role-dependent in their importance.

| Underrated | Overrated | Role-specific |
|---|---|---|
| Value alignment Conscientiousness Low drama Keenness on your organization. | Work experience Interview skills Positive references Known to your network | Communication skills (verbal / written) Quantitative skills Smart/intelligent Detailed/big picture |

---

[150]John, Oliver P., and Sanjay K. Srivastava. "The Big Five Trait Taxonomy: History, Measurement, and Theoretical Perspectives." Handbook of Personality: Theory and Research, January 1, 1999.
[151] Whilst we would expect a conscientious person to have their cover letter proofread, if a piece of writing starts with enough errors, even a friend proofreading will not catch them all.

Some examples of how these traits might play out in specific roles can be found in the online resources at *charityentrepreneurship.com/foundation- program-handbook*

# 9.2. Traits to look for when grantmaking

As with hiring, when it comes to grantmaking, it's important to keep a laser focus on the traits that have the biggest impact on expected performance. But unlike with hiring, you need to vet more than just a person; when it comes to a grant proposal, you need to vet the idea, the plan, *and* the people.

Ultimately, as with hiring, you're working toward a spreadsheet that compares options in terms of the traits that matter most so that you can make a decision. You will compare them to one another and your benchmark to decide which ones to fund. Of course, not every option will need to be scored on the spreadsheet – many can be ruled out beforehand based on the idea (we'll explain how shortly!)

*Example of a grant decision-making spreadsheet*

| What you're vetting: | | Idea | Plan/ People | People | Idea | Idea | Idea | Plan | Idea/ People |
|---|---|---|---|---|---|---|---|---|---|
| Weighting: | | 15% | 15% | 10% | 20% | 10% | 10% | 10% | 10% |
| Grant option | Total score | Cost-effectiveness if successful* | Chance of success | Competence & value alignment | Potential scale (considering limiting factors) | Counterfactuals | Externalities | Feedback loops / M&E | X-factor & red flags |
| A | 7.0 | 9 | 5 | 4 | 7 | 7 | 9 | 7 | 8 |
| B | 6.4 | 7 | 9 | 6 | 7 | 7 | 5 | 3 | 5 |
| C | 6.3 | 10 | 4 | 5 | 5 | 5 | 7 | 5 | 10 |
| D | 6.2 | 7 | 8 | 6 | 5 | 5 | 7 | 5 | 6 |
| E | 6.0 | 5 | 7 | 3 | 8 | 7 | 5 | 5 | 6 |
| F | 5.3 | 4 | 3 | 9 | 6 | 6 | 6 | 5 | 4 |

* Factoring in the strength of evidence

The factors you consider might differ based on your grantmaking strategy (e.g. hits vs. evidence-based). And the number and choice of factors might differ based on how many hours you will spend vetting each application (e.g. scoring 10 factors in an hour is unrealistic). Meanwhile, the weights we apply to each factor might vary based on your strategy, as well as the maturity of the projects you're considering (e.g. for young projects, you might focus less on the plan and more on the people and the idea). It may be helpful to have an 'x-factor' or red flags score for capturing important information or intuitions not captured elsewhere. Explicitly building in a sandboxed place for your intuitions may also help prevent them from coloring your scores for all the other factors.

Example of a grant decision-making spreadsheet for early-stage organizations

| What you're vetting: | | People | People | People | Idea | Idea | Plan | Plan |
|---|---|---|---|---|---|---|---|---|
| Weighting: | | 20% | 20% | 20% | 15% | 15% | 5% | 5% |
| Grant option | Total score | Conscientiousness | Value alignment | Intelligence & epistemics | Theory of change | Evidence base | Concrete plan | Feedback loops / M&E |
| U | 8.0 | 9 | 7 | 8 | 7 | 9 | 7 | 8 |
| V | 7.7 | 9 | 7 | 7 | 7 | 9 | 7 | 7 |
| W | 6.5 | 8 | 8 | 3 | 6 | 8 | 8 | 3 |
| X | 5.9 | 8 | 8 | 3 | 2 | 8 | 8 | 3 |
| Y | 5.3 | 5 | 2 | 6 | 7 | 10 | 1 | 2 |
| Z | 4.8 | 5 | 3 | 5 | 7 | 5 | 3 | 5 |

# 9.2.1. The idea

The first characteristic to look at for a given application is the idea – what is the concept that is being pitched? It's often easy to rule out a large number of grant applications based on a short explanation of the idea – perhaps the idea is outside your foundation's scope, perhaps the estimated cost-effectiveness is far below your benchmark, or perhaps the theory of change is implausible and lacks evidence. When vetting grant applications, 25%-50% can often be ruled out by reading a single page.

## Is it in scope?

Thankfully, some decisions in grantmaking are easy! Are you focused on mental health, but the idea is about factory farming? Are you focused on direct-delivery interventions, but the idea is about policy? Are you focused on mature organizations, but this is a brand-new, one-person organization? Are you focused on India, but this intervention is in Sweden? You don't need to waste your time – simply move on to the next opportunity.

## Is there a tight, well-evidenced theory of change?

Another quick way to get a sense of the quality of an applicant's idea is to assess the strength of their theory of change. Many will be implausible, allowing the application to be dismissed. Those that are plausible will instill different degrees of confidence based on how many questionable steps they have to cause cost-effective impact.

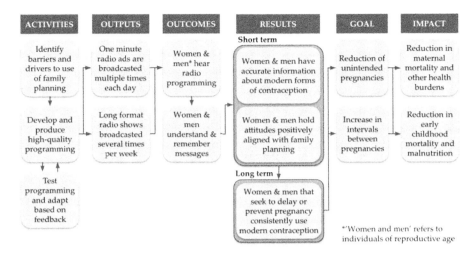

*Example of a theory of change from Family Empowerment Media as an early-stage organization*

**Does a theory of change exist?** It's a bit of a red flag if the applicant doesn't have one, but not necessarily a finishing blow. Sadly, this best practice is not as widespread as it should be, so you should make some allowances for those who have not heard of it. It may be worth asking an otherwise promising applicant to produce one before ruling them out.

**Next, is the theory of change sufficiently detailed,** or does it make large leaps like 'Research → Impact.' If the latter, it's a sign that this applicant is not sufficiently skeptical and rigorous when they think about their own impact. It also makes the theory of change harder to sense-check, as important steps are left implicit.

**Is it well-evidenced?** For each non-obvious step in the theory of change, you should expect to see some evidence, or at minimum, justification for any assumptions being made. When it comes to evidence, for established organizations, this might be a matter of looking at their monitoring and evaluation results. For newer projects, it will be a matter of looking at the broader set of literature.

*Summary:* SMS reminders offer a nudge that works at a minimal cost. Rigorous evidence from seven randomized controlled trials (RCTs) conducted in multiple contexts found vaccine SMS reminders effective at increasing immunization coverage. A meta-analysis of nine RCTs run by Charity Science Health's team found that the average effect on vaccination rates is a 7% increase.

| Study | Primary outcome | Effect size |
| --- | --- | --- |
| Schlumberger et al 2015 | Rate of Pentavalent 3 vaccination | 18% (p<0.001) |
| Haji et al., 2016 | Rate of Pentavalent 3 vaccination | 13% (95 % CI: 5.6–21.26) |
| Eze et al., 2015 | Rate of Pentavalent 3 vaccination | 8.7% (OR 1.47, 1.1 – 2.0) |
| Bangure et al., 2015 | Rate of Pentavalent 3 vaccination | 16.3% (95% CI: 12.5-28.0) |
| Gibson 2017 | Rate of full immunization at 12 months | 4% (RR: 1.04, CI: 0.97-1.12) |
| Domek 2016 (pilot) | Rate of full immunization at 22 weeks | 5.5% (p=.94) |
| Kazi et al., 2018 | Rate of Pentavalent 3 vaccination | 5.3% (p=.31) |

*An example evidence table for Charity Science Health as an early-stage organization*

**When evidence is lacking, how plausible are the assumptions?** In some cases, empirical evidence may be lacking. But assumptions can still be made explicit and justified, which makes them easier to assess. In the 'Research → Impact' example, why do they expect their research to have an impact? Is there an established actor who has agreed to take action based on the research reports? Is there a strong argument for why you should expect that actor's actions to cause a positive impact? What probability can you put in these assumed causal steps playing out as hoped?

**How many steps are there between inputs and impact?** The more independent elements that need to go right for the inputs to cause the impact, the lower the chances that the idea will be successful. For this reason, theories of change that are short and simple (without being over-simplified) are preferable over those that are long and convoluted. Of course, you can't assess the length of a theory of change by counting the steps – you can break down the same causal chain into different numbers of steps, depending on how detailed you choose to be. Nonetheless, when you look at the two example theories of change below (with the same goal and number of steps), it's clear which one is more 'long'/complicated and which is more 'short'/direct. Which do you think is more likely to have any impact at all?

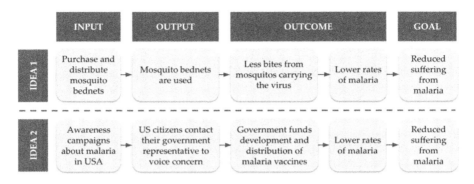

## Does it meet your cost-effectiveness benchmark?

By the time you are investigating specific applications, ideally, you will have a benchmark you can compare them to. Many ideas will quickly fail to reach this benchmark.

Sometimes you'll get your hands on an actual cost-effectiveness estimate from the charity itself (e.g. $253 per DALY) or from your own back-of-the-envelope calculations. This makes comparison with your benchmark a lot easier. Whilst these preliminary cost-effectiveness estimates will be low in accuracy, they're far more likely to be flattering than harsh (given the charity's incentives to impress you and that more rigorous CEAs regress to the mean, as discussed in Chapter 3.2.4.) So if this early cost-effectiveness doesn't meet your bar, you can be fairly confident that a more rigorous one won't either.

In other cases, you won't have hard numbers. However, you will still be able to make an assessment of the likely cost-effectiveness of the idea. For example, in the mental health space, paying for registered psychologists in high-income countries to do one-on-one consultations will almost never be able to compete with using generalist health workers to run group sessions in a lower-income context (given that the costs are orders of magnitude different, but the evidence suggests that the effect size is fairly similar). Ideally, you'll have access to some more concrete information, like the project's budget, to help you make this assessment.

## Other questions about fit for a foundation

So far, we've added three questions to your checklist:

- Is the idea in scope?
- Does it stand a chance of hitting our cost-effectiveness benchmark?
- Is there a tight, well-evidenced theory of change?

In addition to these questions, there will be other questions you can ask about whether the idea is a good fit for your foundation:

- Is the idea one that I could vet with the help of my team?
- Do I understand the concept of this idea enough to know if it was going well or poorly after a year?
- Does this idea have any major risk of negative or significant positive flow-through effects?
- Does this idea hit the minimum bar on other criteria our foundation has?

# 9.2.2. The plan

A good idea is a great start but does not guarantee a well-executed plan. Knowing that malaria bednets have a great evidence base and can be highly cost-effective is different from having a viable and efficient way to get them to the people that need them. The next step in vetting a proposal is to look at the plan: Is it concrete and realistic, with a strong M&E plan?

## How concrete is the plan?

The most common flaw plans have is that they are too vague. We know this has happened when you still don't know how an intervention should work after reading the proposal. This level of vagueness can make it near impossible to actually judge the plan. And if you aren't able to judge whether it's good enough to fund, you have to treat it as if it isn't. Vagueness can often come from the use of buzzwords that don't carry a clear specific meaning. "We will build a sustainable solution with local stakeholders" ticks off a lot of terms that people feel positively about but does not say much about how the intervention will be executed. A concrete plan will give a clear sense of questions like: "Where will the intervention take place? Who, specifically, are the target beneficiaries?" "How many staff will be used to execute the plan?" "What are the steps that make up the plan, and how long will each take?" "How and when will evaluation occur?" A vague plan will leave you with seemingly obvious questions unanswered, like "How will you get local health workers to cooperate?" "How will you get the beneficiaries to trust you enough to use the service?" "What about the customs fees to import thousands of bednets into the country?"

A much less common issue, but one to be aware of, is when a plan is so specific that it's not sufficiently flexible to change in the face of roadblocks or new information. For example, a plan may depend on a very minor detail playing out a certain way or involve irreversible decisions that lock us into a certain course of action.

## How realistic is the plan?

Even if a plan is concrete, it could be unrealistic. For example, if a plan involves the organization working in two countries, one that is much easier to work in (e.g. Ghana) and another that is far more challenging (e.g. South Sudan), and the plan also assumes and depends on progress happening equally quickly in both, it's likely to fail. Another example is a plan involving a very basic fundraising plan that sees a budget doubling each year. These types of examples aren't just red flags regarding the quality of the plan; they also reflect poorly on the people. It suggests that the decision-makers behind the plan might be naive or not understand the context.

One word of caution on realism: Many of our top incubated charities surprised many donors with how much progress they could make in such a short period. We had a policy charity that got a policy passed in a country they had never worked in before within three months and a direct delivery charity that reached 100,000 beneficiaries in their first six months. Rather than relying too heavily on broad heuristics like "a charity cannot cause a policy change in less than 24 months," think more along the lines of "Does each step of this plan seem thoughtfully conceived and believable, given the other steps?" You should expect your current views on what's realistic to be regularly proven wrong by new information, and you should expect to be surprised by what the best charities can achieve. As such, disqualifying every plan that is more ambitious than your expectations would be a mistake.

## How good is the plan for M&E?

Every charity needs to have a way to evaluate whether they're having the desired impact and monitor ongoing performance to make improvements and keep things on track. Even the earliest stage charity should consider what they plan on monitoring and measuring; the absence of such a plan is a cause for concern. When the plan exists, you can assess how much the proposed metrics correspond to causing an impact. Suppose a charity's goal is to reduce malaria. In that case, the existing evidence that using bednets works may be strong enough so that they needn't prioritize measuring the actual impact on malaria (which may be very expensive to measure), but that doesn't mean that it's good enough to just measure how many bednets they buy. How many of those reach their destination? How many of those get used? How many are still in use and in good working condition a year later? How confident are they that the beneficiaries actually live in an area where malaria is an issue in the first place? Does it look like a reasonable amount of time and effort is dedicated to measurement and evaluation (about 10% is a good heuristic)?

The worst thing to see here is no plan at all; the second worst is a plan that does not seem like it could ever show negative results. One of the jobs of a donor is to hold charities accountable, so this will often be an area where there is a need to ask for more work to be done or for plans to be better fleshed out. For more details on what to look for in an M&E plan, refer to Chapter 5.2. which includes a list of quality hurdles.

# 9.2.3. The people (leadership)

The last aspect is, of course, to look at the people leading and executing the project. After establishing a good idea and plan, you need to consider if the team is competent and trustworthy enough to execute it well. For older charities, the best predictor will be the team's past track record. Have they done similar projects in the past? How did those projects go? This is worth about 80% of your focus when assessing the team, with traits of the leadership team making up the remaining 20%. For newer teams, you have to rely almost entirely on people's traits instead and how well they correspond with the predictive traits of other successful leaders and teams.

## Traits for new nonprofit founders (CE's perspective)

Our organization focuses on charities at the earliest stage. So we've spent a significant amount of time considering what makes an early-stage leader. When we select 10-20 individuals out of 2000-5000 applications to join our incubation program, we look for a wide range of capabilities, personality traits, motivations, and skills. We have summarized these into a list of five broad characteristics we look for.

## 1. Ambitious altruism
   a. Puts impact first in their worldview and actions
   b. High bar or no bar for what is enough impact
   c. Keen sense of counterfactuals

## 2. Committed to consequentialism
   a. Is results-oriented: wants to see and measure concrete results
   b. Highly focused, 80/20 mindset
   c. Puts results over other values or metrics like mastery, well-being, vanity, consensus, peer pressure, etc.

## 3. Startup culture fit
   a. Highly conscientious, able to motivate themselves independently of external deadlines
   b. Agile, lean, iterative – improving quickly through Minimum Viable Products, experiments, and fast feedback loops
   c. Resilient to pressure and risk

## 4. Scientific mindset & good epistemic
   a. Believes in, actively seeks, and follows empirical and systematic evidence
   b. Humble and open-minded; not absolutely set on their own idea or cause area
   c. Transparent in their reasoning

## 5. Collaborative personality
   a. Able to communicate effectively with a wide range of stakeholders
   b. Able to work harmoniously with lots of different people as potential co-founders
   c. Appropriately honest and considerate

The important thing here to understand is that no one excels at all of these criteria; we are looking for a combination that comes together in a way that makes it extremely likely that they will be able to build and lead a highly impactful nonprofit startup.

Some other examples of traits that different organizations (from the for-profit sector) think are important for early-stage leaders are available at *charityentrepreneurship.com/foundation- program-handbook.*

## Traits for more established leaders (from Y Combinator)

As mentioned above, if you are vetting leaders of more established organizations, their track record should be your focus. However, it's still worth considering the traits of the individuals themselves. Here are some pointers for how to assess good leadership when considering a project to fund, on the basis of an article[152] by the for-profit startup accelerator, Y Combinator:

1. **Clarity of thought and communication:**
   a. Thought comes first: do they understand what's truly important for the nonprofit, and can they express it in simple terms?
   b. They spend lots of time on internal communications, especially as the organization grows, to ensure that everybody understands the plan; even if they get so large, the leaders do not have personal relationships with the employees.
2. **Judgment about people:**
   a. Good intuition about people: seeing the hidden potential and seeing where ambition exceeds ability
   b. Judgment about initial hiring and promotions (who they give power and responsibility to)
   c. Rectifying mistakes: they know when to fire (use sparingly)
   d. Being able to learn from cases where it went wrong
3. **Personal integrity and commitment:**
   a. Integrity means standing for something meaningful beyond oneself rather than being motivated by narrow personal interests. Specifically the organization's impact.
   b. Being able to admit when they have made a mistake, rather than acting like they are always right. Having the humility to receive critical feedback openly and work to improve.
   c. Avoiding behavior like favoritism, conflicts of interest, inappropriate language, inappropriate work relationships, etc., that erode trust.

---

[152] Ali Rowghani, "How Do You Measure Leadership?" YCombinator, Jan. 19, 2017, accessed Feb. 20, 2023, https://www.ycombinator.com/blog/how-do-you-measure-leadership.

To summarize:

| Early-stage leaders | Late-stage leaders |
|---|---|
| • Ambitious altruism<br>• Committed to consequentialism<br>• Startup culture fit<br>• Scientific mindset and good epistemic<br>• Collaborative personality | • All of the early-stage traits<br>• Clarity of thought and communication<br>• Judgment about people<br>• Personal integrity and commitment |

# 9.2.4. The people (team composition and culture)

Although the leadership of an organization is important, it's also worth looking at the broader culture and composition of the team. The right structure may solve problems, for example, a strong advisory board that offsets a weakness of a cofounder. It might also amplify problems or raise doubts; for example, the way an organization frames itself on its website could cause concerns that it might lack a focus on effectiveness- the team structure may suggest that its focus is all on fundraising and growth rather than executing the intervention and measuring their impact. Maybe the charity idea requires a lot of technical staff they don't have and might have difficulty hiring.

When vetting an organization more thoroughly (maybe because the grant being considered is large), getting closer to their operations can be very valuable, rather than just speaking to their leaders. Maybe it would be possible to have a conversation with some of the more junior members of their team or attend a field visit? Asking to see their org chart can sometimes bring some useful insight. Speaking to some of the organization's partners or stakeholders to get a sense of how they're perceived could also be valuable.

There are millions of different organizations, but they tend to roughly match a small set of archetypes. In our experience, these archetypes make for low-quality grant recipients, so it's worth watching out for them. We discuss a handful of these below:

## Mercenary NGOs

One of the challenges funders face is the power differential between them and NGOs. This can lead to some negative outcomes. In an ideal world, NGOs and funders with similar perspectives on improving the world would match up. The NGO would bring the hours, and the foundation would bring the funding, perfectly complementing each other to bring about the impact. However, instead of funding an NGO that is truly aligned, some funders fall into the pattern of funding NGOs that will do any task in exchange for funding. We call these NGOs "mercenary NGOs," as their actions are primarily determined by the funding available.

It's tempting to think this is fine; surely, it's almost like contracting a for-profit to provide a service? A for-profit surveying company might not care one way or another about the impact of an organization, but nonetheless, be useful to hire. However, unlike a for-profit providing a specific service, NGO grants are often much broader and require a higher level of trust. NGOs' activities tend to be less concrete and measurable, so you can't set up as specific metrics as possible for an average for-profit contract. Additionally, there are costs that you might be willing to pay with an NGO that you expect to be aligned with you long term (e.g. organizational capacity building) but which you would not want to pay for a for-profit or mercenary NGO.

Many NGOs have a strong focus on the growth of budget and staff size. This typically means that when talking to a funder, they will aim to get the largest grant possible for the work being offered. This is similar to the for-profit world, but due to the nonprofit space being a lot less competitive and less transparent, a given action's true cost is often unclear. For instance, how much should an NGO be granted to distribute a medical service? A value-aligned NGO might see the service as fully under their mandate and ask a grantmaker for the minimal amount that could be spent to get it done. However, a less-aligned project that focuses on growth has a strong incentive to instead ask for the most it thinks it can get out of any funder they talk to. This can often result in mercenary-style NGOs asking for the maximum amount a grantmaker can fund in a round and spending roughly that much on the project (plus, of course, other internal costs to the organization). This habit can be particularly damaging in highly-connected spaces: once other organizations see this NGO's outputs per dollar, they will often be less inclined to value cost-effectiveness themselves (maybe even having to raise salaries or other investments to keep up with the new market set by the higher-cost NGO); or be motivated to try to grow more themselves, at the expense of counterfactual impact.

## Capacity-building NGOs

Picture this scenario: A funder makes a large grant to an NGO working in the global vaccination space to build its management capacity. All agree that while the direct progress of the NGO slows down a little, the higher capacity, later on, will more than make up for it.

However, nine months later, a large earthquake hits a nearby region. It receives a ton of attention, and funders flock to fund disaster relief efforts. Our original funder sees this and realizes that it is not the highest impact thing to work on; the cost-effectiveness does not compare to the vaccination work. But the NGO, which has been offered triple the funding it has never received before, gives in to the temptation of the money and pivots to work on the earthquake, taking the newly developed management team with it. The vast bulk of the organization's resources gets moved to the new, better-funded project. The funder feels burned, having spent resources with long-term impact in mind and not seeing the intended results of the investment come to fruition.

While it could be easy to blame the NGO, the funder should have been skeptical from the start. Some research would have shown that the NGO had only started working in the vaccination space due to COVID contracts being the easiest activity to get funding for at the time. In fact, such substantial capacity-building had never been a part of the NGOs original plan, and the funder's grant had been part of a pretty large change of direction.

## Territorial NGOs

Getting good done *should* be the highest priority for NGOs, and whose name gets the credit should be of far less importance. In reality, many funding-motivated NGOs are highly focused on their reputation and are protective over the space they cover. They discourage other NGOs from entering 'their' space by staking claim to as many broad areas as possible, even though they don't have the capacity to operate at high effectiveness so broadly. This can prevent other, potentially better, NGOs from working in that area, an unfortunate zero-sum situation. For psychological reasons, NGOs can sometimes be run like for-profits competing for customers rather than as part of a bigger collective effort to solve a problem.

This sort of culture can be net positive for the NGO claiming the space first, but be quite negative for its counterfactual impact on the world. The territorial NGO claims more ground than it really covers and, in practice, causes those areas to be neglected. Territorial NGOs have often forgotten that what really matters is the good done, not who exactly does it. Again, this is a case where the NGO has forgotten that doing well differs from progress on the problem.

## "Improvements-are-always-right-around-the-corner" NGOs

Another category of NGOs is those that don't take accountability for their shortcomings or mistakes, claiming they were just about to change. An example might be an NGO that has never done M&E, but after a funder suggests it, they claim it was already in their plans and were just about to start. Sometimes this really will be true, but you should remember that planning to do something in the future is cheap – past actions are a far better indicator of what you should expect. Particularly with more established organizations, you should be suspicious when a new staff member or organizational pivot is held up as the imminent solution to all past problems. History is the best predictor of the future, and a new hire, even in a leadership role, only has so much ability to change an organization. Patterns get deeply entrenched, and habits tend to stick.

NGOs need to be optimistic about the future to be motivated to move forward. But too much optimism can lead to forgetting errors made in the past or complacency that they won't happen again. You can always find a reason the time things went wrong was a special case and why things will go to plan next time. You should find these arguments unconvincing. Every case is a special case. Organizations need to take ownership of past failures, treating them as indicative of systemic problems that need to be mitigated rather than mere flukes; otherwise, they will repeat them.

# 9.2.5 Summary

- When vetting for staff hires, you should create an explicit list of traits important for the specific role. When doing so, keep in mind: (a) hire generalists first, specialists later, (b) mission alignment is critical for decision-making roles, (c) organization/team fit is underrated, (d) conscientiousness is always important.
- When vetting grants, you need to vet the idea, the plan, and the people. The relative importance of each will depend on the maturity of the project you're considering funding.
- The idea: You can filter out many ideas by asking whether (a) it's in scope and (b) meets your cost-effectiveness benchmark. If it survives this filter, your confidence in the idea will depend on how tight and well-evidenced the theory of change is.
- The plan should be concrete, realistic, and have a strong M&E plan.
- The people: You need to assess both the leadership and the team and its culture:
  - Leadership: Traits the Charity Entrepreneurship looks for include (a) ambitious altruism, (b) commitment to consequentialism, (c) start-up culture fit, (d) scientific mindset & good epistemic, and (e) a collaborative personality. Leaders of more mature organizations need to be particularly strong communicators and demonstrate good judgment about people.
  - Team and culture: Types of dangerous organizations to look out for include (a) mercenary NGOs, (b) capacity-building NGOs, (c) territorial NGOs, and (d) "improvements-are-always-right-around-the-corner" NGOs.

# 10. Designing a best-practice vetting process

Now that you know *what* traits you're vetting for, let's talk about how to do the vetting. This section goes into how to make a specific process for narrowing down a range of applications (whether people or grant applications) to a select few.

## 10.1. Principles for vetting processes

The key to designing an excellent vetting process is to incorporate a few core principles. However, some of these principles are in tension: A few suggest the need for high levels of rigor, whilst others suggest the need for moderation. The challenge is to strike a balance between these principles.

### Keep the end-to-end process length reasonable for applicants

Not everyone can wait three months for a job or grant. The best job applicants might be hired by someone else if the process takes too long. And the best grant applicants might have run out of funding, shut down, missed an important opportunity, or been forced to take funding from another funder that pushes them down a less impactful path.

**A week or two per step is a good rule of thumb:** After the closing date of the application (e.g. the job ad or grant application deadline), getting back to applicants within one to two weeks of them submitting their work in each stage is a good target to aim for. This makes the candidate feel like we respect their time, and the momentum helps keep candidates motivated.

**In grantmaking, a fast process can be a comparative advantage**, allowing you to fund time-sensitive opportunities and support young, small organizations that can't afford to spend many hours on fundraising. It tends to be smaller funders who lean into this comparative advantage, as they are more nimble themselves; they tend to give smaller grants where it's possible to both be sufficiently rigorous and have a fast turnaround time.

**The smaller the grant size, the higher the cost of a time-consuming process.** Say you have a process that gives a $50,000 grant and takes about five hours for most people to complete. At first glance, this might seem like a good deal: Raising $10,000 in funds per hour is worth the organization's time. However, this does not consider the number of applications that do not get funding. Suppose you fund one application for every 100 you get. In that case, you're asking 100 nonprofits to spend time fundraising for an expected return of $100 per hour.

Meanwhile, the time spent fundraising has a dollar cost of its own (the fundraiser's salary) and an opportunity cost in terms of the impact they could have had with that time or money. Given that you'd expect a charity to spend a limited percentage of its budget on fundraising (e.g. 10%), your process would only allow for the fundraiser to be paid $10 per hour; otherwise, applying would mean losing money in expectation. It's pretty easy for an application process to be net negative in expectation for the applicant when the grant size is small. This risk can be reduced with the next principle:

## Apply iterative depth

Any vetting process that involves assessing more than a handful of options should use iterative depth. First, you assess options superficially to rule out the least promising options, then slowly ramp up the rigor as you get further into the process. This has three major advantages:

1. It's more time efficient for you
2. It increases the chances that good applicants will invest time in the process
3. It's more respectful to applicants and saves them time

It may be tempting to not rule out any candidates until you've vetted them to your maximum level of rigor. But you generally have enough information to know which options are in the top third and bottom third quite quickly, and assuming you have a finite amount of time in which to make your hiring or grantmaking decisions, over-investing in the bottom third means you'll have less time to invest in determining which of the top applicants to choose.

Moreover, being overly rigorous too early in the process (e.g. asking for a 20-page report) risks filtering out good applicants. After all, if someone has limited information on how good of a fit they are relative to the many other applicants, it would be irrational for them to spend too much time applying when the chance of them securing that job or grant is comparatively small. As candidates progress further in a process and it becomes more and more likely that they could be a good fit, it becomes progressively more rational for them to spend more time on the process, and thus more reasonable for you to ask this of them.

## It's worth investing a lot of resources in vetting

The process we will go on to recommend may look overly long and intense, but we don't think it is for two main reasons. Firstly, it uses iterative depth, so only a small percentage of applicants will go through the process. Secondly, vetting is extremely important, so investing considerable resources in designing and executing the process is justified.

**Spending time on hiring is worth it**: The people you hire will make or break your organization, so spending time on hiring the right people is time well spent. Given the large variance in employee capability, it's worth investing 20% more time to secure a hire that is 50% more productive or makes 50% better decisions. On top of that, managing a hire who underperforms or causes conflicts within the organization can easily eat up several hours per week of managers' time. It also undermines morale and team cohesion, affecting the performance of everyone around them – not to mention the psychological effects on the team if you ultimately have to let them go. Meanwhile, given the fixed costs involved in hiring (writing the job description, advertising it, onboarding and training a new employee), it is worth investing more effort to secure someone who is a strong fit for the role, and so is likely to stay at your organization for longer – that way you don't have to hire again as soon.

**Spending time on grantmaking is worth it:** There are serious opportunity costs to the grants you make. Each ~ $4,500 could otherwise have saved a life if given to a GiveWell-recommended charity. If you've found an even more impactful benchmark within your foundation's scope, your opportunity cost will end up even higher than that. When the stakes are literally life or death, it's worth investing considerable time in getting it right. We recommend using a rigorous multi-step process once the grant being considered is over $50k and for the time investment to scale with grant size, as discussed in Chapter 7.1.2. We should always keep your benchmark in mind, as discussed in Chapter 5.3.1, so you never make a grant where the opportunity cost exceeds the benefit.

**The process we suggest is less time-consuming than it looks**: Firstly, the process's iterative nature means that while hundreds of people might fill in the initial application form, only very few people will make it to the final steps. Despite the importance of spending time on a good vetting process, we think that most people spend too much time evaluating applicants who do not have a serious chance of getting the job or grant (which wastes their time and ours). The Pareto Principle applies here: We should aim to eliminate about 80% of the options using 20% of the total vetting time.

Secondly, when it comes to creating your vetting process, you can use templates to save time. There is no need to reinvent the wheel. Once you make a great vetting process (or steal CEs!), you can use it repeatedly with minor modifications to continuously improve its efficiency and accuracy.

## Most of your efforts should be spent on 'the middle third.'

Comparing within a cohort of applicants makes your process much more efficient: It's far quicker to decide whether an applicant is in the top, middle or bottom third of applicants in terms of quality than scoring each applicant independently against some abstract standard. The top third can be easily moved on to the next round of the process, and the bottom third can be cut. As a result, most of your time will go into assessing the middle third to determine whether they meet the bar.

Remember though: This 'middle third' idea is just a heuristic. These proportions will change depending on how many people you're hiring or how many dollars you're granting and depending on how numerous and strong the applicants are. What won't change is that the borderline cases will take up most of your efforts.

## Aim to continuously improve and tweak the systems

M&E applies to your vetting processes as well. By measuring which parts of your process are most and least predictive of grantee or employee performance, you can make continuous improvements. You should deweight or remove the least predictive elements and lean into the most predictive ones. You can also run experiments to test completely new elements.

For example, early in the development of the vetting process for our incubation program, we asked a number of our staff to look at the participants in the program and predict who would go on to found a charity after the program and which charities would have a high impact. The results varied significantly between different staff, with some having predictions negatively correlated with results (-0.3) and others being very strongly correlated (0.89). Different staff used different heuristics, and we could then compare which was more predictive. For example, it turned out that people who placed more weight on test tasks in the application process predicted outcomes better than average, and people who weighted CVs more heavily performed worse.

CE continues experimenting with different sets of multiple-choice questions in our application process to see which are most predictive. We've gotten to the point where, in a recent vetting round, all but one of the successful applicants scored in the top 10% on these multiple-choice questions. To take things a step further, we're dividing these questions into categories (e.g. personality, values, epistemic) to see whether some categories are more predictive.

## Use quantitative scoring with rubrics for consistency

Explicit quantitative scoring makes for more consistent comparisons between candidates. Yes, giving an applicant's test task or project's theory of change a 7 out of 10 is not an objective measure, but it's a lot more precise than "bad," "fine," "good," or "great."

The idea of assigning scores is not that an average score of, e.g. 7 corresponds literally to something in the world, nor can you take it at face value that a candidate scoring an 8.6 is a better fit than someone scoring an 8.2. Instead, the point is that scores (a) will help you put candidates into a rough order, (b) will force you to be more intentional in your evaluation, (c) will be a useful memory aid later on when you consider a candidate's performance on previous steps of the process, and (d) will allow for better calibration between different scorers and more precise conversations about applicants' strengths and weaknesses.

The best practice is to build a structured rubric to assist with scoring. This will increase the consistency of any individual's scoring and the calibrating of scoring between multiple team members. Here is a simple example of a rubric for an interview question:

| Question | <5 | 6-7 | 8-9 | 10 |
|---|---|---|---|---|
| What cause area do you focus on and why? | Chosen for unclear reasons. | Selection involved some reasoning | Solid reasoning plus numerical quantification of options | Selection involved multiple strong specific methodologies (e.g. CEA, WFM & experts) |

It will be hard to know what a good versus bad applicant looks like the first time a vetting process is run. Hence, a shortcut for that very first round is to score through comparison (e.g. give the first applicant a 5 and score the rest relative to them). Over time, better insights will be gained into the quality range of answers and what makes the best answers better than the worst, allowing you to build and refine your rubrics.

## Be more lenient in earlier steps

Some pieces of information will allow you to confidently rule an applicant out very early in the process. But beyond those, the general principles should be that you are more lenient in earlier steps of the process where you have fewer data points about an applicant. This is for two reasons: firstly, there will be some variance in an applicant's performance and in the accuracy of the vetting process, so there's a decent chance that an applicant just falling short of the quality benchmark in the first couple steps of the process is due to random chance rather than genuinely low quality. The more data points you have, the more confident you can be that your average score for an applicant reflects their quality. Secondly, you won't be able to test every trait that matters in each step of the vetting process. So underperformance in one step might show you the weakest point of an overall high-quality applicant (e.g. their social skills are weak, so they perform worse in an interview, but their other strengths more than make up for this).

### Watch out for cognitive biases.

There is strong enough evidence that cognitive biases affect people's hiring and vetting accuracy that it would be hubris for anyone to assume they and their process are immune. Some specific biases to look out for:

1. Bias about who the applicant is (anonymization helps and is easy to do on the first rounds)
2. Regression to the mean when marking, i.e. people often rank the first few applicants they look at really highly or really poorly
3. Halo-effect between steps and traits, i.e. people's scores for supposedly independent variables (like different traits we're assessing or performance on different steps of the process), tend to be influenced by the overall sense of the applicant's quality

### Get multiple perspectives on the hardest calls

Asking a colleague or trusted advisor to double-check your judgment can improve the robustness of the process. Especially towards the later, high-stakes stages of the process, it helps to have more than one person give ratings independently, combine the scores, and discuss deviations. This can be a great time for an advisor or board member to get involved. The areas where our assessments converge and deviate will clarify the crux of the decision.

## 10.2. Structuring the vetting processes

In this chapter, we will introduce default processes for vetting that are structured, systematic, scientific, and standardized. They will help to vet applications for the traits discussed in Chapter 9 and will incorporate the principles we laid out in Chapter 10.1. We will provide different processes for hiring, grantmaking, and selecting advisors, but they have a lot in common. These default processes are a starting place and should be adjusted according to need based on things like the size of the grants being given, the maturity of the organizations being funded, or the seniority or technicality of the roles.

# 10.2.1. Vetting process for hiring

Let's look at a rough seven-step process that should help narrow down from thousands of job applications to a top few.

| | Step | Time spent vetting per applicant (avg)* | Rough suggested weightings | Time investment for applicant (avg) |
|---|---|---|---|---|
| 0 | Job description | - | - | 10 mins to read |
| 1 | Application form | 2 to 10 mins | ~10% | 15 to 60 mins |
| 2 | Test task 1 | 5 to 15 mins | ~25% | 3-4 hours |
| 3 | Interview 1 | 10 to 25 mins | ~15% | 30 mins to 2 hours |
| 4 | Test task 2 | 10 to 20 mins | ~30% | 3-4 hours |
| 5 | Interview 2 | 90 to 120 mins | ~20% | 60 mins to 5 hours** |
| 6 | Reference check | 30 to 60 mins | Variable: Focus on red flags | 30 mins |
| 7 | Giving feedback to top applicants | 30 mins | - | 15 mins |

*The more important the role, the more time should be invested in each step*

**The interview itself may only last 60 minutes, but the applicant may spend hours preparing for it*

Each step has proven value for predicting applicant quality. But some steps (like test tasks) have far stronger predictive power than others (like reviewing CVs). However, the order of the steps is determined largely by how time-intensive they are for applicants and for you to review. The most time-intensive steps are taken later when you have significantly narrowed down the pool of applicants.

For grantmaking, we recommend using each step of the vetting process to help populate a weighted-factor model that scores each applicant on the traits you vet for (discussed in Chapter 9). When it comes to hiring, we find that it works well enough to score applicants on their performance at each step of the process. This is because, unlike grant applications which are often very strong on some traits and quite weak

CHOOSING WHO TO HIRE AND WHO TO FUND

on others, we find that job applicants' performance on different traits tends to be more closely correlated, such that each step is broadly predictive of overall quality (albeit with some steps indexing more heavily on certain types of skills, like verbal communication in interviews).

| Weighting: | 10% | 25% | 15% | 30% | 20% | | |
|---|---|---|---|---|---|---|---|
| Applicant | Application form | Test task 1 | Interview 1 | Test task 2 | Interview 2 | Reference check | Average score |
| A | 7.5 | 7 | 9 | 8.5 | 10 | All clear | 8.4 |
| B | 10 | 8.5 | 7 | 7 | 9 | Red flag | 8.1 |
| C | 6.5 | 7 | 8 | 9 | 7.5 | All clear | 7.8 |
| D | 8 | 8 | 7 | 5 | ✗ | | |
| E | 8 | 4 | ✗ | | | | |
| F | 4 | ✗ | | | | | |

During the first two-three steps of the process, it will often be enough to only look at the candidate's score for that step to decide whether or not to progress them. After that, looking at the weighted average for a more complete picture makes more sense. Looking at the bigger picture will also allow you to get a sense of relative strengths and weaknesses, which you may want to dig into in later steps. We recommend keeping an eye out for red flags throughout the process (e.g. a comment in an interview that suggests they aren't value-aligned) and investigating them.

The final decision will be informed by the average score, but you needn't follow it blindly if other considerations are pushing you in a particular direction.

To screen for the best possible candidates, we recommend following these best practices for each step of the process:

**Job descriptions:** The goal of a job description is to make it clear to as many strong candidates as possible that the role might be a good fit for them whilst minimizing the number of people that apply for whom the role is a bad fit (so that you don't have to waste time vetting them). To achieve this, the first thing you need to do is to provide enough detail for people to understand what the role actually entails. This sounds easy, but it's amazing how uncommonly it's achieved. Be specific, and avoid buzzwords and jargon like the plague. The second thing is to strike the right balance when it comes to 'selling the role.' People tend to assume that the more applications received, the better, but this is far from the truth. Vetting inappropriate applicants wastes time and the process of applying wastes theirs. So whilst it makes sense to advertise the exciting aspects of the role, don't overplay them or hide the downsides. Keep in mind that the successful applicant will know the downsides eventually. So you're better off hiring someone who understands and is comfortable with them. Someone who comes in thinking the role is more glamorous or senior than it is will likely only be disappointed and leave after six months, leaving you to start hiring again.

**Application forms:** The best application forms can allow you to rule out 50-75% of applications, using less than an hour of applicant time and just a few minutes of your own time per application. To do this, we recommend two types of questions: The first are questions that generate standardized data, like from a set of multiple-choice questions. You can refine these over time to generate a predictive score of applicant quality that doesn't require any vetting time. The second is short-answer questions that allow you to test things like the applicant's mission alignment, conscientiousness, clarity of reasoning, and communication skills. Ideally, some of the questions prompt the applicant to think through their fit for the role more carefully (allowing inappropriate ones to filter themselves out). The application form is also a good place to capture information for later use, like their CV and logistical information (like when they can start and where they'd be based). You may wish to break the scoring of the application form down, assigning a weight to each part: their CV, their predictive score based on multiple choice questions, and their short answer questions.

**Test tasks:** This is the first step where you ask for substantial time from the candidate. Between self-filtering and the application form, ideally, you will have ruled out the most clear cases and are now looking for deeper information. The point of test tasks is to give the applicant a better sense of what the job involves and to test their ability to do it. The challenge here is finding a discrete piece of work that an outsider can work on with minimal context or inside knowledge. Provide whatever resources you can (e.g. links to relevant reading or to internal documents) to allow them to showcase their ability. One goal we have when designing test tasks is to minimize the amount of new work the applicant needs to do that won't be useful to them beyond the job application. For example, if hiring a copywriter, we may be able to ask them to provide an example of their writing rather than having them write something new just for this application. If hiring a grantmaker, you could ask them to write a one-pager on which cause area they think is most important to fund, which will both test relevant traits and be something they ought to be thinking about as aspiring grantmaker already.

**Interviews:** When it comes to interviews, we strongly recommend using a standardized set of questions, with a scoring rubric for each question. This improves consistency and leads to more meritocratic, less charisma-dominated hiring decisions. You should lean into the comparative advantages of the interview medium: interviews allow us to test verbal communication skills and applicants' ability to think on their feet. We find we can better understand their value alignment and whether they have a collaborative personality through interviews. The fact that the applicant has to answer in real-time gives them less opportunity to craft their answers to match what you want to hear. And the visibility of their body language and tone of voice makes it harder for them to hide their motivations.

**Reference check:** The purpose of references is to look into key uncertainties and possible red flags. Just keep in mind that most references the applicant provides will be overwhelmingly positive about them, so you will have to ask some smart questions to get at the truth. Questions like "How would you score them on a scale of 1 to 10... why not a 10?" will get more honest responses than just asking for someone's weaknesses. People do not like lying directly on reference checks, but exaggerating the positives and skimming over the negatives is pretty common. Getting to specifics and questions with no good answer, like "Which person did this person struggle most with?" will get you far closer to the truth.

**Giving feedback:** Most applicants will want some feedback, and the more time you've asked them to invest in the process, the more you owe it to them. We recommend giving verbal feedback to the strongest applications that weren't successful and sharing a more general write-up for other applications, like common reasons why applicants didn't pass an interview or an example of an excellent test task.

## 10.2.2. Vetting process for grantmaking

Grantmaking vetting processes require a lot more variety than hiring ones due to the high variance of factors like open vs. closed applications, grant size (and therefore the total amount of vetting time that's appropriate), and the maturity of the grantee organizations. Nonetheless, the same set of design principles apply.

374　　DESIGNING A BEST-PRACTICE VETTING PROCESS

Here is an example structure, followed by tips for designing the steps:

| Step | | What we're focusing on vetting |
|---|---|---|
| 0 | Call for applications | N/A, but aim for self-filtering |
| 1 | Application form | (a) Rule applications out based on the idea (Does it match your scope? Is cost-effectiveness in the right ballpark?)<br>(b) For those that pass this, add them to a WFM and give preliminary scores based on their answers and their website (if they have one). For example, you might be able to give a preliminary score for value alignment (based on their organizational values), track record, evidence base, or counterfactuals (who would they seek funding from if not from you?) |
| 2 | Project proposal | • Idea – Theory of change, Evidence base, Potential scale, Counterfactuals<br>• Plan – Chance of success, Feedback loops / M&E, Externalities |
| 3 | Interview | • People – Value alignment, Quality of leadership, Communication skills, Organizational culture |
| 4 | Deeper analysi | • Investigating areas of uncertainty by doing things like:<br>  ○ Cost-effectiveness analyses<br>  ○ Digging into the evidence base<br>  ○ Testing the idea/plan with an advisor<br>  ○ Follow-up interviews, including with other members of the team<br>  ○ Conducting a site visit to test the people (team competence, culture) and the plan (by getting a sense of the reality on the ground) |
| 5 | Giving feedback | - |

**Call for applications:** As with a job description in hiring, the aim here is to be crystal clear on who will likely be a good fit for the foundation to save everybody's time.

- Be explicit about what you're looking for: Which cause areas or types of interventions will you consider funding? What ballpark of cost-effectiveness are you looking for? Are you looking for speculative ideas that could be big hits or opportunities with a strong evidence base? What countries are you looking to fund interventions in? What metrics do you measure impact in? What is your minimum and maximum grant size? What are some organizations or past grants you're excited about?
- Be explicit about how you expect to engage with grantees: Will you be very hands-off or deeply involved in grantees' operations? What follow-up reporting do you expect from successful grantees? Are you interested in funding promising projects long-term or once-off?

Suppose your grantmaking system is more closed (i.e. no open applications). In that case, you still need to make it as clear as possible (likely on your website) what you're looking for, so other organizations can know whether to reach out.

**Project proposal:** As with test tasks in hiring, ideally, the applicant can use something they've created for other applications. For this reason, you can be somewhat flexible on the format (e.g. slide deck vs. written document). You can feel free to be prescriptive on what content you want to see, especially if it's content that a charity ought to have already, like a theory of change, a summary of evidence, a cost-effectiveness analysis, a one-year plan, or an M&E plan.

**Deeper analysis:** This is the most flexible step, aimed at digging into any uncertainties you have left. A lot of the work here will be done on your end, with some back and forth to the applicant to request further details. Depending on grant size, this could be as short as a quick phone call or as long as creating a detailed CEA from scratch and sending someone to conduct a field visit. Because of iterative depth, you'll only need to conduct this for a small percentage of applicants.

When it comes to scoring, unlike hiring, where you score the applicant on their performance in each step of the process, you'll be gradually filling in scores in your weighted-factor model for the traits that you're vetting for. You will be able to decide who makes it through to the next step based on their weighted average score, which will get more accurate as you refine your previous scores and score new traits later on.

*Example: a grant application scoresheet after the proposal step (i.e. preliminary scores, with some traits not being scored yet)*

## DESIGNING A BEST-PRACTICE VETTING PROCESS

| Weighting: | 30% | 15% | 15% | 10% | 10% | 20% | |
|---|---|---|---|---|---|---|---|
| Grant option | Avg score | Cost-effe ctiveness | Chance of success | Value alignment | Counter-factuals | Extern-alities | M&E |
| A | 7.4 | 9 | 5 | - | 7 | - | 7 |
| B | 6.6 | 7 | 9 | - | 7 | - | 4 |
| C | 6.7 | 10 | 4 | - | 5 | - | 5 |
| D | 7.1 | 7 | 8 | - | 5 | - | 8 |
| E | 4.9 | 3 | 7 | - | 7 | - | 5 |
| F | 4.3 | 4 | 3 | - | 6 | - | 5 |
| Relative confidence | Low | Low | n/a | High | n/a | Med | |

✗ Not good
✗ enough

*Example: a grant application scoresheet at the end of the process (i.e. previous scores have been refined, and all traits have been scored)*

| Weighting: | 30% | 15% | 15% | 10% | 10% | 20% | | |
|---|---|---|---|---|---|---|---|---|
| Grant option | Avg score | Cost-effe ctiveness | Chance of success | Value alignment | Counter-factuals | Extern-alities | M&E | Step eliminated |
| A | 7.7 | 8 | 8 | 6 | 9 | 9 | 7 | n/a - Grant given |
| B | 7.0 | 8 | 9 | 9 | 8 | 5 | 3 | n/a - Grant given |
| C | 5.7 | 6 | 4 | 7 | 7 | 7 | 5 | Deeper analysis |
| D | 5.3 | 7 | 8 | 1 | 5 | 6 | 4 | Interview |
| E | 5.7 | 5 | 7 | - | 7 | - | 5 | Proposal |
| F | 4.3 | 4 | 3 | - | 6 | - | 5 | Proposal |
| Relative confidence | High | High | High | High | High | High | | |

Those with a closed grantmaking process will be tempted to use a less structured process than we've recommended. But we strongly advise being as structured as possible. In particular, we think it's helpful to organize grantmaking into rounds (even if they're only internal) so that we are comparing grant options against one another instead of just assessing them on their own merits in isolation or just compared with a benchmark.

We have a much more detailed explanation of how to set up and execute each step of this vetting process and the hiring process at *charityentrepreneurship.com/foundation-program-handbook.*

## 10.2.3. Vetting process for advisors

Everyone wants to give funders advice. Often, this advice will be informed more by an agenda than given openly, impartially, and transparently. To find advisors you can trust, you will need to use a rigorous process like you do for hiring or grantmaking.

You will need to be creative, informally recreating the stages of a hiring or grantmaking vetting process, as potential advisors likely won't be willing to complete a test task or proposal for you.

It might look something like this (keep in mind that both the order of these steps, their concrete weightings, and time suggestions are speculative and need to be adjusted according to need):

| Step | | Rough time spent vetting per applicant | Rough suggested weightings | Potential advisor time commitment |
|---|---|---|---|---|
| 0 | Needs description* | - | - | - |
| 1 | A list of potential candidates** | 2 to 10 mins | - | - |
| 2 | An idea of the quality of a person's work (i.e. their track record) | 10-60 mins | 30% | - |
| 3 | Conversations with candidates to test their values and personality traits (like interviews) | 30 to 120 min | 30% | 30 to 120 mins |
| 4 | Testing how good their advice is by testing that advice *** | 60 mins | 30% | - |
| 5 | Conversations with others who know them (like reference checks) | 15 to 60 mins | 10% | - |

*What are you looking for advice on? Decision-making in general, on grantmaking processes, managing staff, assessing early-stage charities, or specialist advice on fish or the nonprofit landscape in Asia?*

*\*\*See charityentrepreneurship.com/foundation-program-handbook for a link to an example candidate list.*

*\*\*\* Refer to Chapter 7.2.2 of this book for how-to-test advice advisors give.*

Keep in mind that advisors don't have to be people you know personally to advise you on the specifics of what you're trying to achieve. Advisors can also come in the form of authors, public intellectuals, or organizations with insights that can be applied to your circumstances.

## 10.2.4. Summary

- When designing a vetting process, keep in mind the following principles:
  - o Keep the end-to-end process length reasonable for applicants – you could miss out on the best candidates if the process takes too long.
  - o Apply iterative depth to rule out the least promising options, then slowly ramp up the rigor as you get further into the process.
  - o It is worth investing significant resources into vetting – the people you hire will make or break your organization, and there are serious opportunity costs to the grants you make.
  - o Most of your efforts should be spent on the "middle third" of applicants.
  - o Run continuous experiments to improve your process each time you run it.
  - o Use quantitative scoring with rubrics for consistency.
- Our recommended hiring process includes the following:
  - o A clear job description to attract the right candidates and screen out the wrong ones,
  - o An application form that allows you to rule out 50-75% of the applicants using questions that generate standardized data, like from a set of multiple choice questions, and short-answer questions that allow you to test things like the applicant's mission alignment or their conscientiousness,
  - o Test tasks to give the applicant a better sense of what the job involves and to test their ability to do it,
  - o Interviews to get a better sense of their value alignment and whether they have a collaborative personality. (Utilize a standardized set of questions, with a scoring rubric for each question, for increased consistency),
  - o References to look into key uncertainties and possible red flags
  - o Giving feedback appropriately, according to how much time the applicant has invested in the process at the point of rejection.

It will generally involve scoring each step of the process and progressing those who meet a certain score threshold.

- Our recommended grant vetting process involves gradually filling out a WFM of traits you're vetting for, scoring more traits, and refining your scores as you gather information through the following iterative steps:
  - A call for applications to make it crystal clear who is likely to be a good fit for the foundation, to save everybody's time
  - An application form that allows you to filter many applications out based on the idea and to give preliminary scores to those that remain
  - A project proposal, preferably one the applicant has already written, to get more information on the idea and the plan,
  - An interview to test traits of the people (in particular the leadership)
  - Deeper analysis (like digging into the CEA or the primary evidence) to test any remaining uncertainties. The depth will depend on the size of the grant

# 11. Putting it all into practice

*Yuki[153] put down the fire hose and wiped the sweat off her brow.*

*She looked out over her neighborhood at all the families she had saved that were now back to living their much, she thought.*

*Then, almost imperceptibly, she saw a glimmer, far off in the distance. She took out her binoculars and set her gaze on the horizon. It might be a little blurry, sure, but it was unmistakable. More fires. But this time, they weren't burning houses; they were burning farms and fields - Yuko could even make out some animals running, trapped between two oncoming walls of flames.*

*Yuko felt her pride turn into a sense of responsibility. She knew what she had to do. And this time, she knew deep down that she could do it.*

*She put down her binoculars, took one more look at the happy families behind her, and set off running in the direction of the fires.*

---

A foundation's first year is exciting, but it can sometimes feel overwhelming. This final chapter aims to help you figure out "what next?" and turn theoretical knowledge into real-world impact.

---

[153] Our overwhelmed protagonist from this book's introduction

## 11.1. Learn decision-making skills by doing

You can read all the books in the world about how to play a sport, but without some real-life practice, you will never get good at it. Similarly, many people (including the authors of this book) will try to give you useful grantmaking advice. But at the end of the day, it's impossible to become a great grantmaker without giving some grants, tracking them carefully, and learning from your successes and mistakes. In most domains, poor grants don't risk causing catastrophic negative outcomes – at worst, they just have minimal impact. Small grants consume relatively little of your total donation budget but generate extremely valuable lessons if processed and evaluated with the same rigor you would use for a larger-scale grant.

Each tool we have discussed can be useful when accessing grants, but all of them will require practice. The more experience you gain and the angles of attack you employ, the more confident you can be in your eventual conclusion. Recall that it can be easier to build a high-quality shelf with five tools than with just one; likewise, watch out for relying too heavily on your favorite tool.

Instead of waiting until your first grantmaking decision to figure it all out, you should try to set up some of your decision-making systems beforehand. Build your system to be less forgetful than any individual could be, and send every grant through it. Use rubrics for evaluating individual steps of your process, and make sure these reflect multiple perspectives of looking at a grant opportunity. Don't be afraid of building and using an imperfect system first; improve it as you go along. In time, you will learn what works and what doesn't (every grantmaker does this). Look for occurrences where multiple uncorrelated tools converge to indicate that a particular grant is highly impactful – that is when you know you've found a really exciting opportunity.

## 11.2. Make preliminary decisions

Making the key decisions about your grantmaking approach will be one of the hardest things you have to do as a foundation leader, and it will be tempting to put off deciding at all. Many foundations get paralyzed by indecision on these sorts of issues. They either ramp up their giving without an explicit grantmaking scope, structure or strategy, or never ramp up their giving. Below are some tips to help you pull the trigger.

## Remember that your decisions are written in pencil

The first tip to help you make your key decisions is to keep in mind that they are not written in permanent ink. Indeed, you do not want to radically change your scope every week, but having a re-evaluation point to critically look at your key decisions once a year is nothing to be ashamed of; in fact, it's best practice! Having a point like that means that you are making a call "for now" and not "for forever."

## Timebox your choices.

Making a plan for when you want to make your first grant and what decisions you want to make before then can highly increase your odds of getting started. Maybe you want to do your first granting round within six months of finishing this book, so map out how long that gives you to pick a scope and set up your first draft vetting process. Depending on how much time you dedicate to them, all these steps can be done in as little as a month or take as long as 10 years. Setting up a timeline will keep everything moving forward and keep you accountable for your goals. Sharing your plans with another foundation you respect is another great way to set up accountability.

# 11.2.1. Getting started on scope

Setting a scope often feels like the hardest of the key decisions to make. But you don't have to do it all at once because your first decision doesn't have to be exhaustive. It's also worth remembering that you can always broaden your scope, but it's generally far harder to narrow it down due to social pressures. Narrowing scope often involves disappointing people, e.g. grantmakers you've hired to work on a given topic, organizations you're providing funding to, or admitting you were mistaken to fund that area, to begin with.

For these reasons, starting with a relatively narrow and short-term scope commitment is advisable, e.g. "50% of my grantmaking this year will be focused on high-evidence family planning interventions." This sort of scope will allow you to start to build expertise in the subject matter, as well as in the grantmaking process in general, without closing any doors long term.

When choosing how narrow to set your initial scope, you should consider the amount of funding you plan to spend per year:

| Annual grant budget | Examples of reasonable initial scopes |
|---|---|
| $50,000 | Guided self-help interventions<br>• Interventions in Ecuador<br>• Seed-stage orgs |
| $500,000 | Mental health interventions<br>• Interventions in Africa<br>• Seed-stage and mid-sized organizations |
| $5,000,000 | Global health interventions<br>• Low-income countries<br>• Organizations of any size |
| $50,000,000 | Human welfare interventions<br>• Global<br>•Organizations of any size |

Another great way to set an initial scope is to join a funding circle dedicated to one of the areas you find promising. This can put you into regular contact with other grantmakers in the space and make it easy to "try on" a highly counterfactual niche without committing to staying in it long term.

# 11.2.2. Getting started on structure

### Reminder of what you need to decide

There are a number of important decisions to make regarding structure, but a good place to start is gathering advisors. A reasonable goal is to have five strong advisors who you trust, can speak to at least three times a year, and who have a diverse range of perspectives and expertise. Here is an example of what this group might look like:

| Advisor | Skills | Frequency of communication |
|---|---|---|
| Ying | Measurement and evaluation specialist. Brilliant quantitative thinker | Monthly |
| Kikiope | A more experienced grantmaker with a similar scope | Quarterly |

| Abraham | A charity founder in an area that's outside your scope who understands what strong project execution looks like | Bi-annually |
| Natalia | A creative grantmaker who thinks outside the box and challenges conventions but has defensible strategies and processes | Quarterly |
| Wallace | A hedge fund manager. Smart, highly critical, and honest | Three times a year |

Each of these advisors is likely to bring different tools to the table, answer your questions differently, and ask different questions of their own. This will be far more useful than having five hedge fund managers or five senior leaders from the same foundation or cause area advise you.

# 11.2.3. Getting started on strategy

### Reminder of what you need to decide

Out of the key decisions of scope, structure, and strategy, your strategy is likely the element that will change the most from year to year. You will want to make your strategy clear to the public somewhere on your website and explicitly integrate it into your vetting systems. As a starting point, you can have a lot of impact by taking the lead of a reputable role model or two and applying their strategy to a slightly different scope. Some possible examples are provided below:

| Foundation | Strategy worth cross-applying |
| --- | --- |
| GiveWell | Highly evidence-based and process-based giving, with a specific and transparently-stated benchmark (~6-8x GiveDirectly) • High signaling value for grantee projects |
| Open Philanthropy | Largely hits-based approach across multiple cause areas • Highly specialized and networked team within each cause area, using active, person-based processes and strategies • Gradually broadening to include more cause areas, including through the use of competitions (e.g. Cause Exploration Prize) |

| | |
|---|---|
| EA Animal Welfare Fund | Open applications fund regranting donations from a wide range of donors • Transparent process designed to be accessible to as broad a range of potential grantees applying EA principles as possible • Team comprised of non-full-time leaders of different organizations in the animal welfare and EA space |

By mixing and matching principles from other organizations and grantmakers, you can assemble an initial strategy to start granting and refine with time. Coming up with a one-page strategy document grounded in your values and scope will be deeply helpful when formalizing your process.

# 11.3. Goals for a foundation in its first year

## 11.3.1. Get planning

### Create a three-to-five-year plan.

As your foundation sets off on its journey, it needs to be equipped with a clear plan. This plan will serve as your map and compass to navigate towards doing good in the world. Much like a voyage that ventures into uncharted territory, your map must be updated regularly as you learn new information. Despite the uncertainty ahead, making concrete guesses and writing them down is important. If the plan isn't written down, you will be at risk of heading in a direction that makes no sense in the long term.

A three-to-five-year plan should include the following key elements. Between a paragraph and a page on each of these would be ideal:

- Your long-term vision, including your aspirations for carving out a comparative advantage for your foundation
- Your current scope and early thoughts on your future scope
- Your current and planned organizational structure
- Your top advisors (or what types of advisors you're looking for and how you plan to find them)
- Your strategy for the next 12 months
- The high-level themes of what your organization will focus on each year for the next three-five years
- A detailed timeline for your organization over the next 12 months

- Your initial vetting system for grants (and for hires, if you plan on making any)
- Your measurement, monitoring, and evaluation plan for your grants, with concrete reevaluation time points

# 11.3.2. Get giving

### Make learning grants a foil against inaction & drift

Giving the first grant can be the hardest. There are many options and reasons to do a bit more research. Sadly, you will never quite be sure; and the best way to learn is by giving and carefully tracking your results. Getting into the habit of giving is just as important as giving well. Donating small grants as learning grants and building up the logistical and vetting systems can be a controlled way to build towards bigger things. Having a set benchmark and dispersion goal can keep you moving towards your goal of having an impact, even when life throws obstacles in the way.

# 11.3.3. Get public

### Launch a website; make yourself accountable

When setting up your foundation, think about what an ideal grantee would need to see on your website to figure out that they ought to get in touch. This website can be pretty basic; include one paragraph on your scope, another on your strategy, a team page, and most importantly, an application page or contact form that leads grantees to the first step in your process. The website for the Mental Health Funding Circle that we launched is rudimentary. But it's enough for the public to easily understand what the funding circle is about and to get potential grantees started on the process. The website creation is the easy part of achieving this goal – the majority of the work, which will likely take several months, will be on making preliminary key decisions.

## 11.4. Final remarks

At CE, we pursue a vision of a philanthropic sector where the norm is for foundations to choose their scope carefully and become experts in it over time. A world where funded projects can be defended using the highest forms of evidence. Where foundations are proud of the methodology they have used. In this world, different foundations' focus areas and strategies slot together like puzzle pieces to address the most important problems in the world together, with limited gaps. Foundations make decisions after considering a wide range of complementary but rigorously defendable perspectives. They vet opportunities systematically and consistently and share lessons from successes and failures. In this way, foundations and grantmakers shape both the philanthropic sector and the nonprofit sector- and ultimately, the world we and all other sentient beings live in, to make it the best version it can be. Charities think deeply about their real impact before applying, as they know the funders will do their homework and rarely be convinced by a single anecdote or a glossy website.

Every foundation and grantmaker has a part to play in making this world a reality.

Hopefully, this handbook has given you some tools, processes, and perspectives that you can use to start building your own high-impact foundation or to steer an existing one to become more impactful. We encourage every foundation and grantmaker reading this book to set the bar high. Equipped with the lessons in this handbook, you can set the goal not just to start and run any foundation but to run an excellent one whose impact and influence on the world will be disproportionate to its origins. With thoughtful decisions and a commitment to constant learning and hard work, it is possible to achieve great things for the world that would never have happened without you.

Printed in Great Britain
by Amazon